D1303623

GUIDE TO
CURRENT
BRITISH JOURNALS

Second edition

edited by

DAVID P. WOODWORTH

Lecturer, School of Librarianship, Loughborough

Vol. 2

DIRECTORY

OF

PUBLISHERS

LONDON

THE LIBRARY ASSOCIATION

1973

The Library Association
7 Ridgmount Street, London, WC1E 7AE

© David Woodworth, 1973

Vol. 2.
First edition 1971
Second edition 1973

Vol 1. ISBN: 0 85365 356 9
Vol 2. ISBN: 0 85365 097 7

PRINTED BY Unwin Brothers Limited
THE GRESHAM PRESS OLD WOKING SURREY ENGLAND

Produced by 'Uneoprint'
A member of the Staples Printing Group

INTRODUCTION

Previously published as a separate work this has now more logically been included as an integral part of the main guide. However as the information given is both complementary and supplementary to it the material is so arranged that this volume is self contained and may be purchased as a separate work in its own right and thus be available to those in differing fields who might not wish/need to purchase the complete work.

However careful the preparation, omissions are always possible, and I would be grateful if publishers would contact me with any relevant details such as changes of address, new titles, discontinued works etc. so that future editions can be accurately maintained. It will be noticed that fewer publishers are noted in this edition and this is in part due to amalgamations, winding up of some firms, and failure to trace continued existence of others. Additionally as this work is now an integral part of the main guide I decided in the interests of accuracy to include those publishers *known* to be in existence at the date of going to print.

ARRANGEMENT

(a) Alphabetical listing of publishers and their addresses together with the titles they publish, with a running number, for quick reference purposes, from the index.

(b) Alphabetical index of all titles covered (no inversion) referring to the relevant number of its publisher in the main sequence. Current titles only have been used.

LIMITATIONS

Broadly these are identical with the main work in that while omissions have been kept to a minimum they at present include such categories as: Parish magazines, some 'pin-up' journals, daily press, comics, and some student publications.

1   **A4—PUBLICATIONS LTD.**
Press House
25, High Street
Edenbridge, Kent

Building Materials
Flooring Journal

2   **ABC TRAVEL GUIDES LTD.**
Oldhill
London Road
Dunstable, Beds.

ABC Air Cargo Guide
ABC Guide to International Travel
ABC Rail Guide
ABC World Airways Guide
Inter-City ABC

3   **A.C.M. WEBB (PUBLISHING) LTD.**
60, Fleet Street
London EC4

Squash Player

4   **A.E. MORGAN PUBLICATIONS LTD.**
172, Kingston Road
Ewell, Surrey

Anaesthesia and Analgesia
Dental Practice
Medical Technician

5   **A.H. THROWER LTD.**
44-46, South Ealing Road
Ealing
London W5

Diplomatic Bookshelf

6   **A.J.H. PUBLICATIONS LTD.**
110, Fleet Street
London EC4A 2JL

Fishing News International
Fishing News

7   **A.K. NIELSEN COMPANY LTD.**
Nielsen House
Headington
Oxford OX3 9RX

Nielsen Researcher

8   **A.P. PUBLICATIONS LTD.**
Morley House
Holborn Viaduct
London EC1

Software World

9   **A.S. KERSWILL LTD.**
15, Cochrane Mews
St. John's Wood
London NW8

Vacher's European Companion
Vacher's Parliamentary Companion

10   **ABBOT DUPLICATE BOOK CO. LTD.**
Abbot Works
King's Langley
Herts WD4 8JD

Printers Prophet

11   **ABBOTSBURY PUBLICATIONS**
Abbotsbury
Weymouth
Dorset

Energy and Character

12   **ABERDEEN AND DISTRICT MILK MARKETING BOARD**
Twin Spires
Bucksburn
Aberdeen AB2 GNR

Milk News

13   **ABERDEEN—ANGUS CATTLE**
6, King's Place
Perth

Aberdeen-Angus Review

14   **ABERDEEN CHAMBER OF COMMERCE**
15, Union Terrace
Aberdeen AB9 1HF

Aberdeen Chamber of Commerce Journal

15   **ABERDEEN UNIVERSITY PRESS LTD.**
Farmers Hall
Aberdeen
Scotland AB9 2XT

Philosphy of the Social Sciences
Scottish Historical Review

16   **ABOUT WINE**
36-38, Southampton Street
London WC2E 7HE

About Wine

17   **ABSTAINING MOTORISTS ASSOCIATION**
40, Waterloo Road
Bramhall
Cheshire SK7 2NX

Abstaining Driver

18   **ACADEMIC PRESS**
15, Cavendish Square
London W1M 0HT

Journal of Verbal Learning and Verbal
Behaviour

19   **ACADEMIC PRESS INC. (LONDON) LTD.**
24-28, Oval Road
London NW1

Advancement of Science
Biological Journal of the Linnean Society
Botanical Journal of the Linnean Society
British Polymer Journal
Estuarine and Coastal Marine Science
Experimental Eye Research
Ibis
International Journal of Man-Machine Studies
International Library Review
Journal of Agricultural Engineering Research
Journal of Applied Bacteriology
Journal of Applied Chemistry and Biotechnology
Journal of Biological Education
Journal of Chemical Thermodynamics
Journal of Environmental Management
Journal of Fish Biology
Journal of Molecular and Cellular Cardiology
Journal of Molecular Biology
Journal of Sound and Vibration
Journal of the Institute of Mathematics and its
Applications
Journal of the Science of Food and Agriculture
Journal of Theoretical Biology
Journal of Zoology
Leprosy Review
Medical Laboratory Technology
Pesticide Science
Physiological Plant Pathology
Public Health
Quarterly Journal of Experimental Psychology
Scandinavica
Zoological Journal of the Linnean Society

20 ACCOUNTANTS' PUBLISHING CO. LTD.
27, Queen Street
Edinburgh EH2 1LA

Accountants' Magazine
Accountants Weekly

21 ACHESON COLLOIDS CO.
Plymouth PL4 0SP

Prospects

22 ADDITIONAL CURATES SOCIETY
14, Rothamsted Avenue
Harpenden
Herts

Home Mission News

23 ADMAP PUBLICATIONS LTD.
273A, Kings Road
London SW3

Admap

24 ADMARK PUBLISHING CO. LTD.
Mercury House
103/119, Waterloo Road
London SE1

Advertisers Weekly
Industrial Advertising and Marketing

25 ADULT EDUCATION CENTRE
73, Farnham Road
Guildford

Link

26 ADVERTISING ASSOCIATION
1, Bell Yard
London WC2

Advertising Quarterly

27 ADVERTISING MANAGEMENT LTD.
348, Grays Inn Road
London WC1

Advertising and Marketing Management

28 ADVISORY BODY OF LIBRARIANS
c/o Central Library
Romford, Essex

Loga

29 ADVISORY CENTRE FOR EDUCATION
32, Trumpington Street
Cambridge CB2 1QY

Where

30 AER LINGUS—IRISH AIRLINES
Head Office
Airport
Dublin

Cara

31 AFRICA JOURNAL LTD.
28, Great Queen Street
London WC2

Africa

32 AFRICA PUBLICATIONS TRUST
48, Grafton Way
London W1 5 LB

Africa Digest

33 AFRICA RESEARCH LTD.
1, Parliament Street
Exeter

Africa Research Bulletin

34 AFRICAN BUYER AND TRADER LTD.
Wheatsheaf House
Carmelite Street
London EC4Y OAX

African Development

35 AFRICAN STUDIES ASSOCIATION OF THE UK
c/o Centre of West African Studies
P. O. Box 363
University of Birmingham B15 2SD

Bulletin of the African Studies Association of
the United Kingdom

36 AFRICAN SUCCULENT PLANT SOCIETY
54, Fishponds Road
Hitchin
Herts SG5 1NS

Bulletin of the African Succulent Plant Society

37 AGENDA
5, Cranbourne Court
Albert Bridge Road
London SW11 4PE

Agenda

38 AGRICULTURAL ECONOMICS SOCIETY
Department of Agricultural Economics and
Management
The University
Reading RG6 2AR

Journal of Agricultural Economics

39 AGRICULTURAL EDUCATION ASSOCIATION
Cliftonfield
Shipton Road
York

Agricultural Progress

40 AGRICULTURAL MERCHANT
58, Mark Lane
London EC3R 7NP

Agricultural Merchant

41 AGRICULTURAL PRESS LTD.
161, Fleet Street
London EC4

Agricultural Machinery Journal
Poultry Industry
Poultry World

42 AGRICULTURAL TRUST
The Irish Farm Centre
Naas Road
Dublin 12

Irish Farmers' Journal

43 AGUDAS ISRAEL OF GREAT BRITIAN
97, Stamford Hill
London N16

Jewish Tribune

44 AIR AGE PUBLICATIONS LTD.
1, Temple Chambers
London, EC4

Helicopter World

45 AIR-BRITAIN (HISTORIANS) LTD.
Stone Cottage
Great Sampford
Saffron Walden
Essex

Air-Britain Digest
Air Britain News

46 AIR RAID PROTECTION INSTITUTE CO.
316, Vauxhall Bridge Road
London SW1

Journal of the Institute of Civil Defence

47 AIR TRANSPORT AND TRAVEL INDUSTRY
TRAINING BOARD
Staines House
158-162, High Street
Staines
Middx.

Air and Travel Training World

48 AKROS PUBLICATIONS
14, Parklands Avenue
Penwortham
Preston, Lancs.

Akros

49 ALAN EXLEY LTD.
P.O. Box 1
Battle, Sussex

Horse World
Livestock Farming

50 ALAN OSBORNE AND ASSOCIATES
1/113 Blackheath Park
London SE3

Protection

51 ALBION PRESS
50 Pawson's Road
Croydon
Surrey CR0 2QF

Spearhead

52 ALCHEMIST PUBLICATIONS
25 Oxford Street
London W1

Journal of Hospital Pharmacy

53 ALDEN AND BLACKWELL (ETON) LTD.
Eton College
Windsor SL4 6DF

Etoniana

54 ALDRIDGE PRESS LTD.
7, Queen Square
Brighton

Wholesale Confectioner

55 ALL ENGLAND NETBALL ASSOCIATION
26, Park Crescent
London W1N 4ER

Netball

56 ALLIANCE PARTY OF NORTHERN IRELAND
6, Cromwell Road
Belfast BT7 1JW

Alliance

57 ALPINE CLUB
74, South Audley Street
London W1Y 5FF

Alpine Journal

58 ALPINE GARDEN SOCIETY
Lye End Link
St John's
Woking
Surrey

Quarterly Bulletin of the Alpine Garden
Society

59 ALUMINIUM FEDERATION
Broadway House
Carthorpe Road
Five Ways
Birmingham B1J 1TN

Aluminium for Schools

60 AMALGAMATED POWER ENGINEERING LTD.
Bedford

Apex

61 AMALGAMATED UNION OF BUILDING TRADE
WORKERS
Crescent Lane
Clapham
London SW4

Building Worker

62 AMALGAMATED UNION OF ENGINEERING WORKERS
Onslow Hall
Little Green
Richmond
Surrey

Tass Journal

63 AMATEUR BASKET BALL ASSOCIATION
P.O. Box 1 W3
Leeds 16

Basketball

64 AMATEUR ENTOMOLOGISTS SOCIETY
c/o 355, Hounslow Road
Hanworth
Feltham, Middx

Bulletin of the Amateur Entomologists
Society

65 AMATEUR ROWING ASSOCIATION
Embankment
London SW15

Rowing

66 AMATEUR YACHT RESEARCH SOCIETY
Hermitage
Newbury, Berkshire

A.Y.R.S. Airs

67 AMBASSADOR PUBLISHING SERVICES LTD.
49, Park Lane
London W1

Ambassador
British Hosiery and Knitwear

68 AMBIT
17, Priory Gardens
London N6

Ambit

69 AMERICAN CHAMBER OF COMMERCE (UK)
75 Brook Street
London W1Y 2EB

Angle-American Trade News

70 AMPLEFORTH ABBEY
Ampleforth College
Yorks YO6 4EN

Ampleforth Journal

71 AN CHOMHAIRLE NÁISIÚNTA DRÁMAÍOCHTA
6 Sraíd Fhearchair
Dublin 2

Ardán

3

72 **AN COMUNN GAIDHEALACH**
Abertarff House
Inverness

Sruth

73 **AN COSANTÓIR**
Red House
Infirmary Road
Dublin 7

An Cosantóir

74 **ANBAR PUBLICATIONS LTD.**
P. O. Box 23
Wembley HA9 8DJ

Anbar Management Services Bibliography
Accounting and Data Processing Abstracts
Marketing and Distribution Abstracts
Personnel and Training Abstracts
Top Managment Abstracts

75 **ANCIENT MONUMENTS SOCIETY**
33, Ladbroke Square
London W11 5NT

Transactions of the Ancient Monuments
Society

76 **ANCIENT ORDER OF FORESTERS**
136, High Street
Southampton

Foresters Miscellany

77 **ANDERSONIAN NATURALISTS OF GLASGOW**
c/o Dept. of Botany
The University
Glasgow G12 8QQ

Glasgow Naturalist

78 **ANGLESEY ANTIQUARIAN SOCIETY AND FIELD CLUB**
c/o 22, Lon Ganol
Menai Bridge

Transactions of the Anglesey Antiquarian
Society and Field Club

79 **ANGLIA ECHO NEWSPAPERS LTD.**
2-6, High Street
Haverhill, Suffolk

Liberal News
Sound and Picture Tape Recording

80 **ANGLO-ARAB ASSOCIATION**
West End House
Hills Place
London W1R 1A6

Arab World

81 **ANGLO-BYELORUSSIAN SOCIETY**
230, Strand
London WC2

Journal of Byelorussian Studies

82 **ANGLO-CHILEAN SOCIETY**
3, Hamilton Place
London W1

Chilean News

83 **ANGLO-DANISH SOCIETY**
7, St. Helen's Place
London EC2

Denmark

84 **ANGLO-SPANISH LEAGUE OF FRIENDSHIP**
Anglo-Spanish Society
5, Cavendish Square
London W1M 9HA

Anglo Spanish Society Quarterly Review

85 **ANGLO/WELSH REVIEW AND DOCK LEAVES**
Ty Newydd
Lodge Hill
Caerleon
Newport, Mon NP61DA

Anglo Welsh Review

86 **ANTHROPOSOPHICAL SOCIETY IN GREAT BRITIAN**
Rudolf Steiner House
35, Park Road
London NW1 6XT

Anthroposophical Quarterly

87 **ANTI-APARTHEID MOVEMENT**
89, Charlotte Street
London WIP 2DQ

Anti-Apartheid News

88 **ANTIQUARIAN HOROLOGICAL SOCIETY**
28, Welbeck Street
London W1M 7PG

Antiquarian Horology

89 **ANTIQUE AND GENERAL ADVERTISING LTD.**
The Old Town House
High Street
Wendover, Bucks

Antiques
Antiques in Britain
Antiques World

90 **ANTIQUE COLLECTOR LTD.**
Victoria Chambers
16, Strutton Ground
Victoria Street
London SW1

Antique Collector

91 **ANTIQUE COLLECTOR'S CLUB**
Clapton
Woodbridge, Suffolk

Antique Collecting

92 **ANTIQUE FINDER LTD.**
34/40, Ludgate Hill
London EC4

Antique Finder

93 **APPLIED PROBABILITY TRUST**
Dept. of Probability and Statistics
University
Sheffield S3 7RH

Advances in Applied Probability
Journal of Applied Probability

94 **APPLIED SCIENCE PUBLISHERS LTD.**
22, Rippleside Commercial Estate
Barking, Essex.

Applied Acoustics
Biological Conservation
Build International
Environmental Pollution
Fibre Science and Technology
International Journal of Bio-medical
Computing
International Journal of Pressure Vesels and
Piping

Pressure Vessels and Piping
Proceedings of the Royal Institution of Great Britain

95   APPRENTICE
c/o Magdalen College
Cambridge

Apprentice

96   APPROACH MAGAZINE PUBLISHING CO.
St. Peter's College
Oxford

Approach Magazine

97   APPROACHES
Casa Garcia Moreno
1, Waverley Place
Saltcoats
Scotland KA215AY

Approaches

98   ARAB HORSE SOCIETY
Sackville Lodge
Lye Green
Crowborough, Sussex

Arab Horse Society News

99   ARAB REPORT AND RECORD
84, Chancery Lane
London WC2A 1DL

Arab Report and Record

100   ARAWAK PRESS LTD
The Penthouse
Glenwood House
Dorking
Surrey

West Indian Review

101   ARCHAEOLOGY ABROAD SERVICE
31-4, Gordon Square
London WC1 HOPY

Archaeology Abroad

102   ARCHIGRAM
59, Aberdare Gardens
London NW6

Archigram

103   ARCHITECTURE AND PLANNING INFORMATION SERVICE
Science Library
Queen's University of Belfast
Belfast BT9 5EQ

APIS Bulletin

104   ARCHITECTURAL AND PLANNING PUBLICATIONS LTD.
4, Catherine Street
Aldwych
London WC2B 5JN

Built Environment

105   ARCHITECTURAL PRESS LTD.
9-13, Queen Anne's Gate
London SW1H 9BY

Architects Journal
Architectural Review

106   ARCHITECTURAL RADICALS, STUDENTS-EDUCATORS GROUP
c/o David Wild
20, Chalcot Road
London NW1 8LL

ARse

107   ARCHITECTURAL SOCIETY
Queen's University of Belfast
Department of Architecture
Queen's University of Belfast
Belfast BT7 1NN

Big A

108   ARENA PUBLICATIONS
325, Streatham High Road
London SW16

Athletic's Arena Internátional

109   ARGUS PRESS LTD.
12/18, Paul Street
London EC2

Photoplay
Scale Models

110   ARMS AND ARMOUR SOCIETY
c/o 17, St. Charles Square
London W10 6EF

Journal of the Arms and Armour Society

111   ARMY CADET FORCE ASSOCIATION
58, Buckingham Gate
London SW1

Cadet Journal and Gazette

112   ART INFORMATION REGISTRY LTD.
Burlington House
Piccadilly
London W1V 9AG

Airmail

113   ART LIBRARIES SOCIETY
St. Albans School of Art Library
7, Hatfield Road
St. Albans, Herts

Arlis Newsletter

114   ART SALES INDEX LTD.
Pond House
Weybridge
Surrey

Art Sales Index

115   ARTHRITIS AND RHEUMATISM COUNCIL
8, Charing Cross Road
London WC2

Arc

116   ARTHUR HEIGHWAY PUBLICATIONS LTD.
110, Fleet Street
London EC4

Self Service Times and Modern Marketing

117   ARTIST PUBLISHING CO. LTD.
46, Charlotte Street
London W1

Artist

118   ARTS INFORMATION REGISTRY
71, Stepney Green
London E1

Catalyst

119 ASHIRE PUBLISHING LTD.
10, Laystall Street
London EC1

Mine and Quarry
Mining and Minerals Engineering

120 ASLIB
3, Belgrave Square
London SW1

Aslib Book List
Aslib Information
Aslib Proceedings
Aslib Transport and Planning Group Newsletter
Forthcoming International Scientific and
Technical Conferences
Journal of Documentation
Program

121 ASSEMBLIES OF GOD IN GREAT BRITAIN AND
IRELAND
106-114, Talbot Street
Nottingham NG1 5GH

Redemption Tidings

122 ASSOCIATED BRITISH MACHINE TOOL MAKERS
LTD.
17, Grosvenor Gardens
London SW1

Machine Tool Engineering

123 ASSOCIATED NEWSPAPERS GROUP LTD.
Carmelite House
Camelite Street
London EC4 YOJA

Weekend

124 ASSOCIATED SOCIETY OF LOCOMOTIVE
ENGINEERS AND FIREMEN
9, Arkwright Road
London NW3

Locomotive Journal

125 ASSOCIATION FOR PROMOTING RETREATS
Church House
Newton Road
London W2

Vision

126 ASSOCIATION FOR SCIENCE EDUCATION
College Lane
Hatfield, Herts

Education in Science

127 ASSOCIATION FOR SCOTTISH LITERARY STUDIES
c/o Department of English Literature
University of Aberdeen
Taylor Building
Old Aberdeen
Scotland

Scottish Literary News

128 ASSOCIATION FOR SPECIAL EDUCATION
Publications Dept.
Beaconwood
Bordon Hill
Stratford-on-Avon

Research in Special Education

129 ASSOCIATION OF ACROBATICS
27, Bridge Way
Twickenham TW2 7JL

Acrobatics

130 ASSOCIATION OF AGRICULTURE
78, Buckingham Gate
London SW1E 6PE

Association of Agriculture Journal

131 ASSOCIATION OF ARTS CENTRES IN SCOTLAND
216, Strathearn Road
Edinburgh EH9 2AB

Trends and Topics

132 ASSOCIATION OF ASSISTANT LIBRARIANS
c/o Central Library
Manor Park Road
Sutton, Surrey

Assistant Librarian

133 ASSOCIATION OF ASSISTANT LIBRARIANS
Devon and Cornwall Branch
Public Library
Plymouth

Outpost

134 ASSOCIATION OF BEAUTY THERAPISTS
4, Berkeley Mews
Portman Square
London W1

Beauty Therapy Journal

135 ASSOCIATION OF BLIND CHARTERED
PHYSIOTHERAPISTS
204, Great Portland Street
London W1

Braille Journal of Physiotherapy
Braille Physiotherapists Quarterly

136 ASSOCIATION OF BRITISH ADOPTION AGENCIES
27, Queen Anne's Gate
London SW1

Child Adoption

137 ASSOCIATION OF BRITISH DENTAL SURGERY
ASSISTANTS
Bank Chambers
3, Market Place
Poulton
Blackpool, Lancs

British Dental Sugery Assistant

138 ASSOCIATION OF BRITISH LAUNDERERS AND
CLEANERS LTD.
22, Lancaster Gate
London W2

ABLC Journal

139 ASSOCIATION OF BRONZE AND BRASS FOUNDERS
69, Harborne Road
Birmingham 15

Association of Bronze and Brass Founders
Bulletin

140 ASSOCIATION OF CASHIERS
Old Rectory
Tallington
Stamford, Lincs

Cashier

141 ASSOCIATION OF CERTIFIED ACCOUNTANTS
22, Bedford Square
London WC1 B 3HS

Certified Accountant

142 ASSOCIATION OF CHILD CARE OFFICERS
Oxford House
Derbyshire Street
London E2

Social Work

143 ASSOCIATION OF CHRISTIAN TEACHERS
47, Marylebone Lane
London W1M 6AX

Spectrum

144 ASSOCIATION OF CLINICAL BIOCHEMISTS
7, Warwick Court
London WC1

Annals of Clinical Biochemistry

145 ASSOCIATION OF COMMONWEALTH UNIVERSITIES
36 Gordon Square
London WC1

A.C.U. Bulletin of Current Decumentation
Bulletin of Current Documentation

146 ASSOCIATION OF COST ENGINEERS
33, Ovington Square
London SW3

Cost Engineer

147 ASSOCIATION OF DISPENSING OPTICIANS
22, Nottingham Place
London W1M 4AT

Dispensing Optician

148 ASSOCIATION OF HOSPITAL AND WELFARE
ADMINISTRATIONS
Bensted House
Faversham, Kent

Bulletin

149 ASSOCIATION OF HOSPITAL TREASURERS
c/o Sherwood Hospital
Hucknall Road
Nottingham NG5 1PD

Hospital Service Finance
Industrial Equipment News
What's New

150 ASSOCIATION OF INDUSTRIAL AND COMMERCIAL
EXECUTIVE ACCOUNTANTS LTD.
4-9, Wood Street
London EC2

Executive Accountant

151 ASSOCIATION OF INTERNATIONAL ACCOUNTANTS
Temple Chambers
Temple Avenue
London EC4

International Accountant

152 ASSOCIATION OF JEWISH REFUGEES IN GREAT
BRITAIN
8, Fairfax Mansions
London NW3 6JY

AJR Information

153 ASSOCIATION OF MASTER UPHOLSTERERS
4, Sutherland Avenue
London W9

Monthly Bulletin

154 ASSOCIATION OF MEDICAL RECORDS OFFICERS
Shotley Bridge General Hospital
Consett
Co. Durham

Medical Record

155 ASSOCIATION OF MEDICAL SECRETARIES
22, Manchester Street
London W1

Medical Secretary

156 ASSOCIATION OF MEN OF KENT AND KENTISH
MEN
Cornwallis House
Pudding Lane
Maidstone

Kent

157 ASSOCIATION OF MINING, ELECTRICAL AND
MECHANICAL ENGINEERS
c/o 34, Great James Street
London WC1

Mining Technology

158 ASSOCIATION OF MUNICIPAL CORPORATIONS
36, Old Queen Street
London SW1

Municipal Review

159 ASSOCIATION FOR PETROLEUM ACTS ADMINIS-
TRATION
Teesside Fire Brigade Headquarters
Park Road South
Middlesbrough
Teesside TS5 6LG

Bulletin

160 ASSOCIATION OF POLISH MERCHANTS AND IN-
DUSTRIALISTS
47, Earls Court Road
London W8 6EE

Wiadomosci Gospodarcze

161 ASSOCIATION OF PSYCHIATRIC SOCIAL WORKERS
Oxford House
Derbyshire Street
London E2

British Journal of Psychiatric Social Work

162 ASSOCIATION OF PUBLIC ADDRESS ENGINEERS
LTD.
6, Conduit Street
London W1R 9TG

Public Address

163 ASSOCIATION OF PUBLIC ANALYSTS
325, Kennington Road
London SE11

Journal of the Association of Public Analysts

164 ASSOCIATION OF PUBLIC HEALTH INSPECTORS
19, Grosvenor Place
London SW1

Environmental Health

165 ASSOCIATION OF PUBLIC LIGHTING ENGINEERS
78, Buckingham Gate
London SW1E 6PF

Public Lighting

166 ASSOCIATION OF RECOGNISED ENGLISH LAN-
GUAGE SCHOOLS
43, Russell Square
London WC1B 5DH

A.R.E.L.S. Journal

167 ASSOCIATION OF SCHOOL NATURAL HISTORY
SOCIETIES
c/o Seaford College
Petworth, Sussex

Starfish

168 ASSOCIATION OF SCIENTIFIC TECHNICAL AND
MANAGERIAL STAFFS
15, Half Moon Street
London W1

A.S.T.M.S. Gains
A.S.T.M.S. Journal

169 ASSOCIATION OF SUPERVISORY AND EXECUTIVE
ENGINEERS
Wix Hill House
West Horsley
Surrey

Electrical Supervisor

170 ASSOCIATION OF TEACHERS IN COLLEGES AND
DEPARTMENTS OF EDUCATION
3, Crawford Place
London W1H 2BN

Education for Teaching

171 ASSOCIATION OF TEACHERS IN TECHNICAL
INSTITUTIONS
Hamilton House
Mabledon Place
London WC1

Technical Journal

172 ASSOCIATION OF TEACHERS OF DOMESTIC
SCIENCE
Hamilton House
Mabledon Place
London WC1H 9BB

Housecraft

173 ASSOCIATION OF TEACHERS OF GERMAN
27, Wood Lane End
Adeyfield
Hemel Hempstead, Herts

Treffpunkt

174 ASSOCIATION OF TEACHERS OF MANAGEMENT
c/o Dept. of Management Polytechnic
77, Whitworth Street
Manchester 1

Management Education and Development

175 ASSOCIATION OF TEACHERS OF MATHEMATICS
Market Street Chambers
Nelson
Lancs BB9 7LN

Mathematics Teaching

176 ASSOCIATION OF TEACHERS OF PRINTING AND
ALLIED SUBJECTS
132, Cheviot Road
West Norwood
London SE27

ATPAS Bulletin

177 ASSOCIATION OF TEACHERS OF RUSSIAN
c/o Dept. of Russian and Soviet Studies
University of Lancaster
Bailrigg, Lancaster

Journal of Russian Studies

178 ASSOCIATION OF UKRAINIANS IN GREAT BRITAIN
49, Linden Gardens
London W2 4HG

Ukrainian Review

179 ASSOCIATION OF UNIVERSITY TEACHERS
Bremar House
Sale Place
London W2

A.U.T. Bulletin

180 ASTON MARTIN OWNERS CLUB
47, Lenchen Road
London W13

A.M.

181 ASTRIAN PUBLIC RELATIONS LTD.
344, South Lambeth Road
London SW8

Yoga and Health

182 ATHOL PUBLICATIONS
Athol Street
Douglas
I.O.M.

Fate and Horoscope

183 ATKINSON VEHICLES LTD.
Walton-le-Dale
Preston PR5 4AS

Seddon Atkinson Magazine

184 ATLANTIC INFORMATION CENTRE FOR
TEACHERS
23/25, Abbey House
8, Victoria Street
London SW1H 9LA

Crisis Paper
World and the School
World Survey

185 ATLANTIC PRESS
122, Grand Buildings
Trafalgar Square
London WC2N 5EP

New Poetry

186 ATLAS PUBLISHING LTD.
80, Kennington Park Place
London SE11

Golf Weekly

187 ATOMIC WEAPONS RESEARCH ESTABLISHMENT
Aldermaston
Reading RG7 4PR

A.W.R.E. News

188 AUDIO-VISUAL LANGUAGE ASSOCIATION
Department of Modern Languages
University of Salford
Salford 5

Audio-Visual Language Journal

189   AVENUE PUBLISHING CO.
      18, Park Avenue
      London NW11

          British Journal of Social Psychiatry and
             Community Health
          International Journal of Social Psychiatry

190   AVON COSMETICS LTD.
      Nunn Mills Road
      Northampton

          Contact

191   AYRSHIRE ARCHAEOLOGICAL AND NATURAL
HISTORY SOCIETY
      c/o Ayr Public Library
      12, Main Street
      Ayr

          Ayrshire Archaeological and Natural History
             Society Collections

192   AYRSHIRE CATTLE SOCIETY
      1, Racecourse Road
      Ayr

          Ayrshire Cattle Society's Journal

193   B.A.R.C. NEWS
      Sutherland House
      5-6, Argyll Street
      London W1

          B.A.R.C. News

194   B.B. BOOKS
      1 Spring Bank
      Salesbury
      Blackburn
      Lancs BB1 GEU

          B.B. Book Issues
          Global Tapestry Journal and Vegan Action
          P.M. Newsletter
          Vegan Action Newsletter

195   B.B.C. PUBLICATIONS
      35, Marylebone High Street
      London W1

          Listener

196   B.E.A.M.A.
      8, Leicester Street
      Leicester Square
      London WC2

          Domestic Electrical Appliance Industry
             Statistics

197   BED BUSINESS JOURNALS LTD.
      Park House
      Park Street
      Croydon CR9 1UA

          Business Equipment Digest
          Business Equipment Guide
          Datascene
          Repro
          Reproduction

198   B.E.M.A. LTD.
      Royal London House
      Queen Charlotte St
      Bristol BS1 4E2

          BEMA Bulletin

199   B.P.S. EXHIBITIONS LTD.
      6, London Street
      London W2

          Foodpack

200   B.S.C. FOOTWEAR LTD.
      Sunningdale Road
      Leicester LE3 1UR

          Shoebiz

201   B. EDSALL AND CO. LTD.
      36, Eccleston Square
      London SW1V 1PF

          Health Visitor
          Journal of Alcoholism

202   BABCOCK AND WILCOX LTD.
      Cleveland House
      St. James's Square
      London SW1Y 4LN

          Circulator

203   BABYLONIAN JEWRY
      11 Russell Road
      London W14

          Scribe

204   BADMINTON ASSOCIATION OF ENGLAND
      24, The Charter Road
      Woodford Green, Essex

          Badminton Gazette

205   BAILLIERE, TINDALL AND CASSELL LTD.
      7/8 Henrietta Street
      London WC2 8QE

          Age and Ageing
          Animal Behaviour
          Animal Behaviour Monographs
          British Journal of Diseases of the Chest
          British Veterinary Journal
          International Journal of Psychoanalysis
          Rheumatology and Physical Medicine

206   BAKELITE XYLONITE LTD.
      Enford House
      139 Marylebone Road
      London NW1 5QE

          Crosslink

207   BALINT SOCIETY
      150, Lady Margaret Road
      Southall
      Middx

          Journal of the Balint Society

208   BANBURY HISTORICAL SOCIETY
      c/o Banbury Museum
      Marlborough Road
      Banbury
      Oxon

          Cake and Cockhorse

209   BANDSMAN'S PRESS LTD.
      210, Strand
      London WC2

          British Bandsman

210   BANK OF ENGLAND
      Economic Intelligence Dept.
      London EC2R 8AH

          Bank of England Quarterly Bulletin

211   BANK OF ENGLAND
      London EC2R 8AH

          Bank of England Statistical Abstract

212 BANKER LIMITED
   Bracken House
   Cannon Street
   London EC4P 4BY

   Banker

213 BAPTIST MISSIONARY SOCIETY
   93, Gloucester Place
   London W1H 4AA

   Quest
   Wonderlands

214 BAPTIST TIMES LTD.
   4, Southampton Road
   London WC1B 4AB

   Baptist Times

215 BAPTIST UNION OF GREAT BRITAIN AND IRELAND
   4, Southampton Row
   London WC1B 5AB

   Baptist Quarterly

216 BAPTIST UNION OF IRELAND
   3, Fitzwilliam Street
   Belfast BT9 6AW

   Irish Baptist Historical Society Journal

217 BARCLAYCARD MAGAZINE
   94, St. Pauls' Churchyard
   London EC4M 8EH

   Barclaycard Magazine

218 BARCLAYS BANK INTERNATIONAL LTD.
   54, Lombard Street
   London EC3P 3AH

   Barclays International Quarterly
   Barclays International Review

219 BARCLAY'S BANK TRUST CO. LTD.
   Juxon House
   94, St. Paul's Churchyard
   London EC4M 8EH

   Money Matters

220 BARCLAYS BANK LTD.
   54, Lombard Street
   London EC3P 3AH

   Barclays Review
   Spread Eagle

221 BAROQUE PRESS
   28, James Street
   London W1M 5HS

   Image

222 BARRIE AND JENKINS LTD.
   2, Clements Inn
   London WC2

   Cambridge Review

223 BARTLE AND SON LTD.
   Station Road
   Scunthorpe, Lincs

   Retort

224 BASIL BLACKWELL AND MOTT LTD.
   5, Alfred Street
   Oxford OX1 4HB

   American Philosophical Quarterly
   Analysis
   British Journal of Educational Studies
   Bulletin of the Oxford University Institute of
      Economics and Statistics
   Business Economist

   Didaskalos
   French Studies
   German Life and Letters
   International Political Science Abstracts
   Journal for the Theory of Social Behaviour
   Journal of Common Market Studies
   Journal of Industrial Economics
   Medium Aevum
   Metaphilosophy
   Mind
   R and D Management
   Ratio
   Transactions of the Philological Society

225 BATH AND CAMERTON ARCHAEOLOGICAL
   SOCIETY
   61, Pulteney Street
   Bath

   Camertonia

226 BATH UNIVERSITY PRESS
   Claverton Down
   Bath

   Technology and Society

227 BATISTE PUBLICATIONS LTD.
   203/209, North Gower Street
   London NW1

   Electrical Wholesaler
   I.H.V.E. Journal
   Screen Printing and Point of Sale News

228 CYRIL BEASTALL
   92, Westbrook Avenue
   Margate, Kent

   Skating World

229 BEAT INSTRUMENTAL
   58, Parker Street
   London WC2 B5QB

   Beat Instrumental and International Recording
      Studio

230 BEE RESEARCH ASSOCIATION
   Hill House
   Chalfont St Peter
   Gerrards Cross
   Bucks SL9 ONR

   Apilcultural Abstracts
   Bee World
   Journal of Apicultural Research

231 LIONEL BEER
   15, Freshwater Court
   Crawford Street
   London W1H 1HS

   Spacelink

232 BEHAVIOURAL ENGINEERING ASSOCIATION
   Dept. of Mental Health
   Queen's University
   Belfast

   Behavioural Engineering Association Conference
      Proceedings

233 BELFAST NATURAL HISTORY AND PHILOSOPHICAL
   SOCIETY
   7, College Square North
   Belfast 1

   Proceedings and Reports: Belfast Natural
      History and Philosophic Society

234 BENHAM AND CO. LTD.
   Colchester

   Proceedings of the Geologists Association

235 BENJAMIN DENT PUBLICATIONS LTD.
40, New Oxford Street
London WC1

Fabric Forecast
Fashion Forecast

236 BENN BROTHERS LTD.
74, Dryman Road
Bearsden, Glasgow

Commercial Grover
Forestry and Home Grown Timber

237 BENN BROTHERS LTD.
Lyon Tower
125, High Street
Colliers Wood
London SW19

British Trade Journal and Export World
Chemist and Druggist
Domestic Gas
Education Equipment
Fire Protection Review
Gas Marketing and Domestic Gas
Gas World
Gifts
Hardware Trade Journal
Industrial and Commercial Gas
Junior Education Equipment
Marine and Air Catering
Mercantile Guardian
Paper
Printing World
Shipping World and Shipbuilder
Sports Trader
University Equipment

238 BENN BROTHERS LTD.
25, New Street Square
London EC4 A 3JA

Builders Merchants Journal
Cabinet Maker and Retail Furnisher
Carpet and Floor Covering News
Chemical Age International
Leather
Leathergoods
Nurseryman and Garden Centre
Printing Trades Journal
Sports and Recreation Equipment
Timber Trades Journal
Wood

239 BENTHAM-MOXON TRUST
Royal Botanic Gardens
Kew
Richmond, Surrey

Curtis's Botanical Magazine
Hooker's Icones Plantarum

240 BERKSHIRE ARCHAEOLOGICAL SOCIETY
c/o 'Turstins'
High Street
Upton
Didcot, Berks

Berkshire Archaeological Journal

241 C.J.J. and M.F. BERRY
North Gaye
The Avenue
Andover, Hants

Amateur Winemaker

242 BERTRAND RUSSELL PEACE FOUNDATION LTD.
Gamble Street
Forest Road West
Nottingham NG7 4ET

Spokesman

243 BIBLE CHURCHMEN'S MISSIONARY SOCIETY
157, Waterloo Road
London SE1 8XN

Mission

244 BIBLIOGRAPHIC PRESS LTD.
10, Montague Place
Worthing
Sussex BN11 3BG

British Geological Literature

245 BICYCLE POLO ASSOCIATION OF GREAT BRITAIN
c/o 2, Crossways
Tatsfield
Westerham, Kent

Bi-Polo News

246 BILL FREEDMAN LTD.
33, Henrietta Street
London WC2

Theatre Nights

247 BILLBOARD PUBLICATIONS
7, Carnaby Street
London W1

Music Week

248 P. BILLINGSLEY
24, Riglett Crescent
London W12

Ronin

249 BIOCHEMICAL SOCIETY (PUBLICATIONS)
P.O. Box 32
Commerce Way
Whitehall Industrial Estate
Colchester, Essex

Annals of Applied Biology
Biochemical Journal

250 BIODETERIORATION INFORMATION CENTRE
University of Aston in Birmingham
80, Coleshill Street
Birmingham B47PF

Biodeterioration Research Titles
International Biodeterioration Bulletin

251 BIOMEDICAL INFORMATION PROJECT
Dept. of Physiology University
Sheffield S10 2TN

Biological Rhythms
Cell Membranes
Cyclic Amp
Enzyme Regulation
Ferritin
Intestinal Absorption and Related Topics
Nerve Cell Biology
Neurophysiology
Radioimmunoassay
Renal Physiology
Renal Transplantation and Dialysis
Ribosomes

252 JAMES BIRD
102, Finchale Green
Spennymoor
Co. Durham

Writers Journal

253 BIRD PUBLICATIONS LTD.
27, Albermarle Street
London W1X 3FA

Instant Cookery

254 BIRDS AND COUNTRY
79, Surbiton Hill Park
Surbiton, Surrey

Birds and Country

255 BIRKETT PRESS LTD.
64, Kingsway
London WC2

European Reviews

256 BIRMINGHAM AND WARWICKSHIRE ARCHAEOLO-
GICAL SOCIETY
Birmingham and Midland Institute
Margaret Street
Birmingham

Transactions of the Birmingham and Warwickshire Archaeological Society

257 BIRMINGHAM CHAMBER OF COMMERCE AND
INDUSTRY
75, Harborne Road
Edgbaston
Birmingham B15 3DH

Midlands Industry and Commerce

258 BIRMINGHAM POETRY CENTRE
Birmingham and Midland Institute
Margaret Street
Birmingham 3

Muse Magazine

259 BIRTH CONTROL CAMPAIGN
233, Tottenham Court Road
London W1P 9AE

Birth Control Campaign Bulletin

260 BITMAN
141, Westbourne Park Road
London W11 1BQ

Bitman

261 BLACK COUNTRY SOCIETY
49, Victoria Road
Tipton, Staffs

Blackcountryman

262 BLACK FLAG
10, Gilbert Place
London WC1

Black Flag

263 BLACK VOICE
31, Belgrade Road
London N16

Black Voice

264 BLACKFACE SHEEP BREEDERS' ASSOCIATION
24, Beresford Terrace
Ayr KA7 2EL

Blackface Sheep Breeders' Association
Journal

265 BLACKFRIARS PRESS PERIODICALS LTD.
P.O. Box 80
Smith Dorrien Road
Leicester

Motorists Guide to New and Used Car Prices

266 BLACKWELL SCIENTIFIC PUBLICATIONS
Osney Mead
Oxford OX2 OEL

African Journal of Medical Sciences
Anaesthesia

British Journal of Haematology
Cell and Tissue Kinetics
Clay Minerals
Clinical Allergy
Clinical and Experimental Immunology
Clinical Endocrinology
Clinical Science
East African Wildlife Journal
Freshwater Biology
Geophysical Journal of the Royal Astronomical
Society
Immunology
Journal of Animal Ecology
Journal of Applied Ecology
Journal of Biosocial Science
Journal of Ecology
Journal of Food Technology
Journal of Microscopy
Journal of Reproduction and Fertility
Journal of the Society of Cosmetic Chemists
Lichenologist
Mammal Review
Monthly Notices of the Royal Astronomical
Society
New Phytologist
Postgraduate Medical Journal
Proceedings of the Malacological Society of
London
Quarterly Journal of the Royal Astronomical
Society
Science Progress
Sedimentology
Weed Research

267 BLAKEHAM PRODUCTIONS
23, Denmark Street
London WC2H 8NA

Hi-Fi For Pleasure

268 BLANDFORD PRESS LTD.
167, High Holborn
London WC1U 6PH

Business Travel World
Catering and Hotel Management
Display International
Freight News Weekly
Glass Age
Junior Age
Pram Retailer
Shop Fitting International

269 BLUE DOG PUBLICATIONS
Basement
37, Andover Road
Winchester, Hants

Black Eggs

270 BLUE RAT
64, Constance Road
Twickenham, Middx

Blue Rat

271 D. BOADELLA
Abbotsbury
Dorset

Character and Energy

272 BODLEIAN LIBRARY
Oxford OX1 3BG

Bodleian Library Record

273 BOND STREET PUBLISHERS
124, New Bond Street
London W1A 4LJ

Writer

274 BOOK COLLECTING AND LIBRARY MONTHLY
 42, Trafalgar Street
 Brighton, Sussex

 Book Collecting and Library Monthly

275 BOOKSELLER
 152, Buckingham Palace Road
 London SW1

 Book Tokens News

276 BOOSEY AND HAWKES MUSIC PUBLISHERS LTD.
 295, Regent Street
 London W1

 Tempo

277 BORDER LIFE PUBLICATIONS LTD.
 27, Channel Street
 Galashiels
 Selkirk

 Border Life

278 BOTANICAL SOCIETY OF EDINBURGH
 Royal Botanic Garden
 Edinburgh 3

 Transactions of the Botanical Society of
 Edinburgh

279 BOTANICAL SOCIETY OF THE BRITISH ISLES
 c/o British Museum (Natural History)
 London SW7

 B.S.B.I. Abstracts
 Watsonia

280 BOUME SOCIETY
 52, Buxton Lane
 Caterham
 Surrey

 Local History Records

281 BOUVERIE PUBLISHING CO. LTD.
 2/3 Salisbury Court
 Fleet Street
 London EC4Y 8AB

 Maternal and Child Care
 Nursery World
 Probe

282 BOW PUBLICATIONS LTD.
 240, High Holborn
 London WC1

 Crossbow

283 BOWMAKER LTD.
 Bowmaker House
 Lansdowne
 Bournemouth BH1 3LG

 Bowmaker Magazine

284 BOXING WORLD
 17, Shaftesbury Avenue
 London W1

 Boxing World

285 BOYNE VALLEY PUBLISHING CO.
 30, James Street
 Drogheda
 Co. Louth

 Photoscene

286 BOY'S BRIGADE
 Brigade House
 Parson's Green
 London SW6

 Boy's Brigade Gazette

287 BRADFORD HISTORICAL AND ANTIQUARIAN
 SOCIETY
 Mechanics Institute
 Bridge Street
 Bradford 1

 Bradford Antiquary

288 H. W. BRADNICK
 22, Cross Street
 London N1

 Buttons
 Millinery and Boutique

289 BRANCH LINE SOCIETY
 18, Higher Drive
 Risley, Surrey

 Branch Line News

290 BRAND BROKERS LTD.
 P.O. 102, Normandy House
 St. Helier
 Jersey
 Channel Islands

 Trade Market

291 BRANT WRIGHT ASSOCIATES LTD.
 P.O. Box 22,
 Ashford, Kent

 Horological Journal

292 BRAZILIAN CHAMBER OF COMMERCE IN GREAT
 BRITAIN
 35 Dover Street
 London W1X 3RA

 Brazil Journal

293 BRAZILIAN EMBASSY
 Commercial Section
 15 Berkeley Street
 London W1X 5AE

 Brazilian Bulletin

294 BRETON INFORMATION BUREAU
 9 Br Cnoc Sion
 Ath Cliath 9
 Eire

 Breton News

295 BREWER'S GUILD PUBLICATIONS LTD
 8, Ely Place
 London EC1N 6SD

 Brewer

296 BREWING INDUSTRY RESEARCH FOUNDATION
 Nutfield
 Redhill
 Surrey

 Bulletin of Current Literature

297 BREWING PUBLICATIONS LTD.
 19, Briset Street
 London EC1

 Brewing Review

298 BRICK DEVELOPMENT ASSOCIATION
3-5 Bedford Row
London WC1R 4BU

Brick Bulletin

299 BRIGHTON FOLK DIARY
Brighton
Sussex

Brighton Folk Diary

300 BRISTOL AND GLOUCESTERSHIRE ARCHAEOLO-
GICAL SOCIETY
45A, Henley Grove
Henleaze
Bristol BS9 4EQ

Transactions of the Bristol and Gloucestershire Archaeological Society

301 BRISTOL & WEST BUILDING SOCIETY
P.O. Box 27
Broad Quay
Bristol BS99 7AX

Outlook

302 BRISTOL AND WEST CHURCH NEWSPAPER CO. LTD.
279, Gloucester Road
Bristol 7

New Contact

303 BRISTOL NATURALISTS SOCIETY
City Museum
Bristol 8

Proceedings of the Bristol Naturalists Society

304 BRITAIN AND ISRAEL
15, Uxbridge Street
London W8

Britain and Israel

305 BRITTAIN PRESS LTD.
Classified House
New Bridge Street
London EC4

Car Advertiser

306 BRITANNIC ASSURANCE CO. LTD.
Moor Green
Birmingham B13 8QF

Britannic Magazine

307 BRITISH ACTORS' EQUITY ASSOCIATION
(incorporating The Variety Artistes' Federation)
8, Harley Street
London W1N 2AB

Equity

308 BRITISH AGRICULTURAL AND GARDEN MACHINERY
ASSOCIATION
Penn Place
Rickmansworth
Herts

Agricultural and Garden Machinery Service

309 BRITISH AGRICULTURAL HISTORY SOCIETY
Museum of English Rural Life
The University
Whiteknights
Reading RG6 2AG

Agricultural History Review

310 BRITISH AIR MAIL SOCIETY
c/o Hon Secretary T. C. Marvin
3, Lankton Close
Beckenham
Kent BR3 2D2

Air Mail News

311 BRITISH ALUMINIUM CO. LTD.
Norfolk House
St. James's Square
London SW1

B.A. News

312 BRITISH AMERICAN ALUMNI
c/o 17 Queen's Road
Beckenham
Kent BR3 4JN

Griffin

313 BRITISH AND AMERICAN FILM HOLDINGS
Film House
142, Wardour Street
London W1V 4BR

Cinema and T.V. Today

314 BRITISH AND FOREIGN BIBLE SOCIETY
146, Queen Victoria Street
London EC4V 4BX

Word in Action

315 BRITISH AND IRISH COMMUNIST ORGANISATION
10, Athol Street
Belfast 12

Irish Communist

316 BRITISH ANTARCTIC SURVEY
30, Gillingham Street
London SW1 H1Y

British Antarctic Survey Bulletin

317 BRITISH ARACHNOLOGICAL SOCIETY
c/o Pearl Tree House
The Green
Blennerhasset
Carlisle CA5 3RE

Bulletin of the British Arachnological Society
Newsletter of the British Arachnological
Society

318 BRITISH ASSOCIATION FOR COMMERCIAL AND
INDUSTRIAL EDUCATION
16, Park Crescent
London W1N 4AP

B.A.C.I.E. Journal
B.A.C.I.E. News

319 BRITISH ASSOCIATION FOR THE ADVANCEMENT OF
SCIENCE
3, Sanctuary Buildings
20, Great Smith Street
London SW1

B.A. Record

320 BRITISH ASSOCIATION OF ACCOUNTANTS AND
AUDITORS
2/4, Chiswick High Road
London W4

Registered Accountant

321 BRITISH ASSOCIATION OF BLIND ESPERANTISTS
10, Windsor Avenue
Gatley
Cheadle
Cheshire SK8 4DU

Ĉe Ni

322 BRITISH ASSOCIATION OF COLLIERY MANAGE-
MENT
317 Nottingham Road
Basford
Nottingham

National Newsletter of the British Association
of Colliery Management

323 BRITISH ASSOCIATION OF HOTEL ACCOUNTANTS
c/o 13, Southampton Place
London WC1A 2AR

Hotel Accountant

324 BRITISH ASSOCIATION OF INDUSTRIAL EDITORS
2a, Elm Bank Gardens
London SW13

Communication

325 BRITISH ASSOCIATION OF NUMISMATIC SOCIETIES
6, Handside Close
Welwyn Garden City
Herts

Cunobelin

326 BRITISH ASSOCIATION OF ORGANISERS AND LEC-
TURERS IN PHYSICAL EDUCATION
Dept. of Physical Education
St. Pauls College
Cheltenham GL50 4AZ

Bulletin of Physical Education

327 BRITISH ASSOCIATION OF REMOVERS
279, Grays Inn Road
London WC1X 85Y

Removals and Storage

328 BRITISH ASSOCIATION OF RETIRED PERSONS
1, Albyn Place
Edinburgh EH2 4NG

British Association of Retired Persons: Members' Quarterly Bulletin

329 BRITISH ASSOCIATION OF SOCIAL WORKERS
42, Bedford Square
London WC1B 3DP

British Journal of Social Work
Parliament and Social Work
Social Work Today

330 BRITISH ASSOCIATION OF SPORT AND MEDICINE
c/o 39, Linkfield Road
Mountsorrel
Loughborough
Leics

British Journal of Sports Medicine

331 BRITISH BEER-MAT COLLECTORS SOCIETY
142, Leicester Street
Wolverhampton
Staffs WU6 0PS

Beer-mat Magazine

332 BRITISH CANAL UNION
36, St Mary's Place
Newcastle 1

Canoeing in Britain

333 BRITISH CARTOGRAPHIC SOCIETY
c/o Tamesa House
Chertsey Road
Shepperton
Middx

Cartographic Journal

334 BRITISH CAST IRON RESEARCH ASSOCIATION
Alvechurch
Birmingham B48 7QB

B.C.I.R.A. Journal
Russian Castings Production

335 BRITISH CERAMIC PLANT AND MACHINERY MANU-
FACTURERS ASSOCIATION
P.O. Box 9
Sunbury, Middx.

British Ceramic Review

336 BRITISH CERAMIC RESEARCH ASSOCIATION
Queen's Road
Penkhull
Stoke-on-Trent

In Fact

337 BRITISH CERAMIC SOCIETY
Shelton House
Stoke Road
Shelton
Stoke-on-Trent ST4 2DR

Transactions and Journal of the British Ceramic Society

338 BRITISH CHESS MAGAZINE LTD.
9, Market Street
St Leonards-on-Sea
Sussex

British Chess Magazine

339 BRITISH CHICKEN GROWERS ASSOCATION
High Holborn House
52/54, High Holborn
London WC1

British Chicken Growers Association Bulletin

340 BRITISH COKE RESEARCH ASSOCIATION
Chesterfield
Derbyshire S42 6JS

Coke Review

341 BRITISH COMPUTER SOCIETY
29 Portland Place
London W1N 4AP

Computer Bulletin
Computer Journal

342 BRITISH CORRESPONDENCE CHESS ASSOCIATION
c/o D.J. Rogers
90, Park Drive
London W3 8NB

Correspondence Chess

343 BRITISH COUNCIL
59, New Oxford Street
London WC1A 1BP

British Book News

344 BRITISH COUNCIL
Medical Department
97-99, Park Street
London WC1A 1BP

British Medical Bulletin
British Medicine

345 BRITISH COUNCIL FOR REHABILITATION OF THE
DISABLED
Tavistock House South
Tavistock Square
London WC1H 9LB

Rehabilitation

346   BRITISH DEAF AND DUMB ASSOCIATION
          3, Compton Street
          Carlisle CA1 1HU

          British Deaf News

347   BRITISH DEER SOCIETY
          c/o Deer Museum
          Low Hay Bridge
          Bouth by Ulverston
          Lancs

          Deer

348   BRITISH DENTAL ASSOCIATION
          64, Wimpole Street
          London W1M 8AL

          British Dental Journal

349   BRITISH DIRECT MAIL ADVERTISING ASSO-
       CIATION
          110, St Martins Lane
          London WC2

          British Direct Mail Advertising Association
          Newsletter

350   BRITISH DISPLAY SOCIETY
          Alderman House
          37, Soho Square
          London W1Y 5DG

          B.D.S.News

351   BRITISH DRAMA LEAGUE
          9/10, Fitzroy Square
          London W1P 6AE

          Drama

352   BRITISH EGG ASSOCIATION
          High Holborn House
          52/54, High Holborn
          London WC1

          British Egg Association Newsletter

353   BRITISH EPILEPSY ASSOCIATION
          3/6, Alfred Place
          London WC1E 7ED

          Candle

354   BRITISH ESPERANTO ASSOCIATION
          140, Holland Park Avenue
          London W11

          British Esperantist

355   BRITISH EUROPEAN AIRWAYS
          West London Air Terminal
          Cromwell Road
          London SW7

          B.E.A.Magazine

356   BRITISH EXPORT GAZETTE
          Flat 2
          1f Oval Road
          Regents Park
          London NW1

          British Export Gazette

357   BRITISH FALCONER'S CLUB
          c/o 94, High Street
          Saxilby
          Lincoln LN1 2H9

          Falconer

358   BRITISH FEDERATION OF FILM SOCIETIES
          81, Dean Street
          London

          Film

359   BRITISH FEDERATION OF MASTER PRINTERS
          11, Bedford Row
          London WC1R 4DX

          Members Circular

360   BRITISH FILM INSTITUTE
          81, Dean Street
          London W1

          Sight and Sound

361   BRITISH FIRE SERVICES ASSOCIATION
          86, London Road
          Leicester LE2 5DJ

          Journal of the British Fire Services Asso-
          ciation

362   BRITISH FLOWER INDUSTRY ASSOCIATION
          35, Wellington Street
          Covent Garden
          London WC2

          British Flower Industry Association Journal

363   BRITISH FOOD MANUFACTURING INDUSTRIES
       RESEARCH ASSOCIATION
          Randalls Road
          Leatherhead, Surrey

          B.F.M.I.R.A.Abstracts
          F.M.F.Review

364   BRITISH FRIESIAN CATTLE SOCIETY
          Scotsbridge House
          Rickmansworth
          Herts WD3 3BB

          British Friesian Journal

365   BRITISH GLIDING ASSOCIATION
          75, Victoria Street
          London SW1

          Sailplane and Gliding

366   BRITISH GO ASSOCIATION
          60, Wantage Road
          Reading, Berks RG3

          British Go Journal

367   BRITISH GOAT SOCIETY
          Rougham
          Bury St.Edmonds
          Suffolk

          British Goat Society Monthly Journal

368   BRITISH GOLF GREENKEEPERS ASSOCIATION
          Addington Court Golf Club
          Addington
          Croydon

          British Golf Greenkeepers

369   BRITISH GRASSLAND SOCIETY
          c/o Grassland Research Institute
          Horley
          Maidenhead, Berks

          Journal of the British Grassland Society

370   BRITISH GYPSUM LTD.
          Ferguson House
          15-17, Marylebone Road
          London NW1 5JE

          Newsday

371 BRITISH HARDWARE PROMOTION COUNCIL LTD.
19-21, Hatton Garden
London EC2

Homecare

372 BRITISH HEART FOUNDATION
57, Gloucester Place
London W1H 4DH

Heart

373 BRITISH HERPETOLOGICAL SOCIETY
c/o Zoological Society of London
Regents Park
London NW1

British Journal of Herpetology

374 BRITISH HOSIERY JOURNAL
53, Regent Road
Leicester

British Hosiery Journal

375 BRITISH HOTELS, RESTAURANTS AND CATERERS
ASSOCIATION
20, Upper Brook Street
London W1Y 2BN

British Hotelier and Restaurateur

376 BRITISH HYDROMECHANICS RESEARCH ASSOCI-
ATION
Cranfield
Bedford

Channel
Fluid Power Abstracts
Fluid Sealing Abstracts
Fluidics Feedback
Industrial Aerodynamics Abstracts
Pumps and Other Fluids Machinery Abstracts
Tribos

377 BRITISH INDUSTRIAL AND SCIENTIFIC FILM
ASSOCIATION
193/7, Regent Street
London W1

British National Film Catalogue

378 BRITISH INSTITUTE OF ARCHAEOLOGY AT
ANKARA
140, Cromwell Road
London SW7

Anatolian Studies

379 BRITISH INSTITUTE OF INTERNATIONAL AND
COMPARATIVE LAW
32, Furnival Street
London EC4A 1JN

International and Comparative Law Quarterly

380 BRITISH INSTITUTE OF MANAGEMENT
Management House
Parker Street
London WC2B 5PT

Management Abstracts

381 BRITISH INSTITUTE OF RADIOLOGY
32, Welbeck Street
London W1M 7PG

British Journal of Radiology

382 BRITISH INSTITUTE OF RECORDED SOUND
29, Exhibition Road
London SW7

Recorded Sound

383 BRITISH INTERNAL COMBUSTION ENGINE RE-
SEARCH INSTITUTE LTD.
111-112, Buckingham Avenue
Slough, Bucks SL1 4PH

Abstracts from Technical and Patent Publications

384 BRITISH INTERPLANETARY SOCIETY
12, Bessborough Gardens
London SW1V 2JJ

Journal of the British Interplanetary Society
Spaceflight

385 BRITISH IRIS SOCIETY
72, South Hill Part
London NW3 2SN

British Iris Society Newsletter

386 BRITISH ISRAEL WORLD FEDERATION
6, Buckingham Gate
London SW1

New Vision

387 BRITISH JAZZ SOCIETY
10, Southfield Gardens
Twickenham, Middx

Jazz Times

388 BRITISH JEWELLERY AND GIFTWARE FEDERA-
TION LTD.
St. Dunston's House
Casey Lane
London EC2

Britannia
British Jeweller and Watch Buyer
Buyers Guide

389 BRITISH JOINT CORROSION GROUP
14, Belgrave Square
London SW1X 8PS

British Corrosion Journal

390 BRITISH KINEMATOGRAPHY SOUND AND TELE-
VISION SOCIETY
40A, Chagford Street
London NW1

British Kinematography Sound and Television

391 BRITISH LANDRACE PIG SOCIETY
18, Yorkersgate
Malton
Yorkshire YO17 0AL

British Landrace Pig Journal

392 BRITISH LAWN TENNIS LTD.
'Lowlands'
Wenhaston, Suffolk IP19 9DY

Lawn Tennis

393 BRITISH LEATHER MANUFACTURERS RESEARCH
ASSOCIATION
Milton Park
Egham, Surrey TW20 9UQ

B.L.M.R.A. Journal

394 BRITISH LEYLAND MOTOR CORPORATION LTD.
P.O. Box 33
Coventry CU4 9DB

High Road

395   BRITISH LICHEN SOCIETY
      c/o Dept. of Botany
      British Museum (National History)
      Cromwell Road
      London SW1 5BD

        British Lichen Society Bulletin

396   BRITISH LIGHTING INDUSTRIES LTD.
      52, Lawrence Road
      London N15

        Lighting Journal

397   BRITISH LIMBLESS EX-SERVICE MEN'S ASSOCI-
    ATION
      Frankland Moore House
      185-187, High Road
      Chadwell Heath
      Romford, Essex

        Blesmag

398   BRITISH MEDICAL ASSOCIATION
      B.M.A. House
      Tavistock Square
      London WC1H 9JR

        Annals of the Rheumatic Diseases
        Archives of Disease in Childhood
        B.M.A. News
        British Heart Journal
        British Journal of Industrial Medicine
        British Journal of Medical Education
        British Journal of Preventive and Social
          Medicine
        British Medical Journal
        Cardiovascular Research
        Gut
        Journal of Clinical Pathology
        Journal of Medical Genetics
        Journal of Neurology, Neurosurgery and
          Psychiatry
        Medical and Biological Illustration
        Thorax

399   BRITISH MEDICAL STUDENTS ASSOCIATION
      B.M.A. House
      Tavistock Square
      London WC1

        Scope

400   BRITISH MENSA LTD.
      13, George Street
      Wolverhampton
      Staffs.

        British Mensa Activities Bulletin

401   BRITISH MODEL SOLDIER SOCIETY
      16, Charlton Road
      Kenton
      Harrow, Middx.

        Bulletin

402   BRITISH MOTORCYCLISTS FEDERATION LTD.
      225, Coventry Road
      Ilford, Essex

        Motorcycle Rider

403   BRITISH MOUNTAINEERING COUNCIL
      26, Park Crescent
      London W1N 4EE

        Mountain Life

404   BRITISH MUSEUM
      Bloomsbury
      London WC1

        British Museum Quarterly

405   BRITISH MUSEUM
      N.R.L.S.I. (Holborn Division)
      25, Southampton Buildings
      London WC2

        Periodicals News

406   BRITISH MUSEUM
      (Natural History)
      Cromwell Road
      London SW7 5BD

        Bulletin of the British Museum (Natural
          History)
        Bulletin of the British Museum (Natural His-
          tory) Geology Series
        Bulletin of the British Museum (Natural His-
          tory) Historical Series
        Bulletin of the British Museum (Natural His-
          tory) Mineralogy Series

407   BRITISH MUSEUM SOCIETY
      6a, Bedford Square
      London WC1

        British Museum Society Bulletin

408   BRITISH MUSIC HALL SOCIETY
      1 King Henry Street
      London N16

        Call Boy

409   BRITISH MYCOLOGICAL SOCIETY
      c/o Broom's Barn Experimental Station
      Higham
      Bury St. Edmunds
      Suffolk

        Bulletin of the British Mycological Society

410   BRITISH NATIONAL BIBLIOGRAPHY
      7/9, Rathbone Street
      London W1P 2AL

        British Education Index
        See also 699

411   BRITISH NATURALISTS ASSOCIATION
      'Willowfield'
      Boyneswood Road
      Four Marks
      Alton, Hants

        Country-side

412   BRITISH NATUROPATHIC AND OSTEOPATHIC
    ASSOCIATION
      6, Netherhall Gardens
      London NW3

        British Naturopathic Journal and Osteopathic
          Review

413   BRITISH NON-FERROUS METALS RESEARCH
    ASSOCIATION
      Easton Street
      London NW1 2EU

        B.N.F. Abstracts

414   BRITISH NUMISMATIC SOCIETY
      Warburg Institute
      Woburn Square
      London WC1H CAB

        British Numismatic Journal

415   BRITISH OPTICAL ASSOCIATION
      65, Brook Street
      London W1Y 2DT

        British Journal of Physiological Optics

416   BRITISH OPTICAL ASSOCIATION AND ASSOCIATION
       OF OPTICAL PRACTITIONERS
       Ophthalmic Optician

417   BRITISH ORIENTEERING FEDERATION
       18, Doneraile Street
       London SW6 6EN

       Orienteer

418   BRITISH ORNITHOLOGISTS CLUB
       c/o 24, Creighton Avenue
       London N10

       Bulletin of the British Ornithologists Club

419   BRITISH ORTHOPTIC SOCIETY
       Tavistock House North
       Tavistock Square
       London WC1

       British Orthoptic Journal

420   BRITISH OVERSEAS AIRWAYS CORPORATION
       Air Terminal
       Victoria
       London SW1

       B.O.A.C. News

421   BRITISH OXYGEN CO. LTD.
       Hammersmith House
       Hammersmith
       London W6

       Pennant

422   BRITISH PAPER AND BOARD MAKERS ASSO-
       CIATION
       3, Plough Place
       Fetter Lane
       London EC4

       Paper Technology

423   BRITISH PARACHUTIST ASSOCIATION LTD.
       Artillery Mansions
       75, Victoria Street
       London SW1H 0HW

       Sport Parachutist

424   BRITISH PELARGONIUM AND GERANIUM SOCIETY
       129, Aylesford Avenue
       Beckenham
       Kent BR3 3RX

       Pelargonium News

425   BRITISH PHILATELIC ASSOCIATION
       446, Strand
       London WC2R 0RA

       Philately

426   BRITISH PHILLUMATIC SOCIETY
       16, Santley House
       Baylis Road
       London SE1 7RD

       B.P.S. Magazine

427   BRITISH PHYCOLOGICAL SOCIETY
       Dept. of Botany
       University
       Leeds LS2 9JT

       British Phycological Journal

428   BRITISH POST MARK SOCIETY
       42, Corrance Road
       London SW2

       British Post Mark Society Quarterly Bulletin

429   BRITISH PRINTING SOCIETY
       BM/ISPA
       Mono House
       London WC1

       Small Printer

430   BRITISH PTERIDOLOGICAL SOCIETY
       46, Sedley Rise
       Loughton, Essex

       British Fern Gazette

431   BRITISH RACING AND SPORTS CAR CLUB
       Empire House
       Chiswick High Road
       London W4 5TW

       British Racing News

432   BRITISH RECORDS ASSOCIATION
       The Charterhouse
       Charterhouse Square
       London EC1

       Archives

433   BRITISH RED CROSS SOCIETY
       9, Grosvenor Crescent
       London SW1X 7EJ

       Crosstalk
       Junior Journal

434   BRITISH RHEUMATISM AND ARTHRITIS ASSO-
       CIATION
       1, Devonshire Place
       London W1N 2BD

       B.R.A. Review

434A   BRITISH ROAD SERVICES LTD.
       Northway House
       High Road
       London N20 9ND

       Hotline

435   BRITISH SAFETY COUNCIL
       Chancellor's Road
       London W6 9RS

       Safety and Rescue

436   BRITISH SCHOOL OF ARCHAEOLOGY IN JERUSA-
       LEM
       2, Hinde Mews
       Marylebone Lane
       London W1M 5RN

       Levant

437   BRITISH SHIP RESEARCH ASSOCIATION
       Wallsend Research Station
       Wallsend, Northumberland

       Journal of Abstracts

438   BRITISH SOCIAL BIOLOGY COUNCIL
       69, Eccleston Square
       London SW1

       Biology and Human Affairs

439   BRITISH SOCIETY FOR EIGHTEENTH CENTURY
       STUDIES
       c/o Dept. of English
       University College
       Gower Street
       London WC1

       British Society for Eighteenth Century Studies
       Newsletter

440 BRITISH SOCIETY FOR MUSIC THERAPY
48, Lanchester Road
London N6 4TA

British Journal of Music Therapy

441 BRITISH SOCIETY FOR SOCIAL RESPONSIBILITY
IN SCIENCE
70, Great Russell Street
London WC1

Bulletin of the British Society for Social Responsibility in Science
Science for People

442 BRITISH SOCIETY FOR STRAIN MEASUREMENT
281, Heaton Road
Newcastle-on-Tyne NE6 5BB

Strain

443 BRITISH SOCIETY OF DOWSERS
19, High Street
Eydon
Daventry
Northants N11 6PP

Journal of the British Society of Dowsers

444 BRITISH SOCIETY OF RHEOLOGY
c/o Fuller's Earth Union Ltd.
Patteson Court
Nutfield Road
Redhill, Surrey

Bulletin of the British Society of Rheology

445 BRITISH SOCIETY OF SCIENTIFIC GLASSBLOWERS
c/o 53A, Kennel Ride
Ascot, Berks

Journal of the British Society of Scientific
Glassblowers

446 BRITISH SOVIET FRIENDSHIP SOCIETY
36, St John's Square
London EC1

British-Soviet Friendship

447 BRITISH SPELEOLOGICAL ASSOCIATION
Duke Street
Settle, Yorks

Bulletin of the British Speleological Association
Journal of the British Speleological Association
Proceedings of the British Speleological Association
Speleological Abstracts

448 BRITISH STANDARDS INSTITUTION
2, Park Street
London W1

B.S.I. News

449 BRITISH STANDARDS INSTITUTION
Maylands Avenue
Hemel Hempstead
Herts

Quarterly Bulletin

450 BRITISH STATIONERY AND OFFICE EQUIPMENT
ASSOCIATION
6 Wimpole Street
London W1

New Stationer

451 BRITISH STEEL CORPORATION
33, Grosvenor Place
London SW1

British Steel

452 BRITISH STEEL CORPORATION
Corporate Laboratories
Hoyle Street
Sheffield S3 7EY

Steel User News

453 BRITISH STEEL CORPORATION
Special Steels Division
The Mount
P.O. Box 64
Broomhill
Sheffield S10 2PZ

Special Steels Review

454 BRITISH STEELMAKER LTD.
Stamford House
Turnmill Street
London EC1

British Steelmaker

455 BRITISH SULPHUR CORPORATION LTD.
Parnell House
25, Wilton Road
London SW1V 1NH

Fertilizer International
Nitrogen
Phosphorus and Potassium
Statistical Supplement
Sulphur

456 BRITISH TAR INDUSTRY ASSOCIATION
132-135, Sloane Street
London SW1X 9BB

Road Tar

457 BRITISH TIMKEN LTD.
Duston
Northampton NN5 6UL

Timken

458 BRITISH TOURIST AUTHORITY
64, St James' Street
London SW1A 1NF

In Britain

459 BRITISH TOY MANUFACTURERS ASSOCIATION
LTD.
Regent House
89, Kingsway
London WC2B 6RS

British Toys

460 BRITISH TRUST FOR ENTOMOLOGY LTD.
41, Queen's Gate
London SW7

Entomologist

461 BRITISH TRUST FOR ORNITHOLOGY
Beech Grove
Tring, Herts

Bird Study

462 BRITISH UNIDENTIFIED FLYING OBJECT
RESEARCH ASSOCIATION
15, Freshwater Court
Crawford Street
London W1H 1HS

BUFORA Journal

463 BRITISH UNITED SHOE MACHINERY CO. LTD.
P.O. Box 88
Belgrave Road
Leicester LE4 5BX

Unison

464 BRITISH URBAN AND REGIONAL INFORMATION
SYSTEMS
County Planning Dept
Alpha House
120, Kings Road
Reading RG1 3DN
Berks

BURISA Newsletter

465 BRITISH VETERINARY ASSOCIATION
7, Mansfield Street
London W1M 0AT

Veterinary Record

466 BRITISH WATERFOWL ASSOCIATION
The High House
Epping, Essex

Waterfowl

467 BRITISH WATERWAYS BOARD
Melbury House
Melbury Terrace
London NW1 6JX

Waterways News

468 BRITISH WATERWORKS ASSOCIATION
34, Park Street
London W1

British Water Supply

469 BROMLEY OFFICE SUPPLIES AND PRINTING CO.
LTD.
39-41, East Street
Bromley, Kent

N.C.C. Members Newsletter

470 BRONTË SOCIETY
Old Parsonage
Howarth
Keighley, Yorks

Transactions of the Brontë Society

471 BROOK MOTORS LTD.
Publicity Dept
Empress Works
Huddersfield HD1 3LJ

Brook '72
Brook Magazine

472 BROOKLANDS PRESS LTD.
44, Hatton Garden
London EC1N 8AE

Diecasting and Metal Moulding
Disposables and Nonwovens
Heating, Ventilating and Air Conditioning News

473 BROWN, KNIGHT & TRUSCOTT LTD.
11-12, Bury Street
London EC3A 5AP

Local Government Chronicle

474 BROWN SON AND FERGUSON LTD.
52, Darnley Street
Glasgow G41 2SG

Nautical Magazine

475 BROWNING SOCIETY OF LONDON
c/o Prof. A. N. Kincard
29, Southmoor Road
Oxford OX2 6RF

Browning Society Notes

476 BROWN'S GEOLOGICAL INFORMATION SERVICE
LTD.
160, North Gower Street
London NW1 2ND

Brown's Geological Information Bulletin
Bulletin of the Geological Society of Great
Britain

477 BRYNMILL PUBLISHING CO. LTD.
130, Bryn Road
Brynmill
Swansea SA2 0AT

Human World

478 BUCKLEY PRESS LTD.
The Butts
Half Acre
Brentford, Middlesex

Aquarist and Pondkeeper

479 BUCKLEY PRESS LTD.
12/13, Henrietta Street
London WC2E 8LP

Post Magazine and Insurance Monitor
Reinsurance

480 BUDDHIST SOCIETY
58, Eccleston Square
London SW1V 1PH

Middle Way

481 BUILDER GROUP
4, Catherine Street
London WC2B 5JN

Building

482 BUILDING AND CONTRACT JOURNALS LTD.
32, Southwark Bridge Road
London SE1

Architect and Building News

483 BUILDING SOCIETIES INSTITUTE
Fanhams Hall
Ware, Herts

Building Societies Institute Quarterly
Building Society Affairs
Building Society Statistics

484 BUNHILL PUBLICATIONS LTD.
4, Ludgate Circus
London EC4

Abstracts on Hygiene
Aircraft Engineering
Tropical Diseases Bulletin

485 BUREAU OF HYGIENE AND TROPICAL DISEASES
Keppel Street
London WC1

Abstracts on Hygiene
Tropical Diseases Bulletin

486 BURLINGTON MAGAZINE
258-268, Grays Inn Road
London WC1

Burlington Magazine

487   BURLINGTON PUBLISHING CO. (1942) LTD.
     Cordwallis Estate
     Clivemont Road
     Maidenhead, Berks

       Dog's Life

488   BURNHAM-ON-CROUCH LOCAL HISTORY SOCIETY
     12, Granville Terrace
     Burnham-on-Crouch
     Essex

       Bulletin, Burnham-on-Crouch Local History
       Society

489   BUSINESS AND FINANCE LTD.
     P.O. Box 320,
     Botanic Road
     Glasnevin
     Dublin 9

       Business and Finance

490   BUSINESS ARCHIVES COUNCIL
     63, Queen Victoria Street
     London EC4

       Business Archives

491   BUSINESS EXPANSION LTD.
     54, The Grove
     London W5

       Advertising and Marketing

492   BUSINESS PUBLICATIONS
     Mercury House
     Waterloo Road
     London SE1

       Business Management
       Data Systems
       Dataweek
       European Journal of Marketing
       Personnel Management

493   BUTTERWORTHS
     88, Kingsway
     London WC2B 6AB

       All England Law Reports
       British Union Catalogue of Periodicals
       Combustion and Flame
       Howard Journal of Penology and Crime Pre-
         vention
       New Law Journal
       Pure and Applied Chemistry
       Tropical Agriculture

494   F. W. BYERS
     59, Gurney Court Road
     St. Albans, Herts

       Entomologists Record

494A   BYRON JOURNAL
     6, Gertrude Street
     London SW10 0JN

       Byron Journal

495   C. CZARMIKOW LTD.
     Sugar Production Brokers
     Plantation House
     Mincing Lane
     London EC3

       Confectionery and Tobacco News
       Sugar Review

496   C. F. HODGSON AND SON LTD.
     23, Pakenham Street
     London WC1

       Bulletin of the London Mathematical Society
       Journal of the London Mathematical Society

497   CIBA-GEIGY (UK) LTD.
     Plastics Division
     Duxford
     Cambs CB2 4OA

       Technical Notes

498   CADBURY SCHWEPPES LTD.
     Bournville
     Birmingham 30

       Bournville Reporter
       Cocoa Growers' Bulletin

499   CAERNARVONSHIRE COUNTY RECORD OFFICE
     County Offices
     Caernarvon

       Caernarvonshire Record
       Office Bulletin

500   CALDER AND BOYARS LTD.
     18, Brewer Street
     London W1

       Gambit

501   CAMBORNE-REDRUTH NATURAL HISTORY
     SOCIETY
     c/o 'Shang-ri-la'
     Reskadinnick
     Camborne
     Cornwall

       Journal of the Camborne-Redruth Natural His-
       tory Society

501A   CAMBORNE SCHOOL OF MINES
     Camborne
     Cornwall

       Camborne School of Mines Journal

502   CAMBRIAN ARCHAEOLOGICAL ASSOCIATION
     c/o Edleston House
     Queen's Road
     Aberystwyth
     Cards

       Archaeologia Cambrensis

503   CAMBRIDGE INSTITUTE OF EDUCATION
     Shaftesbury Road
     Cambridge

       Cambridge Journal of Education

504   CAMBRIDGE MEDICAL PUBLICATIONS LTD.
     435/437, Wellingborough Road
     Northampton NW1

       Journal of International Medical Research

505   CAMBRIDGE UNIVERSITY PRESS
     P.O. Box 92,
     London NW1

       Annals of Human Genetics
       Archaeometry
       Biological Reviews of the Cambridge Philoso-
         phical Society
       British Journal for the Philosophy of Science
       British Journal of Nutrition
       British Journal of Political Science
       British Journal of Psychology
       British Journal of Psychology, Medical Section
       British Journal of Social and Clinical Psycho-
         logy
       Cambridge Law Journal
       Camparative Studies in Society and History
       Experimental Agriculture
       Genetical Research
       Historical Journal
       International Journal of Middle East Studies
       Journal of African History

Journal of Agricultural Science
Journal of American Studies
Journal of Anatomy
Journal of Cell Science
Journal of Ecclesiastical History
Journal of Embryology and Experimental
Morphology
Journal of Experimental Biology
Journal of Fluid Mechanics
Journal of General Microbiology
Journal of General Virology
Journal of Hygiene
Journal of Latin American Studies
Journal of Linguistics
Journal of Modern African Studies
Journal of Physiology
Journal of Plasma Physics
Journal of Social Policy
Journal of the Marine Biological Association of
the United Kingdom
Journal of West African Languages
Language-Teaching Abstracts
Mariner's Mirror
Modern Asian Studies
New Testament Studies
Parasitology
Proceedings of the Cambridge Philosophical
Society
Proceedings of the Nutrition Society
Quarterly Reviews of Biophysics
Religious Studies
Scottish Journal of Theology
Shakespeare Survey
Slavonic and East European Review
Transactions of the British Bryological Society
Transactions of the British Mycological Society
Transactions of the Cambridge Bibliographical
Society

506 CAMBRIDGESHIRE AND ISLE OF ELY NATURA-
LISTS TRUST LTD.
1, Brookside
Cambridge

Nature in Cambridgeshire
Newsletter: Cambridgeshire and Isle of Ely
Naturalists Trust

507 CAMBRIDGESHIRE LIFE LTD.
2, Crown Yard
St Ives
Huntingdonshire

Cambridgeshire, Huntingdon and Peterborough
Life
Northamptonshire and Bedfordshire Life

508 CAMPAIGN FOR COMPREHENSIVE EDUCATION
123, Portland Road
London W11

Comprehensive Education

509 CAMPAIGN FOR NUCLEAR DISARMAMENT
14, Grays Inn Road
London WC1

Sanity

510 CAMPING AND SPORTS EQUIPMENT LIMITED
4, Spring Street
London W2 3RB

C.S.E. News

511 CAMPING CLUB OF GREAT BRITAIN AND IRELAND
11, Lower Grosvenor Place
London SW1

Camping and Caravanning

512 CANDOUR PUBLISHING CO.
Forest House
Liss, Hants

Candour

513 CANNING PUBLICATIONS
28, Monument Street
London EC3

Canning and Packing
Tin-Printer and Box Maker

514 CANOE-CAMPING CLUB
15, Whalley Road
Hale
Atrincham

Canoe-Camper

515 CAPE ASBESTOS CO. LTD.
114, Park Street
London W1

Cape News

516 CAR AND MOTORCYCLE DRIVERS' ASSOCIATION
LTD
110, Bridge Road
Litherland
Liverpool L21 6PU

CAMDA News

517 CARAVAN CLUB LTD.
65, South Molton Street
London W1Y 2AB

En Route

518 CARDIFF AND DISTRICT CONSUMER GROUP
c/o Chairman
7, Bryngwyn Road
Cyncoed
Cardiff

Newsletter of Cardiff and District Consumer
Group

519 CARDIFF MEDICAL SOCIETY
c/o Royal Infirmary
Cardiff

Scientific Proceedings of the Cardiff Medical
Society

520 CARDIFF NATURALISTS SOCIETY
National Museum of Wales
Cathays Park
Cardiff CF1 3NP

Cardiff Naturalists' Society Reports and
Transactions
Transactions of the Cardiff Naturalists Society

521 CARDIGANSHIRE ANTIQUARIAN SOCIETY
26, Alban Square
Aberaeron

Ceredigion

521A CAREERS RESEARCH AND ADVISORY CENTRE
Cambridge

Further Education

522 CARIBBEAN UNIVERSITIES PRESS
Ginn and Company Ltd.
18, Bedford Row
London WC1R 4EJ

Journal of Caribbean History

523 CARRIERS PUBLISHING CO. LTD.
Blenheim House
Battersea High Street
London SW11

Roads and Road Construction

524 CARSON AND COMERFORD LTD.
19-21 Tavistock Street
London WC2

Stage and Television Today

525 CASE CON
Basement
110, Lansdowne Way
London SW8

Case Con

526 CATENIAN ASSOCIATION
8, Chesham Place
London SW1

Catena

527 CATHOLIC BIBLICAL ASSOCIATION OF GREAT
BRITAIN
St. Mary's
Strawberry Hill
Twickenham
London

Scripture Bulletin

528 CATHOLIC COMMUNICATIONS INSTITUTE OF
IRELAND
Pranstown House
Booterstown Avenue
Co. Dublin

Catholic Communications Institute of Ireland
Weekley News Index
Catholic Communications Institute of Ireland
Abstract of Periodicals

529 CATHOLIC FIRESIDE LTD.
Station Road
Hinckley, Leics

Catholic Fireside

530 CATHOLIC HERALD LTD.
67, Fleet Street
London EC4

Catholic Herald

531 CATHOLIC RECORD SOCIETY
c/o 114, Mount Street
London W1

Recusant History

532 CAVE DIVING GROUP OF GREAT BRITAIN
c/o 40, Ralph Road
Bristol 7

Cave Diving Group Newsletter

533 CAVE RESEARCH GROUP
Lindum
The Homend
Ledbury
Herefordshire

Newsletter of the Cave Research Group of
Great Britain
Transactions of the Cave Research Group of
Great Britain

534 CELTIC LEAGUE
34, Gray Street
Glasgow G3 7TY

A'bhratach Ur

535 CELTIC LEAGUE
9, Br Cnoc Sion
Ath Cliath 9
Eire

Celtic News

536 CEMENT AND CONCRETE ASSOCIATION
52, Grosvenor Gardens
London SW1W 0AQ

Cement Technology
Concrete
Magazine of Concrete Research
Precast Concrete

537 CENTRAL ASIAN RESEARCH CENTRE
16, Parkfield Street
London N1 0PR

U.S.S.R. and Third World

538 CENTRAL COUNCIL FOR BRITISH NATURISM
Sheepcote
Orpington
Kent BR5 4ET

British Naturism

539 CENTRAL COUNCIL FOR THE DISABLED
34, Eccleston Square
London SW1

C.C.D. Bulletin

540 CENTRAL COUNCIL OF CHURCH BELL RINGERS
c/o Seven Corners Press Ltd.
Onslow Street
Guildford, Surrey

Ringing World

541 CENTRAL COUNCIL OF THE SCOTTISH WOMEN'S
RURAL INSTITUTES
42, Heriot Row
Edinburgh EH3 6EU

Scottish Home and Country

542 CENTRAL OFFICE OF INFORMATION
Reference Division
Hercules Road
London SE1

Economic Progress Report
Survey of Current Affairs

543 CENTRAL READER'S BOARD
Church House
Dean's Yard
Westminster
London SW1

Reader

544 CENTRE FOR BUSINESS RESEARCH
Manchester Business School
Booth Street West
Manchester M15 6PB

Centre for Business Research Newsletter

545 CENTRE FOR INFORMATION ON THE TEACHING
OF ENGLISH
Moray House College of Education
Holyrood Road
Edinburgh EH8 8AQ

Teaching English

546 CENTRE FOR SCOTTISH STUDIES
King's College
University
Aberdeen AB9 2UB

Northern Scotland

547 CERES
269a, Portobello Road
London W11

Ceres

548 CERTIFIED BAILIFF'S ASSOCIATION OF ENGLAND
AND WALES
26, Park Place
Stevenage, Herts

Bailiff Journal

549 CHAIR FRAME MANUFACTURERS ASSOCIATION
4, Sutherland Avenue
London W9

Weekly Circular

550 D. CHALONER
8, Granville Road
Cheadle Hulme
Cheshire SK8 5QL

One

551 CHANDLER PUBLICATIONS LTD.
Ivy Hatch
Sevenoaks, Kent

Agricultural and Veterinary Chemicals and
Agricultural Engineering

552 CHAPMAN
10, Spottiswoode Road
Edinburgh EN9 1BQ

Chapman

553 J. V. CHAPMAN
College of Preceptors
2/3 Bloomsbury Square
London WC1

Education Today

554 CHAPMAN AND HALL
11, New Fetter Lane
London EC4P 4EE

Histochemical Journal
Journal of Materials Science
Journal of Neurocytology
Opto-Electronics

555 CHARLES CLARKE LTD.
19/23, Boltro Road
Haywards Heath
Sussex

Welsh Pony and Cob Society Journal

556 CHARLES KNIGHT AND CO. LTD.
11-12, Bury Street
London EC3A 5AP

Knight's Industrial Reports
Local Government Studies

557 CHARRINGTON, GARDNER, LOCKET AND CO. LTD.
Tower House
40 Trinity Square
London EC3P 3AA

Charrilock

558 CHARTERED INSTITUTE OF PATENT AGENTS
Staple Inn Buildings
High Holborn
London WC1V 7PZ

CIPA

559 CHARTERED INSTITUTE OF TRANSPORT
80, Portland Place
London W1N 4DP

Chartered Institute of Transport Journal

560 CHARTERED INSURANCE INSTITUTE
20, Aldermanbury
London EC2V 7AY

Journal of the Chartered Insurance Institute

561 CHARTERED SOCIETY OF PHYSIOTHERAPY
14, Bedford Row
London WC1

Physiotherapy

562 CHARTERHOUSE GROUP LTD.
1, Paternoster Row
St. Pauls
London EC4P 4HP

Business Forecast

563 CHATER AND SCOTT LTD.
530, High Road
Chiswick
London W4

Transport Bookman

564 CHAUCER PUBLISHING CO. LTD.
Chaucer House
13-4, Cork Street
London W1A 2AF

Human Context

565 CHELSEA COLLEGE STUDENT UNION
Manresa Road
London SW3

Science Chelsea

566 CHEMICAL SOCIETY
Burlington House
London W1V 0BN

Aliphatic Alicyclic and Saturated Heterocyclic
Chemistry
Alkaloids
Amino-acids Peptides and Proteins
Annual Reports on the Progress of Chemistry
Aromatic and Heteroaromatic Chemistry
Biosynthesis
Carbohydrate Chemistry
Chemical Communications
Chemical Society Reviews
Chemical Thermodynamics
Chemistry in Britain
Dialectric and Related Molecular Processes
Education in Chemistry
Electrochemistry
Electron Spin Resonance
Electronic Structure and Magnetism of
Inorganic Compounds
Fluorocarbon and Related Chemistry
General Discussions of the Faraday Society
Index of Reviews in Organic Chemistry
Inorganic Chemistry of the Transition Ele-
ments
Inorganic Reaction Mechanisms
Journal of the Chemical Society
Journal of the Chemical Society: Dalton
Transactions
Journal of the Chemical Society: Faraday
Transactions I
Journal of the Chemical Society: Faraday
Transactions II
Journal of the Chemical Society: Perkin
Transactions I
Journal of the Chemical Society: Perkin
Transactions II

Mass Spectrometry
Nuclear Magnetic Resonance
Organic Compounds of Sulphur, Selenium and
  Tellurium
  (Specialist Periodical Reports)
Organometallic Chemistry
Organophosphorus Chemistry
  (Specialist Periodical Reports)
Photochemistry
Russian Chemical Reviews
Russian Journal of Inorganic Chemistry
Russian Journal of Physical Chemistry
Spectroscopic Properties of Inorganic and
  Organometallic Compounds
Surface and Defect Properties of Solids
Symposia of the Faraday Society
Terpenoids and Steroids

567   CHESHAM PRESS
      18, Germain Street
      Chesham, Bucks

      Cormorant

568   CHESHIRE AND NORTH WALES NEWSPAPER CO.
      LTD.
      8, Bridge Street
      Chester

      Cheshire and North Wales Deesider

569   CHESHIRE FOUNDATION FOR THE SICK
      'Greenacres'
      39, Vesey Road
      Sutton Coldfield
      Warwicks

      Cheshire Smile

570   CHESHIRE HISTORY NEWSLETTER
      c/o Watergate House
      Watergate Street
      Chester CH1 2LW

      Cheshire History Newsletter

571   CHESS PLAYER
      12, Buston Avenue
      Carlton
      Nottingham NG4 1PT

      Chess Player

572   CHEST AND HEART ASSOCIATION
      Tavistock House North
      Tavistock Square
      London WC1H 9JE

      Health Horizon
      Hope

573   CHIGWELL LOCAL HISTORY SOCIETY
      3, Parndon House
      Valley Hill
      Loughton
      Essex

      Transactions: Chigwell Local History Society

574   CHILDREN'S RIGHTS PUBLICATIONS
      24, Manor View
      London N3

      Children's Rights

575   CHINA POLICY STUDY GROUP
      62, Parliament Hill
      London NW3

      Broadsheet

576   CHRISTIAN ACTION PUBLICATIONS
      104/5, Newgate Street
      London EC1A 7AP

      Christian Action
      International Defence and Aid Fund Information
      Service Manual

577   CHRISTIAN ALLIANCE
      157 Waterloo Road
      London SE1 8UU

      Broadsheet

578   CHRISTIAN ENDEAVOUR UNION OF GREAT
      BRITAIN AND IRELAND
      31, Lampton Road
      Hounslow TW3 1JD

      Advance

579   CHRISTIAN SALVESEN LTD.
      50, East Fettes Avenue
      Edinburgh EH4 1 EQ

      Salvesen News

580   CHRISTIAN SOCIALIST MOVEMENT
      Kingsway Hall
      Kingsway
      London WC2

      Christian Socialist

581   CHRISTOPHER DAVITS LTD.
      (Llyfrau'r Dryw)
      Llandybie
      Ammanford
      Carmarthenshire

      Poetry Wales

582   CHURCH ARMY
      185, Marylebone Road
      London NW1 5QL

      Church Army Review

583   CHURCH IN WALES PRESS
      Hickman Road
      Penarth CF6 2YQ

      Y Llan

584   CHURCH IN WALES PUBLICATIONS
      8, Hickman Road
      Penarth
      Glamorgan

      Highlights
      Impact
      Welsh Churchman

585   CHURCH INFORMATION OFFICE
      Church House
      Dean's Yard
      Westminster
      London SW1P 3NZ

      Together

586   CHURCH LAD'S BRIGADE
      58, Gloucester Place
      London W1

      Brigade

587   CHURCH MISSIONARY SOCIETY
      157, Waterloo Road
      London SE1L 8UU

      CMS Magazine
      In
      Pacemaker
      Swift

588   CHURCH MUSIC ASSOCIATION OF GREAT BRITAIN
      28, Ashley Place
      London SW1

        Church Music

589   CHURCH OF ENGLAND BOARD FOR SOCIAL
RESPONSIBILITY OF THE GENERAL SYNOD
      Church House
      Dean's Yard
      Westminster
      London SW1P 3NZ

        Crucible

590   CHURCH OF ENGLAND CHILDREN'S SOCIETY
      Old Town Hall
      Kennington
      London SE11 4QD

        Gateway

591   CHURCH OF ENGLAND NEWSPAPER LTD.
      182, Fleet Street
      London EC4

        Christian Record
        Church of England Newspaper

592   CHURCH OF SCIENTOLOGY WORLD WIDE
      Saint Hill Manor
      East Grinstead
      Sussex

        Freedom

593   CHURCH OF SCOTLAND
      121, George Street
      Edinburgh EH2 4YN

        Life and Work

594   CHURCHES OF GOD IN GREAT BRITAIN AND
IRELAND
      16, Newel Road
      Ballymorey
      Co. Antrim

        Standard of Truth

595   CHURCHILL/LIVINGSTONE
      104, Gloucester Place
      London W1

        Transactions of the Ophthalmological Societies
         of the United Kingdom

596   CINEMA RISING LTD.
      12/13, Little Newport Street
      London WC2

        Cinema Rising

597   CIRCLE BOOKS
      16, Davenant Road
      Oxford OX2 8BX

        Er
        Free Form
        Informer

598   CIRCLE PUBLICATIONS LTD.
      47, Hertford Street
      London W1

        Corsetry and Underwear
        Knitwear and Stockings

599   CIRCUIT MAGAZINE
      8, Chelmsford Square
      London

        Circuit Magazine

600   CISTERCIAN ORDER
      Caldey Abbey
      Caldey Island
      Off Tenby
      Pembrokeshire

        Cistercian Studies

601   CITY MAGAZINES
      Aldwych House
      81, Aldwych
      London WC2B 4NL

        Angling
        Boxing News
        Competitors Journal and Money Matters
        Motor Cyclist Illustrated
        Trader

602   CITY MUSEUMS AND ART GALLERIES DEPT.
      Albert Square
      Dundee

        Taymag

603   CITY OF EXETER MUSEUMS AND ART GALLERY
      Devon

        Exeter Museums Bulletin

604   CITY OF LONDON PHONOGRAPH AND
GRAMOPHONE SOCIETY
      10, South Street
      Caversham
      Reading, Berks.

        Hillandale News

605   CITY MAGAZINES LTD.
      Aldwych House
      81, Aldwych
      London WC2

        Antique Dealer and Collectors Guide
        Licensed Bookmaker and Betting Office
        Proprietor

606   CITY TEMPLE
      Cowbridge Road
      Cardiff

        World Pentecost

607   CITY UNIVERSITY
      St. John Street
      London EC1V 4PB

        Quest

608   CIVIC TRUST FOR THE NORTH EAST
      34/35, Saddler Street
      Durham

        Amenity

609   CIVIC TRUST FOR THE NORTH WEST
      56, Oxford Street
      Manchester M1 6EU

        Contact

610   CIVIL SERVICE CHRISTIAN UNION
      27, Jacqueline Gardens
      Billericay, Essex

        Service

611   CIVIL SERVICE DEPARTMENT
      Management Services
      Whitehall
      London SW1A 2AZ

        O & M Bulletin

612   CIVIL SERVICE MOTORING ASSOCIATION LTD.
4, Norris Street
Haymarket
London SW1

Civil Service Motoring

613   CIVIL SERVICE UNION
17-21, Hatton Garden
London EC1

Whip

614   CLARENDON PRESS
Oxford

Eastern Churches Review

615   CLARKE AND HUNTER (LONDON) LTD.
Armour House
Bridge Street
Guildford, Surrey

Parks, Golf Courses and Sports Grounds
Swimming Pool Review

616   CLASSIFIED MEDIA LTD.
101, Hatton Garden
London EC1

Management by Objectives

617   THE CLIQUE LTD.
170, Finchley Road
London NW3

Book Market
Clique

618   CLIVE BINGLEY (JOURNALS) LTD.
16, Pembridge Road
London W11

New Library World

619   CLOTHING INSTITUTE
17/18, Henrietta Street
London WC2E 8QN

Clothing Institute Journal
Clothing Research Journal

620   CLUB AND INSTITUTE UNION LTD.
Club Union House
251/256, Upper Street
London N1

Club and Institute Journal

621   COAL TAR RESEARCH ASSOCIATION
Oxford Road
Gomersal
Cleckheaton
Yorks BD19 4HH

Coke and Chemistry U.S.S.R.
Review of Coal Tar Technology

622   COAL UTILISATION COUNCIL
19, Rochester Row
London SW1P 1LD

C.U.C. News
New Domestic Appliances

623   COATES BROS. INKS LTD.
Easton Street
London WC1X 0DP

Inklings

624   COATES GROUP OF COMPANIES
Easton Street
London WC1X 0DP

Drawdown

625   COATS PATONS LTD.
155, St. Vincent Street
Glasgow G2 5PA

News Reel

626   COBALT INFORMATION CENTRE
7 Rolls Buildings
Fetter Lane
London EC4

Cobalt

627   COBB-THORNTON PUBLISHING LTD.
60, Fleet Street
London EC4

Export Times

628   COCKBURN ASSOCIATION
41, Castle Street
Edinburgh EH2 3BG

Cockburn Association Newsletter

629   COCOA, CHOCOLATE AND CONFECTIONERY
ALLIANCE
11, Green Street
London W1Y 3RF

Alliance Journal

630   COFFEE PROMOTION COUNCIL LTD.
10, Eastcheap
London EC3

Coffee News

631   THE COLLECTOR LTD.
58, Frith Street
London W1V 6BY

Book Collector

632   COLLEGE OF EDUCATION
V.A. Dept.
Chadwick Street
Bolton BL2 1JW

Vocational Aspect of Education

633   COLLEGE OF PSYCHIC STUDIES
16, Queensberry Place
London SW7

Light

634   COLLEGE OF TEACHERS OF THE BLIND
Church Road North
Wavertree
Liverpool L15 6TQ

Teacher of the Blind

635   COLLINS AND FRENCH LTD.
45, South Street
Chichester, Sussex

Motor Industry

636   COMMERCIAL RABBIT ASSOCIATION
Tyning House
Shurdington
Cheltenham
Glos.

Quarterly Newsletter

637   COMMITTEE FOR FREEDOM IN MOZAMBIQUE,
ANGOLA AND GUINE
631, Caledonian Road
London N7

Guerrilleiro

638 COMMISSION FOR LITURGY
   Diocese of Southwark
   Archbishops House
   St. George's Road
   London SE1

   Liturgy Bulletin

639 COMMITTEE OF LONDON CLEARING BANKERS
   10, Lombard Street
   London EC3

   Monthly Statement of Balances of London
      Clearing Banks

640 COMMITTEE OF THE CAMBRIAN LAW REVIEW
   Dept. of Law
   University College, Wales,
   Aberystwyth

   Cambrian Law Review

641 COMMON BROTHERS LTD.
   Exchange Buildings
   Quayside
   Newcastle-on-Tyne NE1 3AB

   Common Crier

642 COMMON LAW REPORTS LTD.
   49, Park Lane
   London W1Y 3LB

   Eurolaw Commercial Intelligence
   European Law Digest

643 COMMONWEALTH AGRICULTURAL BUREAUX
   Farnham Royal
   Slough SL2 3BN

   Animal Breeding Abstracts
   Bulletin of Entomological Research
   Dairy Science Abstracts
   Field Crop Abstracts
   Forestry Abstracts
   Helminthological Abstracts
   Herbage Abstracts
   Horticultural Abstracts
   Index Veterinarius
   Nutrition Abstracts and Reviews
   Plant Breeding Abstracts
   Review of Applied Entomology
   Soils and Fertilizers
   Veterinary Science
   Weed Abstracts
   World Agricultural Economics and Rural
      Sociology Abstracts

644 COMMONWEALTH FORESTRY ASSOCIATION
   18, Northumberland Avenue
   London WC2

   Commonwealth Forestry Review

645 COMMONWEALTH INDUSTRIES ASSOCIATION
   6/14 Dean Farrar Street
   London SW1H 0DX

   Britain and Overseas

646 COMMONWEALTH MYCOLOGICAL INSTITUTE
   Ferry Lane
   Kew
   Richmond
   Surrey TW9 3AF

   C.M.I. Descriptions of Pathogenic Fungi and
      Bacteria
   C.M.I./A.A.B. Descriptions of Plant Viruses
   Bibliography of Systematic Mycology
   Distribution Maps of Plant Diseases
   Index of Fungi
   Review of Medical and Veterinary Mycology
   Review of Plant Pathology

647 COMMONWEALTH PARLIAMENTARY
   ASSOCIATION
   7, Old Palace Yard
   London SW1

   Parliamentarian

648 COMMONWEALTH PRODUCERS' ORGANISATION
   25, Victoria Street
   London SW1

   Commonwealth Producer

649 COMMONWEALTH SECRETARIAT
   Marlborough House
   Pall Mall
   London SW1Y 5HX

   Commonwealth Trade
   Dairy Produce
   Fruit
   Fruit Intelligence
   Grain Bulletin
   Grain Crops
   Hides and Skins Quarterly
   Industrial Fibres
   Meat
   Meat and Dairy Produce Bulletin
   Plantation Crops
   Rice Bulletin
   Tobacco Intelligence
   Tropical Products Quarterly
   Vegetable Oils and Oilseeds
   Weekly Dairy Produce Supplies
   Weekly Fruit Supplies
   Wool Intelligence

650 COMMONWEALTH SOCIETY
   18, Northumberland Avenue
   London WC2

   Commonwealth

651 COMMUNE MOVEMENT
   88, Strathmore Avenue
   Hull

   Communes

652 COMMUNICATIONS GUILD LTD.
   21, Highfield Avenue
   St. Austell
   Cornwall

   Contemporary Communications

653 COMMUNIST FEDERATION OF GREAT BRITAIN
   65, Sisters Avenue
   London SW11

   M.L.Q.

654 COMMUNITY RELATIONS COMMISSION
   10-12 Russell Square
   London WC1

   Education and Community Relations
   New Community

655 COMPOSER'S GUILD OF GREAT BRITAIN
   10, Stratford Place
   London W1N 9AE

   Composer

656 COMPUTER ARTS SOCIETY
   c/o I.C. Ltd.
   Lovelace Road
   Bracknell
   Berks

   Page

657 COMPUTER CONSULTANTS LTD.
P.O. Box 8,
Llandudno

Computer Commentary

658 COMPUTERS FOR PEOPLE
c/o 10, Mornington Crescent
London NW1

Realtime

659 COMUNN NA CANAIN ALBANNAICH
(Scottish Language Society)
27, Lyttleton
East Kilbride
Glasgow

Crann-Tara

660 CONCHOLOGICAL SOCIETY OF GREAT BRITAIN
AND IRELAND
c/o 82, Chelsea Gardens
Chelsea Bridge Road
London SW1

Conchologist's Newsletter
Journal of the Conchological Society of Great
Britain and Ireland

661 CONDÉ NAST PUBLICATIONS LTD.
Belmont Road
Chiswick
London W4

Stitchcraft

662 CONDÉ NAST PUBLICATIONS LTD.
Vogue House
Hanover Square
London W1

Brides and Setting up Home

663 CONFEDERATION OF BRITISH INDUSTRY
21, Tothill Street
London SW1

C.B.I. Education and Training Bulletin
C.B.I. Industrial Relations Bulletin
C.B.I. Industrial Trends Survey
C.B.I. Members Bulletin
C.B.I. Metrication Bulletin
C.B.I. Review
C.B.I. Smaller Firms Bulletin
Fanfare for Britain

664 CONFEDERATION OF IRISH INDUSTRY
28, Fitzwilliam Place
Dublin 2

Economic Review

665 CONNOLLY PUBLICATIONS LTD.
283, Grays Inn Road
London WC1

Irish Democrat

666 CONSERVATIVE CENTRAL OFFICE
32, Smith Square
London SW1

Focus on Local Government

667 CONSTRUCTION INDUSTRY FEDERATION
36, Morehampton Road
Dublin 4

Construction

668 CONSTRUCTION INDUSTRY INFORMATION GROUP
BCM/Box 693,
London WC1V 6XX

C.I.I.G. Bulletin

669 CONSTRUCTION INDUSTRY TRANSLATION AND
INFORMATION SERVICES
30, Baker Street
London W1M 2DS

European Civil Engineering Abstracts

670 CONSTRUCTION PUBLICATIONS LTD.
Elm House
10-16, Elm Street
London WC11 0BP

Consulting Engineer

671 CONSTRUCTION SURVEYORS INSTITUTE
Temple Chambers
Temple Avenue
London EC4

Construction Surveyor

672 CONSUMERS ASSOCIATION
14, Buckingham Street
London WC2N 6DS

Drug and Therapeutics Bulletin
Handyman Which?
Money Which?
Motoring Which
Which?

673 CONTEMPORARY REVIEW CO. LTD.
37, Union Street
London SE1

Contemporary Review

674 CONVEYANCER LTD.
P.O. Box 24,
Warrington WA5 1QT

Conveyancer News

675 CONWAY MARITIME PRESS LTD.
7, Nelson Road
Greenwich
London SE10

East Coast Digest
Model Shipwright

676 COO PRESS LTD.
19, Doughty Street
London

Creative Camera

677 COOKS/MIDLAND BANK
45, Berkeley Street
London W1A 1EB

Cooks' Continental Timetable

678 CO-OPERATIVE MARKETING SERVICES LTD.
Borough Chambers
High Street
Stockport
Cheshire

Co-operative Grocer

679 CO-OPERATIVE PRESS LTD.
418, Chester Road
Manchester M16 9HP

Co-operative Management and Marketing
Scottish Co-operator

680 CO-OPERATIVE UNION LTD.
Holyoake House
Hanover Street
Manchester M6O 0AS

Co-operative Review

681   COPE IN SCOTLAND
       Virginia House
       62, Virginia Street
       Glasgow G1 1PX

       Cope in Scotland

682   COPPER DEVELOPMENT ASSOCIATION
       Orland House
       Mutton Lane
       Potters Bar
       Herts

       Copper Abstracts

683   CORNISH METHODIST HISTORICAL ASSOCIATION
       1, Penventon Terrace
       Redruth
       Cornwall

       Journal of the Cornish Methodist Historical
       Association

684   CORNMARKET PRESS LTD.
       42/3, Conduit Street
       London W1R 0NL

       Higher Education Review

685   CORNWALL ARCHAEOLOGICAL SOCIETY
       c/o Institute of Cornish Studies
       Trevenson House
       Pool
       Redruth, Cornwall

       Cornish Archaeology

686   CORNWELL, GREENE, BERTRAM, SMITH AND CO.
       20, Kingsway
       London WC2B 6LH

       Hotel Tariff Study of Great Britain

687   CORPORATION OF LLOYD'S
       Lime Street
       London EC3M 7HA

       Lloyds List
       Lloyd's Loading List
       Lloyd's Log

688   CORPUS CHRISTI COLLEGE
       Oxford

       Pelican

689   CORRESPONDENTS WORLDWIDE LTD.
       23/25, Abbey House
       8, Victoria Street
       London SW1H 0LA

       Correspondents World Wide

690   CORY ADAMS AND MACKAY
       37, Museum Street
       London WC1

       Studio International

691   COSTUME SOCIETY
       c/o Victoria and Albert Museum
       London SW7

       Costume

692   COTTESWOLD NATURALISTS' FIELD CLUB
       'Bunch of Grapes'
       Painswick
       Glos.

       Proceedings of the Cotteswold Naturalists
       Field Club

693   COTTON RESEARCH CORPORATION
       14, Grosvenor Place
       London SW1X 7JL

       Cotton Growing Review

694   COUNCIL FOR ACADEMIC FREEDOM AND
    DEMOCRACY
       152, Camden High Street
       London NW1

       C.A.F.D. Newsletter

695   COUNCIL FOR BRITISH ARCHAEOLOGY
       8, St Andrews Place
       London NW1 4LB

       British Archaeological Abstracts

696   COUNCIL FOR NATURE
       Zoological Gardens
       Regent's Park
       London NW1 4RY

       Habitat

697   COUNCIL OF BRITISH MANUFACTURERS OF
    PETROLEUM EQUIPMENT
       118, Southwark Street
       London SE1

       Oil and Petrochemical Equipment News
       Petroleum Chemistry USSR

698   COUNCIL OF MAJOR RELIGIOUS SUPERIORS
    (SCOTLAND)
       'Bellfield'
       26, Manse Road
       Edinburgh EH12 7SP

       R.O.C. News

699   COUNCIL OF THE BRITISH NATIONAL
    BIBLIOGRAPHY LTD.
       7 & 9, Rathbone Street
       London W1P 2AL

       British Catalogue of Music
       British National Bibliography
       See also 410

700   COUNCIL OF THE HISTORIC SOCIETY OF
    LANCASHIRE AND CHESHIRE
       c/o Dr M. J. Power
       School of History
       The University
       Liverpool

       Transactions of the Historic Society of
       Lancashire and Cheshire

701   COUNCIL OF THE STOCK EXCHANGE
       14, Austin Friars
       London EC2N 2EU

       Stock Exchange Weekly Official Intelligence

702   COUNCILS AND EDUCATION PRESS LTD.
       10, Queen Anne Street
       London W1

       British Journal of Educational Technology
       Education

703   COUNTRY AND SPORTING PUBLICATIONS
       23-27, Tudor Street
       London EC4

       Sportsworld

704   COUNTRY GENTLEMEN'S ASSOCIATION
       54-62, Regent Street
       London W1

       Country Gentlemen's Magazine

705 COUNTRY LANDOWNERS ASSOCIATION
7, Swallow Street
London W1R 8EN

Country Landowner

706 COUNTY COUNCILS ASSOCIATION
66A, Eaton Square
London SW1W 9BH

County Councils Gazette

707 COUNTY KILDARE ARCHAEOLOGICAL SOCIETY
Tullig
Dublin Road
Naas

Journal of County Kildare Archaeological
Society

708 COUNTY LIBRARIES GROUP OF THE LIBRARY
ASSOCIATION
c/o Central Library
Southgate
Stevenage
Herts.

County Newsletter

709 COUNTY PRESS
County Press Buildings
Bala
N. Wales

Y Faner

710 COUTTS AND CO.
440, Strand
London WC2

Three Crowns

711 COVENTRY AND DISTRICT INFORMATION GROUP
Reference Library
Bayley Lane
Coventry

CADIG Newsletter

712 COVENTRY CHAMBER OF COMMERCE
Station Tower
Station Square
Coventry CV1 2GG

Coventry Commerce

713 COVENTRY CITY FOOTBALL CLUB
Coventry

Sky Blue

714 CRABGRASS PRODUCTIONS
7, Rugby Road
Belfast 7

Crabgrass

715 CRAFTSMEN POTTERS ASSOCIATION OF GREAT
BRITAIN
William Blake House
Marshall Street
London W1

Ceramic Review

716 CRAFTSMAN PUBLICATIONS
87, Lambs Conduit Street
London WC1N 3NA

Reinforced Plastics

717 CRAVEN POTHOLE CLUB
Castle Chambers
Millbridge
Skipton, Yorks

Journal of the Craven Pothole Club

718 CREATION GROUP LTD.
P.O. Box 320
Creation House
Botanic Road
Dublin 9

Property News

719 CREDIT RETAILER LTD.
1, Kenilworth House
Grosvenor Road
London W4 4EJ

Credit Retailer

720 CROFT PUBLISHING CO. LTD.
Unit 4,
Sewell Street Industrial Estate,
Plaistow
London E13

Resale Weekly

721 CRONER PUBLICATIONS LTD.
46/50, Coombe Road
New Malden
Surrey

Croners' Export Digest

722 CROQUET ASSOCIATION
c/o The Hurlingham Club
London SW6

Croquet Gazette

723 CROWN HOUSE PUBLICATIONS LTD.
Crown House
Morden
Surrey

Interior Design

724 CROYDON NATURAL HISTORY AND SCIENTIFIC
SOCIETY LTD.
96A, Brighton Road
South Croydon CR2 6AD

Bulletin of the Croydon Natural History and
Scientific Society
Croydon Bibliographies for Regional Survey
Proceedings of the Croydon Natural History
and Scientific Society

725 CRUISING ASSOCIATION
Chilton Court
Baker Street
London NW1

Cruising Association Bulletin

726 CUCKFIELD BAPTIST CHAPEL
4, Gander Hill
Haywards Heath
Sussex RH16 3RY

Reformation Today

727 CUMBERLAND GEOLOGICAL SOCIETY
c/o 123, High Road
Kells
Whitehaven
Cumberland

Proceedings of the Cumberland Geological
Society

728 CURRENCY JOURNALS LTD.
11, Regency Place
London SW1P 2EA

International Currency Review

729 CURZON-GRANTHAM LTD.
31, St James's Place
London SW1

Report on Spain

730 CYCLISTS' TOURING CLUB
Cotterell House
69, Meadrow
Godalming, Surrey

Cycle Touring

731 'D' TROOP
1st Glasgow Scouts
4, Victoria Circus
Glasgow G12 9LD

'D' Trooper Monthly

732 D. MACLEOD LTD.
45-49, Cowgate
Kirkintillock

Rod and Line

733 D. C. THOMSON CO. LTD.
80, Kingsway East
Dundee

Annabel

734 D. J. MURPHY (PUBLISHERS) LTD.
19, Charing Cross Road
London WC2H 0EY

Light Horse
Pony

735 DR PUBLICATIONS LTD.
103, Brigstock Road
Thornton Heath
Surrey

Water and Waste Treatment

736 DALE REYNOLDS AND CO. LTD.
121, Kingsway
London WC2

Plumbing and Heating Engineer

737 DALESMAN PUBLISHING COMPANY LTD.
Clapham
via Lancaster

Dalesman

738 A. S. DAMERY
Chesterfield House
Bloomsbury Way
London WC1

Knitting and Haberdashery Review

739 DANCE NEWS LTD.
22, Shaftesbury Avenue
London W1V 8AP

Dance News

740 DANCING PATCH PUBLICATIONS
39, Minford Gardens
West Kensington
London W14 0AP

Zero One

741 DANCING TIMES LTD.
18, Hand Court
High Holborn
London WC1

Ballroom Dancing Times
Dancing Times

742 D. DANSIE/B. HARVEY
5, King Harrey Lane
St. Albans
Herts

Auto Accessory International
Auto Accessory Retailer

743 A. DARGAS
8, Alma Terrace
London W8

Mysl Polska

744 DATA PUBLICATIONS LTD.
57, Maida Vale
London W9 1SN

Radio and Electronics Constructor

745 DAVID AND CHARLES (PUBLISHERS) LTD.
South Devon House
Newton Abbot
Devon

Astromomy and Space
History of Education
Industrial Archaeology
Maritime History
Studies in Adult Education
Textile History
Transport History

746 DAVID BROWN TRACTORS LTD.
Meltham
Huddersfield HD7 3AR

David Brown Tractor News

747 DAVID FELDMAN LTD.
102, Leinster Road
Dublin 6

D. F. Newsletter
Stamps of Ireland

748 DELIUS SOCIETY
c/o 45, Redhill Drive
Edgware, Middlesex

Delius Society Newsletter

749 DELTA
12, Hardwick Street
Cambridge CB3 9JA

Delta

750 DELTA
9, Sharrow View
Sheffield S7 1ND

Delta

751 DEMARCO GALLERY
8, Melville Crescent
Edinburgh EH3 7NB

Umbrella

752 JAMES DENNIS
61, Fore Street
Ipswich 1P4 1JL

Record Collector

753 DENTAL TECHNICIAN LTD.
203, Kings Cross Road
London WC1X 9DB

Dental Technician

754 DEPARTMENT OF EDUCATION AND SCIENCE
 Curzon Street
 London W1Y 8AA

  On Course

755 DEPARTMENT OF HEALTH AND SOCIAL
SECURITY LIBRARY
 Alexander Fleming House
 Elephant and Castle
 London SE1

  Current Literature on Community Health and
  Personal Social Services

756 DEPARTMENT OF HEALTH AND SOCIAL
SECURITY
 Ray House
 6/16, St. Andrew Street
 London EC4

  Health Trends
  Prescribers Journal

757 DEPARTMENT OF HEALTH AND SOCIAL SECURITY
 Room 010
 State House
 High Holborn
 London WC1R 4SX

  New Window

758 DEPARTMENT OF THE ENVIRONMENT
 Thames House South
 Millbank
 London SW1P 4QH

  DOE Construction

759 DEPARTMENT OF THE ENVIRONMENT
 2, Marsham Street
 London SW1P 3EB

  DOE World

760 DEPARTMENT OF TOWN PLANNING
 Oxford Polytechnic
 Gypsy Lane
 Headington
 Oxford

  Forma

761 DEPARTMENT OF TRADE AND INDUSTRY
 1, Victoria Street
 London SW1H 0ET

  Coastguard

762 DEPARTMENT OF TRADE AND INDUSTRY
 Technology Reports Centre
 Station House
 St Mary Cray
 Orpington
 Kent BR5 3RF

  R and D Abstracts

763 DEPARTMENT OF TRADE AND INDUSTRY
 Warren Springs Laboratory
 P. O. Box 20,
 Gunnels Wood Road
 Stevenage
 Herts SG1 2BX

  Air Pollution Abstracts

764 DERBYSHIRE ARCHAEOLOGICAL SOCIETY
 35, St. Mary's Gate
 Derby

  Derbyshire Archaeological Journal
  Derbyshire Miscellany

765 DERBYSHIRE COUNTRYSIDE LTD.
 Lodge Lane
 Derby DE1 3HE

  Derbyshire Life and Countryside

766 DERWENT PUBLICATIONS LTD.
 Rochdale House
 128, Theobalds Road
 London WC1X 8RP

  Patents series publications

767 DESIGN COUNCIL
 28, Haymarket
 London SW1Y 4SU

  Design

768 DEVELOPMENT CORPORATION FOR WALES
 15, Park Place
 Cardiff

  Progress Wales

769 DEVON ARCHAEOLOGICAL SOCIETY
 c/o Royal Albert Museum
 Queen Street
 Exeter

  Devon Archaeological Society Proceedings

770 DEVON BEEKEEPERS ASSOCIATION
 Woburnia
 Seaton, Devon

  Beekeeping

771 DICKENS FELLOWSHIP
 The Dickens House
 48, Doughty Street
 London WC1 2LF

  Dickensian

772 DICKENS PRESS LTD.
 161, Queen Victoria Street
 London EC4

  Playfair Cricket Monthly

773 DINERS CLUB OF GREAT BRITAIN
 214, Oxford Street
 London W1

  Signature

774 DIRECTORATE OF NAVAL AIR WARFARE
 Ministry of Defence
 c/o Wykeham Hall
 Lee-on-Solent
 Hant

  Flight Deck

775 DIRECTORATE OF OVERSEAS SURVEYS
 Kingston Road
 Tolworth, Surrey

  Survey Review

776 DISTRICT HEATING ASSOCIATION
 Derbyshire House
 St. Chad's Street
 London WC1

  District Heating Association Journal

777 DIVINE LIGHT MISSION
 3, Woodside Avenue
 London N6

  Divine Light

778 M. DOBBIE ESQ.
      8, Findhorn Avenue
      Hayes, Middx

         Streetword

779 DOG WORLD LTD.
      Press House
      Wotton Road
      Ashford, Kent

         Dog World

780 DOLMEN PRESS
      Dublin

         Journal of the Butler Society

781 DOMESTIC HEATING SOCIETY
      23, Northaw Road
      Cuffley
      Herts

         Domestic Heating and Air Conditioning

782 DOMINION PRESS
      530, Grand Buildings
      Trafalgar Square
      London WC2 N 5BR

         New Secretary

783 DOMINICAN PUBLICATIONS
      St. Saviour's
      Upper Dorset Street
      Dublin 1

         Scripture in Church

784 DOMINION PRESS LTD.
      Grand Building
      Trafalgar Square
      London WC2

         Career
         Career Scotland
         Hospital Career
         London Bride
         Public School Leaver
         School Leaver
         Which Course?

785 RAYMOND DONOVAN
      St Cuthbert's Society
      University
      Durham

         Phalanx

786 DORSET NATURAL HISTORY AND ARCHAEOLOGI-
      CAL SOCIETY
      County Museum
      High West Street
      Dorchester

         Proceedings of the Dorset Natural History
            and Archaeological Society

787 DORSET PUBLISHING CO.
      Milborne Port
      Sherborne
      Dorset

         Dorset

788 D'OYLEY CARTE OPERA TRUST LTD.
      1, Savoy Hill
      London WC2

         Savoyard

789 DRIVE PUBLICATIONS LTD.
      Berkeley Square House
      Berkeley Square
      London W1

         Drive

790 DROP FORGING RESEARCH ASSOCIATION
      Shepherd Street
      Sheffield S3 7BA

         Drop Forging Bulletin

791 DUNDEE CHAMBER OF COMMERCE
      Panmore Street
      Dundee DD1 1ED

         Dundee Chamber of Commerce Journal

792 J. DUNMAN
      27, Bedford Street
      London WC2E 9EE

         Country Standard

793 DURLANCHER PRESS
      258, Altrincham Road
      Manchester MZ2 4AA

         British Journal of Chiropody

794 E AND S HERBERT LTD.
      27, South Lambeth Road
      London SW8

         Dalton's Weekly

795 E. D. O'BRIEN ORGANISATION
      2, Old Burlington Street
      London W1X 2LH

         Zaire Africa

796 E. D. PUBLICATIONS LTD.
      120, Wigmore Street
      London W1

         Automation

797 E. D. U. GAMES (UK) LTD.
      P. O. Box 4,
      London N6 4DF

         Games and Puzzles

798 E. L. I. COMMUNICATIONS LTD.
      4A, Albany Terrace
      Regents Park
      London NW1 4DS

         Film and Society

799 E. M. G. GRAMOPHONES LTD.
      26, Soho Square
      London W1V 6BB

         The Monthly Letter E. M. G.

800 EMI CINEMAS AND LEISURE LTD.
      30/31, Golden Square
      London W1

         Film Review

801 E. R. F. LTD.
      Sun Works
      Sandbach, Cheshire

         Chassis

802 E. S. R. BRISTOL
      St. Lawrence House
      29/31, Broad Street
      Bristol BS1 2HF

         Focus

803 E. V. A. F. SECRETARIAT,
39/40, St. James's Place
London SW1

E. V. A. F. Newsletter

804 EAST ANGLIAN MAGAZINE LTD.
6, Great Colman Street
Ipswich 1P4 2AE

East Anglian Magazine

805 EAST HERTS ARCHAEOLOGICAL SOCIETY
27, West Street
Hertford

East Herts Archaeological Society Newsletter
Hertfordshire Archaeology

806 EAST KENT ROAD CAR CO. LTD.
Station Road West
Canterbury, Kent

East Kent Omnibus

807 EAST LONDON PAPERS CHARITABLE TRUST
History Dept
Queen Mary College
Mile End Road
London E1 4NS

East London Papers

808 EAST MALLING RESEARCH STATION
Maidstone
Kent

Journal of Horticultral Science

809 EAST MIDLAND ALLIED PRESS LTD.
117, Park Road
Peterborough

Angling Times
Boat News
Garden News
Motor Cycle News
Practical Photography
Tackle and Guns
Trout and Salmon
Two Wheeler Dealer

810 EAST MIDLANDS ARTS ASSOCIATION
1, Frederick Street
Loughborough
Leics LE11 3BH

Laurels

811 EAST MIDLANDS GAS BOARD
De Montfort Street
Leicester LE1 9DB

Emgas

812 EAST MIDLANDS GEOLOGICAL SOCIETY
54, Cyprus Road
Mapperley Park
Nottingham NG3 5EB

Mercian Geologist

813 EASTERN ARTS ASSOCIATION
30, Station Road
Cambridge

Eastword

814 EASTERN REGION HOSPITAL BOARD
Vernonholme
Riverside Drive
Dundee

E. R. H. B. Magazine

815 EATON/WILLIAMS PUBLICATIONS
40, Grays Inn Road
London WC1

Triton

816 ECCLES LITHO
North Church Place
Inverness

Inverness Pictorial

817 ECHIDNA EPICS CO. LTD.
307, Portobello Road
London W10

Frendz

818 ECONOMIC AGE LTD.
10 Upper Berkeley Street
London W1

Economic Age

819 ECONOMIC AND SOCIAL RESEARCH INSTITUTE
4, Burlington Road
Dublin 4

Quarterly Economic Commentary

820 ECONOMIC AND SOCIAL SCIENCE RESEARCH
ASSOCIATION
177, Vauxhall Bridge Road
London SW1

E. S. S. R. A. Magazine

821 ECONOMIC AND SOCIAL STUDIES
4, Burlington Road
Dublin 4

Economic and Social Review

822 ECONOMICS ASSOCIATION
101, Hatton Garden
London EC1

Economics

823 ECONOMIC FEATURES LTD.
84/6, Chancery Lane
London WC2A 1DL

Middle East Economic Digest

824 ECONOMIST INTELLIGENCE UNIT LTD.
Spencer House
27, St. James's Place
London SW1A 1NT

European Trends
International Tourism Quarterly
Marketing in Europe
Motor Business
Multinational Business
Paper and Packaging Bulletin
Quarterly Economic Reviews
Retail Business
Rubber Trends

825 ECONOMIST NEWSPAPER CO. LTD.
25, St. James's Street
London SW1

Economist

826 EDINBURGH MEDICAL MISSIONARY SOCIETY
12, Mayfield Terrace
Edinburgh

Healing Hand

827 EDUCATIONAL DRAMA ASSOCIATION
    Drama Centre
    Lea Street South
    Birmingham 5

      Creative Drama

828 EDUCATIONAL INTERCHANGES COUNCIL
    43, Russell Square
    London WC1B 5DG

      Youth Travels

829 EDUCATIONAL PRODUCTIONS LTD.
    27/28, Maunsel Street
    London SW1

      Know Britain

830 EDUCATIONAL PUBLICATIONS LTD.
    East Ardsley
    Wakefield

      Know Britain

831 EDUCATIONAL PUBLISHING CO.
    King Street
    Wrexham

      Teacher in Commerce

832 EDUCATIONAL PUPPETRY ASSOCIATION
    23A, Southampton Place
    London WC1A 2BP

      Puppet Post

833 EDUCATIONAL RESEARCH CENTRE
    St. Patrick's College
    Dublin 9

      Irish Journal of Education

834 EDUCATIONAL RESOURCES LTD.
    6, Hartington Road
    London W4 3UA

      Resources

835 EDWARD ROBERTS LTD.
    Cardiff

      Geology

836 K. EDWARDS
    Broadstairs
    Kent

      Uni Ropa

837 EGYPT EXPLORATION SOCIETY
    2-3, Doughty Mews
    London WC1

      Journal of Egyptian Archaeology

838 ELECTRICAL ASSOCIATION FOR WOMEN
    25, Foubert's Place
    London W1V 2AC

      Electrical Age

839 ELECTRICAL RESEARCH ASSOCIATION
    Cleeve Road
    Leatherhead, Surrey

      Electrostatics Abstracts

840 ELECTORAL REFORM SOCIETY
    6, Chancel Street
    London SE1

      Representation

841 ELECTRICAL CONTRACTORS ASSOCIATION
    55, Catherine Place
    London SW1

      E. C. A. Bulletin
      Electrical Contractor and Retailer

842 ELECTRICAL ELECTRONIC AND TELECOMMUNI-
CATIONS UNION
    Hayes Court
    West Common Road
    Hayes
    Bromley, Kent

      Contact

843 ELECTRICAL, ELECTRONICS, TELECOMMUNICA-
TIONS AND PLUMBING UNION
    Hayes Court
    West Common Road
    Bromley BR2 7AU

      Contact

844 ELECTRICAL POWER ENGINEERS ASSOCIATION
    15, Newgate Street
    London EC1

      Electrical Power Engineer

845 ELECTRICAL RESEARCH ASSOCIATION
    Cleeve Road
    Leatherhead, Surrey

      E. R. A. Abstracts

846 ELECTRIC TRANSPORT DEVELOPMENT
SOCIETY
    101, Woodwater Lane
    Exeter EX2 5NP

      News Sheet, Electric Transport Development
      Society

847 ELECTRICITY COUNCIL
    1, Charing Cross
    London SWIA 2DS

      Circuit News

848 ELECTROPHYSIOLOGICAL TECHNOLOGISTS
ASSOCIATION
    Fleming Memorial Hospital
    Newcastle-on-Tyne

      Proceedings and Journal of the Electrophysio-
      logical Technoligists Association

849 ELGIN SOCIETY
    80, Duncan Drive
    Elgin 1U30 2NA

      Elgin Society Newsletter

850 ELIM PUBLICATIONS BOARD
    P. O. Box 38
    Cheltenham
    Glos.

      The Elim Evangel

851 ELIZABETHAN
    6 Landsdown
    Stroud, Glos

      Elizabethan

852 ENCOUNTER LTD.
    25, Haymarket
    London SW1

      Encounter

853   ELLIOTT PUBLICATIONS LTD.
       9, Queen Victoria Street
       Reading RG1 1SY

         Craft Teacher News

854   EMBASSY OF REPUBLIC OF INDONESIA
       38, Grosvenor Square
       London W1

         Indonesian News

855   EMBER PRESS
       27, Brook Road
       Epping
       Essex

         Laissez Faire
         Littack

856   EMBROIDERERS GUILD
       73, Wimpole Street
       London W1M 8AX

         Embroidery

857   EMERGENCY MEDICINE
       40, Grays Inn Road
       London WC1

         Emergency Medicine

858   ENGINEER SURVEYOR'S ASSOCIATION
       4, Hall Street
       Manchester 2

         Engineer Surveyor

859   ENGINERING CHEMICAL AND MARINE PRESS
       LTD.
       33-39, Bowling Green Lane
       London EC1

         British Plastics
         Chemical Processing
         Design and Components in Engineering
         European Chemical News
         Machinery Lloyd
         Petroleum Times

860   ENGINEERING INDUSTRIES ASSOCIATION
       15, Walker Terrace
       Prince Consort Road
       Gateshead-on-Tyne 8

         Production Exchange

861   ENGINEERING INDUSTRY TRAINING BOARD
       St. Martin's House
       140, Tottenham Court Road
       London W1P 9LN

         Blueprint
         Skill

862   ENGINEERS DIGEST LTD
       120, Wigmore Street
       London W1

         Engineers Digest

863   ENGINEERS GUILD
       400/403, Abbey House
       2 Victoria Street
       London SW1

         Professional Engineer

864   J. ENGLAND
       'Houndel'
       Ounsdale Road
       Wombourne
       Wolverhampton
       Staffs

         B. A. S. R. A. Journal

865   ENGLISH FOLK DANCE AND SONG SOCIETY
       Cecil Sharp House
       2, Regents Park Road
       London NW1

         English Dance and Song
         Folk Music Journal

866   ENGLISH GOLF UNION
       12A, Denmark Street
       Wokingham
       Berks

         Golf Fixtures

867   ENGLISH GUERNSEY CATTLE SOCIETY
       Giggs Hill Green
       Thames Ditton
       Surrey

         Guernsey Breeders' Journal

868   ENGLISH PLACE-NAME SOCIETY
       University College
       Gower Street
       London WC1

         Journal of the English Place-Name Society

869   ENGLISH-SPEAKING UNION
       Dartmouth House
       37, Charles Street
       London W1X 8AB

         Concord

870   ENVIRONMENT
       17, Ridgmont Road
       Bramhall
       Cheshire

         Environment

871   ENVIRONMENTAL DESIGN GROUP, EDINBURGH
       Dept. of Town and Country Planning
       Heriot-Watt University
       39, Palmerston Place
       Edinburgh

         Zoo

872   EPWORTH PRESS/SPCK
       27, Marylebone Road
       London NW1

         Church Quarterly

873   EQUIPMENT NEWS LTD.
       35, Red Lion Square
       London WC1

         Domestic Heating News
         Lighting Equipment News

874   ERDESDUN POINES
       10, Greenhaugh Road
       South Wellfield
       Whitley Bay
       Northumberland

         Ostrich

875   ERNEST RHODES (PROMOTIONS) LTD.
       276/282, Corn Exchange
       Ferrel Street
       Manchester M4 3HF

         Waste Disposal

876   ESPERANTO TEACHERS ASSOCIATION
       87, Sebastian Avenue
       Shenfield
       Essex

         Esperanto Teacher

877 ESSAYS IN CRITICISM
    Temple House
    Brill
    Aylesbury
    Bucks

       Essays in Criticism

878 ESSEX EDUCATION COMMITTEE
    County Hall
    Chelmsford

       Essex Education

879 ESSEX NATURALISTS TRUST
    9, Bury Fields
    Felsted
    Dunmow, Essex

       Essex Naturalists Trust Bulletin

880 ESSEX SUCCULENT REVIEW
    33, Bridge Avenue
    Upminster
    Essex

       Essex Succulent Review

881 ESTATES GAZETTE LTD.
    151, Wardour Street
    London W1V 4BN

       Estate's Gazette

882 EURAP PUBLISHING CO. (LONDON) LTD.
    71, Oldhill Street
    London N16 6LX

       Continental Film Review

883 EUROMONEY PUBLICATIONS LTD.
    14, Finsbury Circus
    London EC2

       Euromoney

884 EUROMONITOR PUBLICATIONS LTD.
    125, Pall Mall
    London SW1

       Euromonitor Review
       European Marketing Data and Statistics
       Market Research/Great Britain
       Market Research/Germany/Italy/Benelux

885 EUROPEAN BAPTIST FEDERATION
    4, Southampton Row
    London WC1B 4AB

       European Baptist

886 EUROPEAN COMMUNITIES INFORMATION
SERVICE
    23, Chesham Street
    London SW1

       European Studies Teachers Series

887 EUROPEAN ECONOMIC DATA PUBLISHING CO.
LTD.
    32, St. James's Street
    London SW1A 1HR

       Common Market News Letter

888 EUROPEAN INTELLIGENCE LTD.
    Agroup House
    16, Lonsdale Gardens
    Tunbridge Wells
    Kent

       European Intelligence

889 EUROPEAN JUDAISM
    34, Upper Berkeley Street
    London W1

       European Judaism

890 EUROPEAN PHYSICAL SOCIETY
    c/o Church Gate Press
    Leicester

       Europhysics News

891 EUROPEAN PROPERTY OWNERS ASSOCIATION
    51, Brompton Road
    London SW3

       Europroperty Magazine

892 EVANGELICAL PRESBYTERIAN CHURCH
    c/o Evangelical Book Shop
    15, College Square East
    Belfast, BT1 6DD

       Evangelical Presbyterian

893 EVANS BROS LTD.
    Montague House
    Russell Square
    London WC1B 5BX

       Art and Craft in Education
       Child Education
       Child Education Quarterly
       Music Teacher
       Pictorial Education
       Pictorial Education Quarterly
       Teacher's World
       Woodworker

894 EVELEEN BLOOMFIELD ASSOCIATION LTD.
    49, Birchwood Avenue
    Sidcup
    Kent

       Housewives Today

895 EXIT
    22, Bostocks Lane
    Risley, Derbyshire

       Exit

896 EXPERTS PUBLISHERS LTD.
    124, Upton Lane
    London E7

       Prevent

897 EYE TO EYE PUBLICATIONS
    107-111, Fleet Street
    London EC4

       New Sixth

898 EYRE AND SPOTTISWOODE
    2 Serjeants Inn
    Fleet Street
    London EC4

       Glad News

899 EYRE METHUEN-A. B. P. LTD.
    39, Goodge Street
    London W1P 1FD

       Theatre Quarterly

900 F. A. PUBLICATIONS
    14, Ridgeway
    Putnoe
    Bedford

       Further Adventures

901   F. T. BUSINESS PUBLICATIONS LTD.
       (Pearson-Longman)
       388-389, Strand
       London WC2

       Professional Administration

902   FABIAN SOCIETY
       11, Dartmouth Street
       London SW1

       Industrial Relations Bulletin
       Third World
       Venture

903   FACTORY PUBLICATIONS LTD.
       780, Fleet Street
       London EC4

       Light Production Engineering

904   FACTORY PUBLICATIONS LTD.
       89, Blackfriars Road
       London SE1

       Industrial and Process Heating
       Maintenance Engineering

905   FACTORY PUBLICATIONS LTD.
       103/119, Waterloo Road
       London SE1

       Building Maintenance
       Converter

906   FACULTY OF ACTUARIES
       23, St. Andrew Square
       Edinburgh EH2 1AQ

       Transactions of the Faculty of Actuaries

907   FACULTY OF ARCHITECTS AND SURVEYORS
       68, Gloucester Place
       London W1H 3HL

       Portico

908   FACULTY OF BUILDING
       10, Manor Way
       Borehamwood
       Herts WD6 1QQ

       Faculty of Building Review

909   FACULTY PRESS
       88, Regent Street
       Cambridge

       Cytobios
       Microbios

910   FAIR ORGAN PRESERVATION SOCIETY
       65, Market Road
       Thrapston
       Northants

       Key Frame

911   FAIRPLAY PUBLICATIONS LTD.
       51, Bishopsgate
       London EC2

       Fairplay International Shipping Journal

912   MRS B. FAIRWEATHER
       Invercoe House
       Glencoe
       Argyll

       The 1745 Association and Military History
       Society Quarterly Notes

913   FAMILY PLANNING ASSOCIATION
       27/35, Mortimer Street,
       London W1A 4QW

       Family Planning

914   FANCY PRESS LTD
       'Overdale'
       55, Langham Road
       Bowdon
       Atrincham, Cheshire

       Pigeons and Pigeon World

915   FARM BUILDINGS ASSOCIATION
       The Estate Office
       Bratton
       Clovelly
       Okehampton
       Devon EX20 4LB

       Journal of the Farm Buildings Association

916   FARM BUILDINGS CENTRE
       National Agriculture Centre
       Kenilworth
       Warwickshire

       Farm Buildings Digest

917   FARM BUSINESS LTD.
       2, Church Street
       Warwick

       Euro-Farm Business

918   FARM ENGINEERING INDUSTRY PUBLICATIONS
       LTD.
       64A, Lansdowne Road
       South Woodford
       London E18

       Farm Engineering Industry

919   FARM MANAGEMENT ASSOCIATION
       National Agricultural Centre
       Kenilworth
       Warwickshire

       Farm Management

920   FARMERS' UNION OF WALES
       Llys Amaeth,
       Queens Square
       Aberystwith

       Y Tir (The Land)

921   FARMING PRESS LTD.
       Fenton House
       Wharfedale Road
       Ipswich

       Arable Farmer
       Dairy Farmer

922   FARRIER'S JOURNAL PUBLISHING CO. LTD.
       48, Spencer Place
       Leeds LS7 4BR

       Farrier's Journal

923   E. E. FARROW
       Rowan Wood
       Southwell Road
       Benfleet, Essex

       Domestic Heating Engineer

924   FAUNA PRESERVATION SOCIETY
       c/o Zoo
       Regents Park
       London NW1 4RY

       Oryx

925 **FEATHERHALL PRESS LTD.**
Featherhall Avenue
Edinburgh 22

Edinburgh Chamber of Commerce and Manufacturers Quarterly Journal

926 **FEDERATED EMPLOYERS PRESS**
82, New Cavendish Street
London W1M 8AD

Modern Plastering
National Builder

927 **FEDERATION OF BRITISH CREMATION AUTHORI-
TIES**
50, Cannon Street
London EC4N 6LA

Resurgam

928 **FEDERATION OF MERCHANT TAILORS**
19, Hanover Square
London W1R 9DA

F.M.T. News

929 **FEDERATION OF OLD CORNWALL SOCIETIES**
Pengarth
Trewirgie Hill
Redruth, Cornwall

Old Cornwall

930 **FEDERATION OF SYNAGOGUES**
64, Leman Street
London E1

Hamaor

931 **FEDERATION OF ZOOLOGICAL GARDENS OF
GREAT BRITAIN AND IRELAND**
Zoological Gardens
Regents Park
London NW1 4RY

Zoo Federation News

932 **FELINE ADVISORY BUREAU**
The Barn Cottage
Tytherington
Wotton-under-Edge
Glos

Feline Advisory Bureau News Bulletin

933 **FELLOWSHIP OF RECONCILIATION**
9, Coombe Road
New Malden
Surrey KT3 4QA

Newspeace
Reconciliation Quarterly

934 **P. FENELON**
1, Ennafort Grove
Raheny
Dublin 5

Billiard and Snooker Journal

935 **FESTINIOG RAILWAY SOCIETY**
17, Tynymaes
Festiniog
Blaenau Ffestiniog
Merioneth

Festiniog Railway Magazine

936 **FETTER LANE REVIEW**
82, Fetter Lane
London EC4

Fetter Lane Review

937 **A.B. FILBY**
Kenwards
Piltdown
Uckfield, Sussex

Bondholder's Register

938 **FILMS IN LONDON PUBLICATIONS**
59, Temple Chambers
3, Temple Avenue
London EC4Y 0ET

Films Illustrated

939 **FINANCE HOUSES ASSOCIATION**
14, Queen Anne's Gate
London SW1

Credit

940 **FINANCIAL TIMES LTD.**
388-9, Strand
London WC2R 0LT

History Today

941 **FINANCIAL TIMES LTD.**
Bracken House
Cannon Street
London EC4

Apollo
Financial Times—European Law Newsletter

942 **FINANCIAL TIMES/STOCK EXCHANGE COUNCIL**
Old Broad Street
London EC2N 1HP

Stock Exchange Journal

943 **FINESCROLL LIMITED**
De Worde House
283 Lonsdale Road
London SW13 9QW

Air Enthusiast

944 **FINISHING PUBLICATIONS LTD.**
17, Cranmer Road
Hampton Hill
Middx

Metal Finishing Abstracts
Metal Finishing Plant and Processes

945 **FIRE PROTECTION ASSOCIATION**
Aldermary House
Queen Street
London EC4N 1TJ

Fire Prevention Centre
Fire Prevention Science and Technology

946 **FIRTH-VICKERS STAINLESS STEELS LTD.**
Staybrite Works
Weedon Street
Sheffield S9 2FU

Staybrite Chronicle

947 **FISH FRIERS REVIEW LTD.**
Federation House
289, Dewsbury Road
Leeds LS11 5HW

Fish Friers Review

948 **MRS M. FISHER**
Ashton Manor
Northampton NN7 2JL

Growing Point

949 FISK PUBLISHING CO. LTD.
95a, Chancery Lane
London WC2

Mayfair

950 FISONS LTD.
Loughborough
Leics

Gen

951 FISONS LTD.
Fertilizer Division
Harvest House
Felixstowe
Suffolk IP11 7LP

Agtec

952 FIVE OWLS PRESS LTD.
Widbury
67, High Road
Wormley
Broxbourne
Herts EN10 6JJ

Children's Book Review

953 FLEET STREET LETTER LTD.
22, Fleet Street
London EC4 1JH

Fleet Street Letter

954 I. K. FLETCHER
22, Buckingham Gate
London SW1

Theatre Notebook

955 FLOUR ADVISORY BUREAU
21, Arlington Street
London SW1A 1RN

Wheat Flour Bread

956 FLOUR MILLING AND BAKING RESEARCH ASSO-
CIATION
Chorleywood
Rickmansworth
Herts WD3 SJH

Flour Milling and Baking Research Association
Abstracts
Flour Milling and Baking Research Association
Bulletin
Gazette

957 FLUIDRIVE ENGINEERING CO. LTD.
Fluidrive Works
Worton Road
Isleworth, Middx

Fluidrive News

958 FLYFISHER'S CLUB
71, Pall Mall
London SW1

Flyfisher's Journal

959 FLYING SAUCER SERVICE LTD.
21, Cecil Court
London WC2

Flying Saucer Review

960 FOCUS ON SOCIAL WORK AND SERVICE IN SCOT-
LAND
c/o 19, Claremont Crescent
Edinburgh 7

Focus on Social Work and Service in Scotland

961 FODENS LTD.
Elworth House
Elworth Works
Sandbach, Cheshire

Foden News

962 FOLKLORE SOCIETY
c/o University College
Gower Street
London WC1E 6BT

Folklore

963 FOOD TRADE REVIEW LTD.
7, Garrick Street
London WC2E 9AT

Food Trade Review

964 FOOTBALL LEAGUE LTD.
Clifton Drive South
Lytham St. Annes
FY8 1JG
Lancs

League Football

965 FORBES PUBLICATIONS LTD.
Hartree House
Queensway
London W2 4SH

Creative Needlecraft
Home Economics
Nutrition and Food Science

966 FORD MOTOR CO. LTD.
Warley
Brentwood, Essex

Ford Times

967 FORD MOTOR CO. LTD.
Public Relations Dept.
Basildon, Essex

Farm

968 FOREIGN AFFAIRS PUBLISHING CO.
139, Petersham Road
Richmond, Surrey

East-West Digest

969 FOREIGN AND COMMONWEALTH OFFICE
Eland House
Stag Place
London SW1

Overseas Challenge

970 FOREIGN BIRDS
c/o H. B. Wragg
131, Berridge Road East
Nottingham NG7 6HS

Foreign Birds

971 FOREIGN CORRESPONDENTS LTD.
58, Paddington Street
London W1

Eastern World
New Africa

972 FOREMOST PRESS LTD.
P.O. Box 1
Wirral
Cheshire

Healthy Living

973   FORENSIC PUBLISHING COMPANY
      P.O. Box 18
      Bognor Regis PO22 7AA

        Forensic Photography

974   FORENSIC PUBLISHING CO.
      9, Old Bailey
      London EC99 1AA

        Criminologist

975   FORENSIC SCIENCE SOCIETY
      107, Fenchurch Street
      London EC3M 5JB

        Journal of the Forensic Science Society

976   FORESTRY COMMISSION
      Forest Research Station
      Alice Holt Lodge
      Wrecclesham
      Farnham
      Surrey

        Forestry Commission Library Review

977   FORESTRY COMMISSION
      25, Savile Row
      London W1X 2AY

        Elm Newsletter

978   FORTH PUBLISHING GROUP
      45, Moray Place
      Edinburgh EH3 6DD

        Construction Technology
        Property Survey

979   FORTNIGHT PUBLICATIONS LTD.
      15, James Street South
      Belfast BT2 7GA

        Fortnight

980   FORUM
      2, Bramber Road
      London W14 9PB

        Forum

981   FOUNTAIN PRESS
      46, Chancery Lane
      London WC2

        Movie Maker
        Photography

982   FOWLER WRIGHT BOOKS LTD.
      Tenbury Wells
      Worcs

        Life and Worship

983   FRANCIS ANTONY LTD.
      20, East Hill
      St. Austell
      Cornwall

        Budget Price Records
        New Cassettes
        New Records

984   FRANCO-BRITISH SOCIETY
      1, Old Burlington Street
      London W1X 1LA

        Britain-France

985   FRANEY AND CO. LTD.
      Burgon Street
      London EC4

        Temple Bar

986   FRANK CASS AND CO. LTD.
      67, Great Russell Street
      London WC1B 3BT

        Adam
        African Language Review
        Business History
        Journal of Development Studies
        Journal of Imperial and Commonwealth History
        Journal of Jewish Studies
        Middle Eastern Studies

987   FREE CHURCH FEDERAL COUNCIL
      27, Tavistock Square
      London WC1N 9NN

        Free Church Chronicle

988   FREE CZECHOSLOVAK PRESS LTD.
      4, Holland Road
      London W14 8AZ

        F.C.I.—Features and News from behind the
          Iron Curtain

989   FREEDOM PRESS
      84b, Whitechapel High Street
      London E1

        Anarchy

990   FRIARY PRESS
      Dorchester

        Arboricultural Association Journal

991   FRIENDS HISTORICAL SOCIETY
      Friends House
      Euston Road
      London NW1

        Journal of the Friends Historical Society

992   FRIENDS OF CANTERBURY CATHEDRAL
      Flat 1
      8, The Precincts
      Canterbury

        Canterbury Cathedral
          Chronicle

993   FRIENDS OF COVENT GARDEN
      Royal Opera House
      London WC2

        About the House

994   FRIENDS OF THE LIBRARY
      Trinity College
      Dublin

        Long Room

995   FRIENDS PUBLICATIONS LTD.
      Drayton House
      30, Gordon Street,
      London WC1H OBQ

        Friend

996   FUDGE AND CO. LTD.
      Sardinia House
      Sardinia Street
      London WC2A 3NW

        Book Exchange
        Bookdealer

997   FUEL AND METALLURGICAL JOURNALS LTD.
      17-19 John Adam Street
      London WC2

        Colliery Guardian
        Foundry Trade Journal
        Glass
        Glass Journal

Metal Construction
Metal Finishing Journal
Metal Forming
Polymers, Paint and Colour Journal
Sheet Metal Industries
Steel Times
Water and Water Engineering
Works Engineering

998 FULL BUDDHIST TRADITION
100 Roundwood Way
Banstead
Surrey

Western Buddhist

999 FULMER RESEARCH INSTITUTE LTD.
Stoke Poges
Slough
Bucks

Fulmer Research Institute Newsletter

1000 FUR REVIEW LTD.
27, Garlick Hill
London EC4V 2BA

Fur and Leather Review

1001 FUR WEEKLY NEWS LTD.
87/93 Lambs Conduit Street
London WC1

Fur Weekly News

1002 FURNITURE HISTORY SOCIETY
c/o Victoria and Albert Museum
London SW7

Furniture History

1003 FURTHER LEFT
12, Fulham Park Road
London SW6

Further Left

1004 G. BELL AND SONS LTD.
York House
Portugal Street
London WC2A 2HC

Mathematical Gazette

1005 G. J. PALMER AND SONS LTD.
7, Portugal Street
London WC2A 2NP

Church Times

1006 GEC TELECOMMUNICATIONS LTD.
P.O. BOX 53
Telephone Works
Coventry, Warks

GEC Telecommunications

1007 GEC-MARCONI ELECTRONICS LTD.
Marconi House
Chelmsford CH1 1PL

Aerial

1008 GEC-MARCONI LTD.
Baddon Research Laboratories
West Hanningfield Road
Great Baddon
Essex

Marconi Review

1009 GKN SCREWS AND FASTOVERS LTD.
Smethwick
Warley
Worcs

Fastener News

1010 GM PUBLICATIONS
515, Finchley Road
London NW3

Quorum

1011 G. W. FOOTE AND CO. LTD.
103, Borough High Street
London SE1 1NL

Freethinker

1012 GALLOWAY CATTLE SOCIETY
Normandale
Castle-Douglas

Galloway Journal

1013 GALPIN SOCIETY
c/o Rose Cottage
Bois Lane
Chesham Bois
Amersham, Bucks

Galpin Society Journal

1014 GAME CONSERVANCY
Fordingbridge
Hants

Game Conservancy Annual Review
Bulletin of the Game Conservancy

1015 GAMEKEEPERS ASSOCIATION OF THE UK
Pentridge
Salisbury, Wilts

Gamekeepers Gazette

1016 GARAVI GUJARAT PUBLICATIONS
22 Rosoman Street
London EC1R 0NH

Garavi Gujarat

1017 GATESHEAD AND DISTRICT LOCAL HISTORY
SOCIETY
Central Library
Prince Consort Road
Gateshead NE8 4LN

Gateshead and District Local History Society
Bulletin

1018 GEE AND CO. (PUBLISHERS) LTD.
151, Strand
London WC2R 1JJ

Accountant

1019 GEE REPORT
110, Goldhurst Terrace
London NW6

Gee Report

1020 GEMMOLOGICAL ASSOCIATION OF GREAT
BRITAIN
Saint Dunstan's House
2/4, Carey Lane
London EC2V 8AB

Journal of Gemmology and Proceedings of the
Gemmological Association of Great Britain

1021 GENERAL ACCIDENT FIRE AND LIFE ASSURANCE
CORPORATION LTD.
General Buildings
Perth

Gen
Generalities
General's Review

1022 GENERAL ELECTRIC CO. LTD.
1 Stanhope Gate
London W1A 1EH

GEC Journal of Science and Technology

1023 GENERAL GRAMOPHONE PUBLICATIONS LTD.
177-179, Kenton Road
Kenton
Harrow
Middx HA3 0HA

Gramophone

1024 GENERAL PUBLICATIONS
59 Merrion Square
Dublin 2

Science

1024 GENERAL STUDIES ASSOCIATION
Longman's House
Harlow, Essex

Bulletin of the General Studies Association

1025 GEO ABSTRACTS
University of East Anglia
Norwich NOR 88C

Geo Abstracts

1026 GEOGRAPHICAL ASSOCIATION
343, Fulwood Road
Sheffield S10 3BP

Geography

1027 GEOGRAPHICAL SOCIETY OF IRELAND
University College
Dublin 4

Irish Geography

1028 GEOLOGICAL SOCIETY
Burlington House
London W1V 0JU

Memoirs of the Geological Society

1029 GEOLOGICAL SOCIETY OF GLASGOW
Geological Department
University
Glasgow W2

Proceedings of the Geological Society of
Glasgow

1030 GEOLOGISTS ASSOCIATION
(South Wales Group)
Cardiff

Welsh Geological Quarterly

1031 GEORGE BELL AND SONS LTD.
York House
Portugal Street
London WC2

Journal of the Royal Society for the Encourage-
ment of Arts, Manufactures and Commerce.
Journal of the Royal Society of Arts

1032 GEORGE L. HOWE PRESS SERVICE LTD.
85, Elmhurst Drive
Hornchurch
Essex RM11 1PB

Printing and Bookbinding Trade Review

1033 GEORGE OUTRAM AND CO. LTD.
70, Mitchell Street
Glasgow C1

Scottish Field

1034 GEORGE OUTRAM AND CO. LTD.
146, King Street
Castle Douglas
Kirkcudbright
Scotland

Climber and Rambler
Skier

1035 GERARD HOUSE (1965) LTD.
736B, Christchurch Road
Bournemouth

Grace

1036 GERRARD MANN LTD.
1-3, Astoria Parade
Streatham High Road
London Sw16 1PP

Laboratory Equipment Digest

1037 GILBERT AND SULLIVAN SOCIETY
c/o 23, Burnside
Sawbridgeworth
Herts

Gilbert and Sullivan Journal

1038 GILBERTSON AND PAGE LTD.
Tamworth Road
Hertford, Herts

Gamekeeper and Countryside

1039 GIRL ABOUT TOWN CO.
47, Victoria Street
London SW1

Girl About Town

1040 GIRL GUIDES ASSOCIATION
17-19, Buckingham Palace Road
London SW1W 0PT

Brownie
Guider
Ranger
Today's Guide

1041 GLASGOW CHAMBER OF COMMERCE
30, George Square
Glasgow G21EQ

Journal

1042 GLASGOW UNIVERSITY MEDICO-CHIRURGICAL
SOCIETY
The Union
University Avenue
Glasgow W2

Surgo

1043 GLEANER CO. LTD.
122, Shaftesbury Avenue
London W1V 8HA

Jamaican Weekly Gleaner

1044 GLOUCESTERSHIRE COMMUNITY COUNCIL
Community House
College Green
Gloucester

Local History Bulletin

1045 GLOUCESTERSHIRE SOCIETY FOR INDUSTRIAL
ARCHAEOLOGY
c/o 6/7 Montpelier Street
Cheltenham, Glos

G.S.I.A. Journal

1046 JAMES GODDARD AND MIKE SANDOW
Woodlands Lodge
Woodlands
Southampton, Hants

Cypher

1047 GOLD STAR PUBLICATIONS LTD.
Gadoline House
Godstone Road
Whyteleafe
Surrey

New Direction

1048 GOLF COURSE AND CLUBHOUSE MANAGEMENT
184, Fleet Street
London EC4

Golf Course and Clubhouse Management

1049 GOLF WORLD LTD.
South Road
Brighton

Golf Trade Journal
Golf World

1050 GOOD ELF PUBLICATIONS
c/o 18, Clairview Road
Streatham
London SW16

Croydon Separatist
Good EIF
Zerone

1051 GOODLIFFE THE MAGICIAN
Arden Forest Industrial Estate
Alcester
Warwicks

Abracadabra

1052 GOODYEAR TYRE & RUBBER CO.(G.B.) LTD.
Stafford Road
Wolverhampton

Goodyear News
Transportation News

1053 GORDON & BREACH
41/42, William 4th Street
London WC2

Afro-American Studies
Applicable Analysis
Astro-physical Letters
Bibliographies of Chemists
Chemical Engineering Communications
Collective Phenomena
Combustion Science and Technology
Comments on Astrophysics and Space Physics
Comments on Atomic and Molecular Physics
Comments on Contemporary Phychiatry
Comments on Earth Sciences: Geophysics
Comments on Plasma Physics and Controlled
Fusion
Comments on Solid State Physics
Connective Tissue Research
Crystal Lattice Defects

Early Child Development and Care
Earth and Extraterrestrial Sciences
Ecology of Food and Nutrition
Economic Selections
Environmental Biology and Medicine
Ferroelectrics
Fields and Quanta
Fundamentals of Cosmic Physics
Geophysical Fluid Dynamics
International Journal of Computer Mathematics
International Journal of Environmental Analytical Chemistry
International Journal of Environmental Studies
International Journal of Magnetism
International Journal of Neuroscience
International Journal of Non-Destructive Testing
International Journal of Polymeric Materials
International Journal of Sulfur Chemistry
International Journal of Psychology
Intra-Science Chemistry Reports
Journal of Adhesion
Journal of Colour and Appearance
Journal of Connoisseurship and Art Technology
Journal of Coordination Chemistry
Journal of Mathematical Sociology
Journal of Mechanochemistry and Cell Mobility
Journal of Non Metals
Journal of Statistical Computation and Simulation
Journal of Structural Learning
Kybernetes
Linear and Multilinear Algebra
Magnetic Resonance Review
Marine Behaviour and Physilogy
Modern Geology
Molecular Crystals and Liquid Crystals
Particle Accelerators
Philosophy Forum
Phosphorus
Physics and Chemistry of Liquids
Polymer News
Progress of Physics
Radiation Effects
Solid-Liquid Flow Abstracts
Stochastics
Texture
Thin Films
Toxicological and Environmental Chemistry
Reviews
Women's Studies

1054 GOSHEN FELLOWSHIP
c/o 4 Canberra Road
Bexleyheath
Kent DAY 5SG

Zion's Herald

1055 GOVERNMENT AND OPPOSITION LTD.
London School of Economics
Houghton Street
London WC2A 2AE

Government and Opposition

1056 GOWER PRESS
Epping
Essex

Personnel Review

1057 GRANBY PR INTERNATIONAL LTD.
c/o East Midlands Litho Ltd.
Peterborough
Northants.

Boots News

1058 PROFESSOR C.W.J.GRANGER
Dept. of Mathematics
University
Nottingham

Stock Market Research Reviews

1059 GRANITE PUBLICATIONS
29 Craigowen Road
Carrickfergus
N. Ireland

Textiles of Ireland and Linen Trade Circular

1060 GRANTA
21a Silver Street
Cambridge

Granta

1061 GRAPHIC PUBLICATIONS LTD.
47 Dawson Street
Dublin 2

Irish Motor Trader
Modern Irish Printer

1062 GREAT BRITAIN PHILATELIC SOCIETY
14 Medway Crescent
Leigh-on-Sea
Essex SS9 2UY

The G.B. Journal

1063 GREAT NORTH OF SCOTLAND RAILWAY ASSOCI-
ATION
14 Gordon Road
Bridge of Don
Aberdeen AB2 8PT

Great North Review

1064 GREAT OUSE RESTORATION SOCIETY
c/o Bedfordshire County Record Office
Bedford

Lock Gate

1065 GREAT WESTERN SOCIETY LTD.
196 Norwood Road
Southall
Middx.

Great Western Echo

1066 GREATER LONDON ARTS ASSOCIATION
27 Southampton Street
London WC2

Greater London Arts

1067 GREATER LONDON COUNCIL
GLC Bookshop
The County Hall
London SE1 7PB

Development and Materials Bulletin
Quarterly Bulletin of the Research and Intel-
ligence Unit, G.L.C.
Urban Design Bulletin

1068 GREATER LONDON COUNCIL RESEARCH LIBRARY
County Hall
London SE1 7BB

Planning and Transportation Abstracts

1069 GRESHAM PUBLISHING GROUP
1, Great James Street
London WC1

Dream

1070 GROCERS GAZETTE
1, Pudding Lane
London EC3

Grocers Gazette

1071 GROUP FOR THE STUDY OF IRISH HISTORIC
SETTLEMENT
Dept. of Geography
Queen's University
Belfast

Bulletin of the Group for the Study of Irish
Historic Settlement

1072 GROWER PUBLICATIONS LTD.
49, Doughty Street
London WC1N 2LP

The Grower

1073 GRYF LTD.
171, Battersea Church Road
London SW11

Orzel Bialy

1074 GUEST PUBLICATIONS LTD.
318, Earls Court Road
London SW5

Hotel

1075 GUIDEPOSTS ASSOCIATES INC.
Witney Press Ltd.
Marlborough Lane
Witney
Oxon. OX8 7D2

Guideposts

1076 GUILD FOR THE PROMOTION OF WELSH MUSIC
4, Southville Road
Newport
Mon

Welsh Music

1077 GUILD OF FREEMEN OF THE CITY OF LONDON
4, Dowgate Hill
London EC4

Freeman

1078 GUILD OF ST. NICHOLAS
27, Knighton Road
Leicester

Dialogue

1079 GUILD OF ST. RAPHAEL
16, Lincoln's Inn Fields
London WC2A 3ED

Chrism

1080 GUILD OF SURVEYORS
90, Camberwell Road
London SE5

Survey

1081 GUILD OF TEACHERS OF BACKWARD CHILDREN
Minster Chambers
Southwell
Notts

Guild of Teachers of Backward Children

1082 GWASG GWENFFRWD
Talwrn Glas
Afonwen
Caerwys
Flint. CH7 5UB

Fflint
Hanes Gweithwyr Cymru
Hyddgen
Llyfrau Newydd
Welsh Sociologist

1083 GYPSY COUNCIL
14, Princes Avenue
London N3

O Glaso Romano

1084 GYPSY COUNCIL
61, Blenheim Crescent
London W11

Romano Drom

1085 H.A.JOB LTD.
Raleigh Way
Hanworth
Feltham
Middx.

Book of Job

1086 H.C.I.M.A.
191, Trinity Road
London SW17 7HN

Hotel Catering and Institutional Management
Association Journal

1087 H.G.WELLS SOCIETY
125, Markgate Road
Dagenham
Essex

Journal of the H.G.Wells Society

1088 H.I.THOMPSON PRESS LTD.
2, Ellis Street
Sloane Square
London SW1

Accessory and Garage Equipment
Good Motoring

1089 H.K.LEWIS & CO.LTD.
136, Gower Street
London WC1E 6BS

British Journal of Cancer
British Journal of Experimental Pathology

1090 H.P.DREWERY (SHIPPING CONSULTANTS) LTD.
87/91, New Bond Street
London W1Y 9LA

Shipping Statistics and Economics
Shipping Studies

1091 H.R.OWEN LTD.
17, Berkeley Street
London W1

H.R.Owen Ltd.Reports

1092 H.RICHARD SIMMONS LTD.
30/31, Knightrider Street
St. Paul's Churchyard
London EC4

Games and Toys

1093 D.HACKETT
5, Plough Place
Fetter Lane
London EC4

Twentieth Century

1094 HAIGH & HOCHLAND LTD.
Precinct Centre
Oxford Road
Manchester 13

Journal of the British Society for Phenomeno-
logy

1095 HALFORD PUBLISHING CO. LTD.
Spencer Chambers
4, Market Place
Leicester

Shoe Manufacturers Monthly

1096 HALIFAX BUILDING SOCIETY
Permanent Buildings
Halifax
Yorks

Home Owner
Round the Table

1097 IAN HAMILTON
72, Westbourne Terrace
London W2

Review

1098 HAMILTON ADVERTISER
Press Buildings
Hamilton
Lanarkshire

Covenanter

1099 HAMPSHIRE FIELD CLUB
Dept. of Archaeology
University
Southampton

Hampshire Field Club Proceedings

1100 HANOVER BOOKS LTD.
61, Berners Street
London W1P 3AE

Folk Review

1101 HANOVER PRESS
4, Mill Street
London W1

Machine Tools and Tooling

1102 HANSARD SOCIETY FOR PARLIAMENTARY GOVERN-
MENT
162, Buckingham Palace Road
London SW1

Parliamentary Affairs

1103 HANSOM BOOKS
Artillery Mansions
75, Victoria Street
London SW1H OH2

Art and Artists
Books and Bookmen
Dance and Dancers
Films and Filming
Look and Listen
Music and Musicians
Plays and Players
Records and Recording
Seven Arts

1104 HARATON LTD.
31, Old Croft Road
Walton-on-the-Hill
Stafford

Railway Forum

1105 HARKER GEOLOGICAL SOCIETY
c/o Dept. of Geology
University
Hull

Journal of the Harker Geological Society

1106 HARMSWORTH PRESS LTD.
8, Stratton Street
London W1X 6AT

Field

1107 HARPER TRADE JOURNALS LTD.
South Bank House
Black Prince Road
London SE1

Solid Fuel

1108 HARPER TRADE JOURNALS LTD.
22, Cousin Lane
London EC4

Harpers Sports and Games
Wine Butler

1109 HARPER TRADE JOURNALS
Black Prince Road
London SE1

Harpers Wine and Spirit Gazette

1110 HARRIS PUBLICATIONS
16, John Adam Street
London WC2

Philatelic Magazine
Philatelic Trader

1111 J. HARRISON
28, Okehampton Road
Exeter

Suzanne

1112 CLIVE HART
Department of Literature
University of Essex
Wivenhoe Park
Colchester
Essex

A Wake Newsletter

1113 HARVEY & BLYTHE LTD.
Lloyds Bank Chambers
216, Church Road
Hove
Sussex

British Journal of Clinical Practice

1114 J. M. HARVEY
18, Cefn Road
Cardiff CF4 3HS

Balthus

1115 HATTON PRESS LTD.
69, Aldwych
London WC2

Manufacturing Optics International

1116 HAVERING CONSUMER GROUP
c/o 97, Woodfields Drive
Romford
Essex

Havering Consumer Group Magazine

1117 N. HAWKIN
Family History Society of Cheshire
89, Dalebrook Road
Sale
Cheshire

North Cheshire Family Historian

1118 HAYMARKET PUBLISHING LTD.
Gillow House
5, Winsley Street
London W1A 2HG

Autosport
Campaign
Accountancy Age
Car Finder
Computing
8mm Magazine
Flying Review International
Gardeners Chronicle/The Horticultural Trade
Journal
General Practitioner
Hi-Fi Answers
Hi-Fi Sound
Housebuyer
Investors Guardian
Lithoprinter
Marketing
Monthly Index of Medical Specialities
National Newsagent
Popular Hi-Fi
Practical Camper
Practical Caravan
S.R.L. Camera
Textile Production
Wine and Spirit Trade International

1119 HEADLAND POETRY
745, Abbeydale Road
Sheffield S7 2B9

Hallamshire & Osgoldcross Poetry Express

1120 HEADLEY BROTHERS
Invicta Works
Ashford
Kent

Bible Translator
British Journal for the History of Science
British Journal of Psychiatry
Friends Quarterly
Journal of Laryngology and Orology

1121 HEALTH & STRENGTH PUBLISHING CO. LTD.
Halton House
20/23, Holborn
London EC1

Health and Strength

1122 HEALTH EDUCATION COUNCIL
Middlesex House
Ealing Road
Wembley
Middx HAO 1HH

Health Education Journal

1123 HEALTH FOR ALL PUBLISHING CO.
3B, Bedford Park
Croydon CR9 2AT

Health for All

1124 HEALTH FROM HERBS
100, Portland Road
Worthing
Sussex

Health from Herbs

1125 HEARTS OF OAK BENEFIT SOCIETY
155, Charing Cross
London WC2

Hearts of Oak Journal

1126   HEATHCOCK PRESS LTD.
        44, Wellesby Road
        West Croydon CR9 2DY

           Audio Record Review
           Mobile Home

1127   HEATING & VENTILATING PUBLICATIONS LTD.
        103, Brigstock Road
        Thornton Heath
        Surrey

           Heating & Ventilating Review

1128   HEATING & VENTILATING RESEARCH ASSOCIATION
        Old Bracknell Lane
        Bracknell
        Berks

           H.V.R.A. Newsletter
           Thermal Abstracts

1130   W. HEFFER & SONS LTD.
        104, Hills Road
        Cambridge

           Antiquity
           Journal of the International Folk Music Council
           Medico-Legal Journal

1131   HEMSLEY & DISTRICT ARCHAEOLOGICAL SOCIETY
        c/o 22, Station Road
        Hemsley
        York

           Ryedale Historian

1132   HELY THOM LTD.
        P.O. Box 138
        Botanic Road
        Dublin 9

           Irish Law Times and Solicitors Journal

1133   HENDERSON GROUP ONE
        1, Roberts Mews
        Lowndes Place
        London SW1X 8DA

           Equine Veterinary Journal

1134   HENRY DOUBLEDAY RESEARCH ASSOCIATION
        20, Convent Lane
        Bocking
        Braintree
        Essex

           H.D.R.A. Newsletter

1135   HENRY EVAN & CO. LTD.
        53, Paddington Street
        London W1

           Journal of the British Endodontic Society

1136   HENRY GREENWOOD & CO. LTD.
        24, Wellington Street
        London WC2E 7DH

           British Journal of Photography
           Photographic Processor

1137   HENRY PUBLICATIONS LTD.
        3, Marlborough Place
        Brighton
        Sussex

           British Engineer

1138   HENRY WIGGIN & CO. LTD.
        Holmer Road
        Hereford HR4 9SL

           Wiggin Nickel Alloys

1139   H.M. EXCHEQUER
        102, George Street
        Edinburgh 2

           Edinburgh Gazette

1140   H.M. STATIONERY OFFICE
        1st Avenue House
        High Holborn
        London WC1V 6HB

           Annual Estimates of the Population of Scotland
           Annual Report of the Registrar General for
              Scotland
           London Gazette
           Population Projections
           Monthly Digest of Statistics
           Quarterly Return of the Registrar General,
              Scotland
           Registrar General's Annual Estimates of the
              Population of England and Wales and of
              Local Authority Areas
           Registrar General's Quarterly Return for
              England and Wales
           Registrar General's Statistical Review of
              England and Wales
           Registrar General's Weekly Return for England
              Wales
           Weekly Return of the Registrar General, Scot-
              land

1141   HER MAJESTY'S STATIONERY OFFICE
        P.O. Box 569
        London SE1

           Accidents
           Agriculture
           Appropriation Accounts
           Army Orders
           British Aid Statistics
           Building Science Abstracts
           Business Monitor
           Changes in Rates of Wages and Hours of Work
           Civil Judicial Statistics
           Civil Service Statistics
           Contents of Recent Economics Journals
           Department of Employment Gazette
           Economic Trends
           Employment and Productivity Gazette
           Family Expenditure Survey
           First Employment of University Graduates
           Highway Statistics
           Hospital Abstracts
           Housing and Construction Statistics
           Loans From the National Loans Fund
           Financial Statement and Budget report
           Inland Revenue Statistics
           Journal of Administration Overseas
           Kew Bulletin
           Marine Observer
           Meteorological Magazine
           N.A.A.S. Quarterly Review
           N.L.L. Review
           New Earnings Survey
           New Technology
           Overseas Geology and Mineral Resources
           Overseas Trade Statistics of the United King-
              dom
           Plant Pathology
           Plant Varieties and Seed Gazette
           Project
           Public Expenditure
           Registry of Ships
           Report of the Commissioners of H.M. Customs
              and Excise
           Report of the Commissioners of H.M. Inland
              Revenue
           Scottish Agriculture
           Supply Estimates
           Trade and Industry
           Trading Accounts and Balance Sheets

Trends in Education
Tropical Science
Water Pollution Abstracts
Weather Report

1142 H.M.S.O.
Clayton Barracks
Aldershot
Hants

Soldier

1143 HER MAJESTY'S STATIONERY OFFICE
Cardiff

Digest of Welsh Statistics

1144 HER MAJESTY'S STATIONERY OFFICE
80, Chichester Street
Belfast

Appropriation Accounts
Digest of Statistics, Northern Ireland
Northern Ireland Economic Report
Northern Ireland Education Statistics
Report on the Administration of Home Office
Services
Report on the Census of Production of Northern
Ireland
Trading and Other Accounts

1145 H.M. STATIONERY OFFICE
Bankhead Avenue
Sighthill
Edinburgh

Agricultural Statistics Scotland
Civil Judicial Statistics (Scotland)
Criminal Statistics Scotland
Health Bulletin
Housing Return for Scotland
Local Financial Return (Scotland)
Rates and Rateable Value in Scotland
Scottish Abstract of Statistics
Scottish Economic Bulletin
Scottish Fisheries Bulletin
Scottish Health Statistics
Scottish Sea Fisheries Statistical Tables

1146 HERALD PRESS
Arbroath
Claymore

1147 HERALDRY SOCIETY
28, Museum Street
London WC1A 1LH

Coat of Arms

1148 HERE NOW
22, Torquay Parade
Hebburn
Co. Durham

Here Now

1149 HEREFORD HERD BOOK SOCIETY
Hereford House
Hereford

Hereford Breed Journal

1150 HEREFORD PRESS LTD.
117, Cheyne Walk
London SW10

Air Cargo
Freeze

1151 HERTFORDSHIRE AND MIDDLESEX TRUST FOR
NATURE CONSERVATION LTD.
24, Castle Street
Hertford

Grebe

1152 HEYDEN & SON LTD.
Spectrum House
Alderton Crescent
London NW4 3XX

Journal of Thermal Analysis
OMR-Organic Magnetic Resonance
Organic Mass-Spectrometry
X-Ray Spectrometry

1153 HIBERNIA NATIONAL REVIEW LTD.
179, Pearse Street
Dublin 2

Hibernia

1154 HIGHLANDS & ISLANDS DEVELOPMENT BOARD
Bridge House
27, Bank Street
Inverness IV1 1QR

North 7

1155 HILL AND TYLER LTD.
Nottingham

Trade Partners

1156 HILL, SAMUEL & CO. LTD.
100, Wood Street
London EC2

Moorgate & Wall Street

1157 HILMARTON MANOR PRESS
Calne
Wilts

International Auction Records

1158 J. HILTON
1, Frandiwion
Glanrafon Hill
Bangor
N. Wales

Ram

1159 HIRE PURCHASE TRADE ASSOCIATION
3, Berners Street
London W1

Hire Trading

1160 HIRST, KIDD & RENNIE LTD.
172, Union Street
Oldham
Lancs

APPTO

1161 HISPANIC COUNCIL
2, Belgrave Square
London SW1

British Bulletin of Publications on Latin Ame-
rica, the West Indies, Portugal and Spain

1163 HISTORICAL ASSOCIATION
59A, Kennington Park Road
London SE11 4VH

Annual Bulletin of Historical Literature
History
History Teachers Newsletter
Teaching History

1164 HISTORICAL MODEL RAILWAY SOCIETY
c/o 81, Silvia Avenue
Hatch End
Pinner
Middx

H.M.R.S. Journal

1165 HISTORICAL SOCIETY OF THE METHODIST CHURCH
IN WALES
c/o Llys Myfyr
Pwllheli
Caern

Bathafarn

1166 HISTORICAL SOCIETY OF THE PRESBYTERIAN
CHURCH OF WALES
c/o 61, Blaenau Road
Llandybie
Carms SA18 3YT

Journal of the Historical Society of the Presy-
terian Church of Wales

1167 HISTORY OF EDUCATION SOCIETY
c/o Department of Education
University of Cambridge
17, Brookside
Cambridge CB2 1JG

History of Education Society Bulletin

1168 C. E. HODGE
The Wick
Roundwood Avenue
Hutton Mount
Brentwood
Essex

Women Speaking

1169 HODGES FIGGIS & CO. LTD.
Dublin

Hermathena

1170 HOLLAND, HANNEN & CUBITTS LTD.
1, Queen Anne's Gate
London SW1H 9BT

Cubitts Magazine

1171 MISS F. HOLMANS
57, Carter Lane
London EC4

Ethiopia Observer

1172 W. & R. HOLMES
98-100, Holm Street
Glasgow G2 6SN

Library Review

1173 HOLYWELL PRESS LTD.
9, Alfred Street
Oxford

PNEU

1174 HOME OFFICE
60, Rochester Row
London SW1

Intercom

1175 HOME OFFICE POLICE PLANNING ORGANISATION
Horseferry House
Dean Ryle Street
London SW1

Police Research Bulletin

1176 HOME OFFICE PRISON DEPT.
H.M. Borstal
Hewell Grange
Redditch
Worcs

Prison Service Journal

1177 HOME WORDS PRINTING & PUBLISHING CO. LTD.
11, Ludgate Square
London EC4M 7AY

Home Words

1178 HOMEFINDERS (1915) LTD.
199, Strand
London WC2

Homefinder
Homes Overseas

1179 HONEYWELL INFORMATION SYSTEMS LTD.
Honeywell House
Great West Road
Brentford
Middx

Honeywell Computer Journal

1180 HONOURABLE SOCIETY OF CYMM RODORION
118, Newgate Street
St. Pauls
London EC1

Transactions of the Honourable Society of
Cymm Rodorion

1181 HOOVER LTD.
Perivale
Greenford
Middx

Hoover News

1182 HORNCHURCH AND DISTRICT CHAMBER OF COM-
MERCE AND INDUSTRY
c/o 115, Victoria Road
Romford
Essex RM1 2NH

Link

1183 E. R. HORSMAN ESQ.,
Court House
Leigh Road
Eastleigh
Hants SO5 42N

Magistrate

1184 HORTICULTURAL EDUCATION ASSOCIATION
c/o The Elvy and Gibbs Partnership
11, Best Lane
Canterbury
Kent

Scientific Horticulture

1185 HOSIERY & ALLIED TRADES RESEARCH ASSOCI-
ATION
7, Gregory Boulevard
Nottingham NG7 6LD

Hosiery Abstracts

1186 HOSIERY TRADE JOURNAL LTD.
11, Millstone Lane
Leicester

Hosiery Trade Journal
Jersey Fabrics International
Knitting News

1187 HOSPITAL LIBRARIES AND HANDICAPPED
READERS GROUP
Library Association
Scottish Hospital Centre
Crewe Road South
Edinburgh EH4 2LF

Book Trolley

1188 HOSPITAL MEDICINE PUBLICATIONS LTD.
Northwood House
93-99, Goswell Road
London EC1U 7QA

British Journal of Hospital Medicine

1189 HOUSEWIVES TRUST
4th Floor
Bedford Chambers
Covent Garden
London WC2E 8HA

Insight

1190 HOUSING CENTRE TRUST
13, Suffolk Street
Pall Mall East
London SW1Y 4HG

Housing Review

1191 HOVER CLUB OF GREAT BRITAIN
128, Queen's Road
Portsmouth
Hants PO2 7NE

Hover Club News

1192 HOVERMAIL COLLECTORS' CLUB
c/o 30, Milverton Road
Winchester Hants

Hover Cover

1193 HOWEY FOUNDATION
2A, Lebanon Road
Croydon
Surrey

Epoch

1194 P. HOY
97, Holywell Street
Oxford

Fishpaste
French Notes and Queries
In Particular
Journals of Pierre Menard
Notebooks of Pierre Menard
Private Printer and Private Press

1195 HOYT METAL CO. OF LONDON LTD.
Deodar Road
Putney
London SW15 2NX

Hoyt Notched Ingot

1196 HUB PUBLICATIONS LTD.
Youlgrave
Bakewell
Derbyshire

Orbis

1197 HUBBARD COLLEGE OF SCIENTOLOGY
Saint Hill Manor
East Grinstead
Sussex

Auditor

1198 HUDSON PUBLICATIONS LTD.
300, Ashley Road
Parkstone
Poole
Dorset

Chandler and Boatbuilder

1199 HUGHES, SANDERS & HOWARD LTD.
222, Strand
London WC2

Jute and Synthetics Review
World Fibre News

1200 HUGUENOT SOCIETY OF LONDON
Barclays Bank Ltd.
1, Pall Mall East
London SW1

Proceedings of the Huguenot Society of London
Huguenot Society of London Quarto Series

1201 HULTON PUBLICATIONS LTD
Audrey House
Ely Place
London EC1

Garage and Transport Equipment
Production Equipment Digest

1202 STANLEY K. HUNTER
34, Gray Street
Glasgow
Scotland G3 7TY

Scottish Stamp News

1203 HUNTING AND SON LTD.
PO Box ITA
Milburn House
Newcastle on Tyne NE99 ITA

Hunting Fleet Magazine

1204 HUNTING GROUP LTD.
4, Dunraven Street
Park Lane
London W1Y 4HN

Hunting Group Review

1205 M C HYDE
44, The Keep
London SE3 OAF

Chemical Insight

1206 HYDE PARK SOCIALISTS
c/o 48, Gilbey Road
London SW17 0QF

Hyde Park Socialist

1207 ICI LTD.
Millbank
London SW1

ICI Magazine
Endeavour

1208 ICI LTD.
Organics Division
Hexagon House
Blackley
Manchester

Organics News

1209 ICI Fibres Ltd.
Hookstone Road
Harrogate
Yorks

Fibres Post

1210 ICI LTD.
(Agricultural Division)
PO Box 1
Billingham
Teesside TS23 1LB

Billingham Post
Modern Grassland Farming

1211 INSPEC
Institution of Electrical Engineers
Savoy Place
London WC2R OBL

Computer and Control Abstracts
Current Papers in Electrical and Electronics
Engineering
Current Papers in Physics
Current Papers on Computers and Control
Electrical and Electronics Abstracts
Physics Abstracts

1212 IPC BUILDING AND CONTRACT JOURNALS LTD.
40 Bowling Green Lane
London EC1

Architect
Building Equipment and Materials
Contract Journal
Highways Design and Construction
International Construction
Surveyor
Surveyor—Local Government Technology

1213 IPC BUSINESS PRESS
Dorset House
Stamford Street
London SE1

Flight International
International Dyer, Textile Printer, Bleacher
and Finisher
Railway Gazette

1214 IPC CONSUMER INDUSTRIES PRESS
40, Bowling Green Lane
London EC1

Carpets and Textiles
Drapery and Fashion Weekly
Food Processing Industry
Footwear Weekly
Hairdressers Journal
Laundry and Cleaning
Meat
Watchmaker, Jeweller and Silversmith

1215 IPC CONTRACT JOURNALS LTD.
Tower House
Southampton Street
London WC2E 9QX

CJ: International Guide to Used Plant and Equipment

1216 IPC ELECTRICAL-ELECTRONIC PRESS LTD.
Dorset House
Stamford Street
London SE1 9LU

Computer Weekly
Data Processing
Electrical and Radio Trading
Electrical Export Review
Electrical Review
Electrical Times
Electron
Electronics Weekly
Nuclear Engineering International
Water Power
Wireless World

1217 IPC INDUSTRIAL PRESS LTD.
33-39, Bowling Green Lane
London EC1

Cast
Engineering Production
Engineering Materials and Design
Motor Ship
Shipbuilding and Shipping Record

1218 IPC MAGAZINES LTD.
69-76, Long Acre
London WC2

Anglers Mail
Practical Boat Owner
Yachting Monthly

1219 IPC MAGAZINES LTD.
Fleetway House
Farrington Street
London EC4

Amateur Gardening
Audio
Disc
Everyday Electronics
Practical Electronics
Practical Motorist
Practical Wireless
Practical Woodworking
Television

1220 IPC MAGAZINES LTD.
Tower House
Southampton Street
London WC2E 9QX

Amateur Photographer
Country Life
Fabulous 208
Geographical Magazine
Hers
Home Sewing and Knitting
Homemaker
Homes and Gardens
Honey
Horse and Hound
Ideal Home
Look Now
Love Affair
Loving
Mirabelle
Mother
New Musical Express
19
Nova
Nursing Mirror
Petticoat
Practical Householder
Riding
True Magazine
Valentine
Woman
Woman and Home
Woman Bride and Home
Woman's Journal
Woman's Own

1221 IPC SCIENCE AND TECHNOLOGY PRESS LTD.
32, High Street
Guildford
Surrey

Applied Ergonomics
Composites
Cryogenics
Fuel
Futures
Gerontology
Iron and Steel
NDT Info
Non-Destructive Testing
Non-Ionizing Radiation
Optics Technology
Polymer
Process Technology International
Soviet Science Review
Tribology
Ultrasonics
Underwater Science and Technology Informa-
tion Bulletin
Underwater Science and Technology Journal

1222 IPC SPECIALIST AND PROFESSIONAL PRESS
161-166, Fleet Street
London EC4

Motor Cycle

1223 IPC TECHNICAL PRESS
Dorset House
Stamford Street
London SE1 9LU

Materials Handling News
Mechanical Handling
Welding and Metal Fabrication

1225 IPC TRANSPORT PRESS
Dorset House
Stamford Street
London SE1 9LU

ABC Airways
Airports International
International Boat Industry

1226 ISE PUBLICATIONS LTD.
Queensway
Royal Leamington Spa
Warwicks

Sales Engineering

1227 ITT COMPONENTS GROUP
Edinburgh Way
Harlow
Essex

Components Standards

1228 IAN ALLAN LTD.
Terminal House
Shepperton
Middx TW17 8AS

Aircraft Illustrated
Armies and Weapons
Buses
Model Railway Constructor
Modern Railways
Modern Tramway
Railway World
Trains Illustrated

1229 ICE CREAM ALLIANCE LTD.
90/94, Gray's Inn Road
London WC1

Ice Cream and Frozen Confectionery

1230 IDLER
The Old Crown
Wheatley
Oxford

Idler

1231 ILEOSTOMY ASSOCIATION OF GREAT BRITAIN AND IRELAND
149, Harley Street
London W1

IA

1232 ILFORD LTD.
Ilford
Essex

X-ray Focus

1233 ILIFFE TRANSPORT PUBLICATIONS LTD.
Dorset House
Stanford Street
London SE1

ABC Good Transport Guide
Autocar

1234 ILLUMINATING ENGINEERING SOCIETY
York House
199, Westminster Bridge Road
London SE1 7UN

Light and Lighting
Lighting Research and Technology

1235 ILLUSTRATED COUNTY MAGAZINE GROUP LTD.
The Radcliffe Press
Hogg Lane
Radcliffe on Trent
Nottingham

Illustrated Bristol News
Manchester Sketch

1236 ILLUSTRATED COUNTY MAGAZINE GROUP LTD.
19, Piccadilly
Bradford 1

Bradford Bystander

1237 ILLUSTRATED COUNTY MAGAZINE GROUP LTD.
Carr Crofts
Armley
Leeds LS12 3HA

Leeds Graphic

1238 ILLUSTRATED COUNTY MAGAZINE GROUP LTD.
22, Collegiate Crescent
Sheffield 10

Sheffield Spectator

1239 ILLUSTRATED LONDON NEWS AND SKETCH LTD.
10, Elm Street
London WC1

Illustrated London News

1240 ILLUSTRATED NEWSPAPERS LTD.
Elm House
Elm Street
London WC1

Yachting and Boating Weekly

1241 ILLUSTRATED NEWSPAPERS LTD.
49, Park Lane
London W1

Common Market Law Reports

1242 ILLUSTRATED PUBLICATIONS CO. LTD.
12-18, Paul Street
London EC2A 4JS

Mother and Baby

1243 IMPERIAL SOCIETY OF TEACHERS OF DANCING
70, Gloucester Place
London WiH 4AJ

Dance

1244 IMPERIAL TOBACCO GROUP LTD.
Imperial House
1, Grosvenor Place
London SW1X 7HB

Imperial Review

1245 IMRAY, LAURIE, NORIE AND WILSON LTD.
Wych House
St Ives
Huntingdon

Proceedings of the Cambridge Antiquarian Society

1246 IN-PLANT PRINTER LTD.
58, Parker Street
London WC2

In-Plant Printer and Art Materials Buyer

1247   IN TUNE
      150, Hope Street
      Glasgow G2 2TH

        In Tune

1248   INCA BOOKS
      36, Ashmead Road
      London SE8

        Apex One

1249   INCOMES DATA SERVICES LTD.
      140, Great Portland Street
      London W. 1.

        Incomes Data Reports
        Incomes Data Studies

1250   INCORPORATED ASSOCIATION OF ARCHITECTS
      AND SURVEYORS
      29, Belgrave Square
      London SW1

        Architect and Surveyor

1251   INCORPORATED ASSOCIATION OF ASSISTANT
      MASTERS IN SECONDARY SCHOOLS
      Gordon House
      29, Gordon Square
      London WC1H OPT

        AMA

1252   INCORPORATED ASSOCIATION OF COST AND
      INDUSTRIAL ACCOUNTANTS LTD.
      60A, Station Road
      Upminster
      Essex

        Costing

1253   INCORPORATED ASSOCIATION OF ORGANISTS
      9, Hill View
      Milton
      Stoke-on-Trent ST2 7AR

        Organists Review

1254   INCORPORATED BRITISH INSTITUTE OF CERTI-
      FIED CARPENTERS
      37, Soho Square
      London W1

        Journal of the Incorporated British Institute of
          Certified Carpenters

1255   INCORPORATED COUNCIL OF LAW REPORTING
      FOR ENGLAND AND WALES
      3, Stone Buildings
      Lincoln's Inn
      London WC2

        Law Reports
        Weekly Law Reports

1256   INCORPORATED PHONOGRAPHIC SOCIETY
      2-12, Wilson Street
      London EC1

        IPS Journal and Reporters Magazine

1257   INCORPORATED PRACTITIONERS IN RADIO AND
      ELECTRONICS LTD.
      32, Kidmore Road
      Caversham
      Reading RG4 7LU

        IPRE Review

1258   INCORPORATED SOCIETY OF VALUERS AND
      AUCTIONEERS
      3, Cadogan Gate
      London SW1

        Valuer

1259   INDCOM PUBLICATIONS LTD.
      Faversham House
      103, Brigstock Road
      Thornton Heath
      Croydon
      Surrey

        Hardware Review

1260   INDEPENDENT BROADCASTING AUTHORITY
      70, Brompton Road
      London SW3

        ITV Education
        ITV Education News

1261   INDEPENDENT MAGAZINES LTD.
      181, Queen Victoria Street
      London EC4

        Coin Collecting Weekly

1262   INDEPENDENT SCHOOLS ASSOCIATION
      49, Gordon Road
      Whitstable
      Kent

        Independent School

1263   INDEPENDENT TRADE PRESS LTD.
      Wheatsheaf House
      Carmelite Street
      London EC4

        Free Trade Review and Club Management

1264   INDIAN ASSOCIATION
      Gandhi Hall
      Brunswick Road
      Manchester M20 9QB

        Mancunian Indian

1265   INDUSTRIAL CO-PARTNERSHIP ASSOCIATION
      60, Buckingham Gate
      London SW1

        Industrial Participation

1266   INDUSTRIAL DIAMOND INFORMATION BUREAU
      7, Rolls Buildings
      Fetter Lane
      London EC4A 1HX

        Industrial Diamond Review

1267   INDUSTRIAL LOCOMOTIVE SOCIETY
      'Channings'
      Kettlewell Hill
      Woking
      Surrey

        Industrial Locomotive Society Journal

1268   INDUSTRIAL MARKETING RESEARCH ASSOCIATION
      Leomansley House
      Lichfield
      Staffs

        IMRA Journal
        Industrial Marketing Research Abstracts

1269   INDUSTRIAL NEWSPAPERS LTD.
      John Adam House
      17-19, John Adam Street
      London WC2

        Journal of the Institution of Highway
          Engineers

1270 INDUSTRIAL OPPORTUNITIES LTD.
    Homewell
    Havant
    Hants

       Product Licensing Journal and Research Disclosure
       Road Traffic Reports

1271 INDUSRTIAL PUBLICATIONS LTD.
    42, High Street
    Croydon CR0 1NA

       Building Specification

1272 INDUSTRIAL RELATIONS ENTERPRISES LTD.
    286, Kilburn High Road
    London NW6

       Industrial Relations Review and Report

1273 INDUSTRIAL RELATIONS LAW REPORTS
    286, Kilburn High Road
    London NW6

       Industrial Relations Law Reports

1274 INDUSTRIAL ROAD TRANSPORT FREIGHT TRANSPORT ASSOCIATION
    Sunley House
    Bedford Park
    Croydon
    Surrey CR9 1XU

       Freight

1275 INDUSTRIAL SOCIETY
    48, Bryanston Square
    London W1H 8AN

       Industrial Society

1276 INFORMATION FOR EDUCATION LTD.
    School of Education
    University of Liverpool
    19-23, Abercromby Square
    Liverpool

       Technical Education Abstracts

1277 INFORMATION RETRIEVAL LTD.
    1, Falconberg Court
    London W1V 5FG

       Amino Acids, Peptide and Protein Abstracts
       Aquatic Sciences and Fisheries Abstracts
       Behavioural Biology Abstracts
       Biological Membrane Abstracts
       Calcified Tissue Abstracts
       Carbohydrate Metabolism Abstracts
       Chemoreception Abstracts
       Entomology Abstracts
       Genetics Abstracts
       Microbiology Abstracts
       Nucleic Acids Abstracts
       Virology Abstracts

1278 INGERSOLL GROUP LTD.
    202, New North Road
    London N1 7BL

       Tim

1279 INKULULEKO PUBLICATIONS
    39, Goodge Street
    London W1

       African Communist

1280 INLAND REVENUE STAFF FEDERATION
    7, St. George's Square
    London SW1V 2NY

       Taxes

1281 INLAND WATERWAYS ASSOCIATION
    114, Regent's Park Road
    London NW1

       Bulletin of the Inland Waterways Association

1282 INNER LONDON TEACHERS' ASSOCIATION
    Hamilton House
    Mabledon Place
    London WC1H 9BD

       Centre Point

1283 INSIGHT
    306A, Fulham Road
    London SW10

       CTV Report

1284 INSTITUTE FOR INDUSTRIAL RESEARCH AND STANDARDS
    Ballyrum Road
    Dublin 9

       Technology Ireland

1285 INSTITUTE FOR THE COMPARATIVE STUDY OF HISTORY, PHILOSOPHY AND THE SCIENCES
    23, Brunswick Road
    Kingston-on-Thames
    Surrey

       Systematics

1286 INSTITUTE FOR THE STUDY OF CONFLICT
    Rusi Building
    Whitehall
    London SW1

       Conflict Studies

1287 INSTITUTE OF ACTUARIES
    Staple Inn Hall
    High Holborn
    London WC1V 7QJ

       Journal of the Institute of Actuaries

1288 INSTITUTE OF ADMINISTRATIVE MANAGEMENT
    205, High Street
    Beckenham
    Kent BR3 1BA

       Office Management

1289 INSTITUTE OF ARCHAEOLOGY
    3-4, Gordon Square
    London WC1

       Committee for Nautical Archaeology: Newsletter

1290 INSTITUTE OF BANKERS
    10, Lombard Street
    London EC3

       Journal of the Institute of Bankers

1291 INSTITUTE OF BANKERS IN SCOTLAND
    62, George Street
    Edinburgh

       Scottish Bankers Magazine

1292 INSTITUTE OF BATHS MANAGEMENT
    Gifford House
    36/38, Sherrand Street
    Melton Mowbray
    Leics LE13 1XJ

       Baths Service

1293 INSTITUTE OF BIOLOGY
    41, Queens Gate
    London SW7

       Biology

1294 INSTITUTE OF BOOK KEEPERS AND RELATED
DATA PROCESSING
418-422, Strand
London WC2

    Book-Keepers Journal

1295 INSTITUTE OF BREWING
33, Clarges Street
London W1

    Journal of the Institute of Brewing

1296 INSTITUTE OF BRITISH FOUNDRYMEN
137/139, Euston Road
London NW1

    British Foundryman

1297 INSTITUTE OF BRITISH GEOGRAPHERS
1, Kensington Gore
London SW7 2AR

    Area
    Institute of British Geographers, Transactions

1298 INSTITUTE OF BUILDING
Englemere
Kings Ride
Ascot, Berks

    Building Technology and Management

1299 INSTITUTE OF CAREERS OFFICERS
c/o Kent Training College for the Youth Employ-
ment Service
College Road
Hextable
Swanley
Kent

    Careers Quarterly

1300 INSTITUTE OF CERTIFIED AMBULANCE
PERSONNEL
5, Grove Terrace
London NW5 1PH

    Ambulance

1301 INSTITUTE OF CHARTERED ACCOUNTANTS IN
ENGLAND AND WALES
56/66, Goswell Road
London EC1M 7AB

    Accountancy
    Accounting and Business Research

1302 INSTITUTE OF CHARTERED ACCOUNTANTS IN
IRELAND
7, Fitzwilliam Place
Dublin 2

    Accountancy Ireland

1303 INSTITUTE OF COMPANY ACCOUNTANTS
11, Portland Road
Edgbaston
Birmingham B16 9HW

    Company Accountant

1304 INSTITUTE OF CONTEMPORARY HISTORY
4, Devonshire Street
London W1

    Wiener Library Bulletin

1305 INSTITUTE OF COST AND MANAGEMENT
ACCOUNTANTS
63, Portland Place
London W1N 4AB

    Management Accounting

1306 INSTITUTE OF CRAFT EDUCATION
23, Brinborn Drive
Darlington

    Practical Education

1307 INSTITUTE OF CREDIT MANAGEMENT
3, Berners Street
London W1

    Credit Management

1308 INSTITUTE OF DATA PROCESSING
418-422, Strand
London WC2

    Data Processing Practitioner

1309 INSTITUTE OF DIRECTORS
10, Belgrave Square
London SW1

    Director

1310 INSTITUTE OF EDUCATION
48, Old Elvet
Durham

    Durham Research Review

1311 INSTITUTE OF FUEL
18, Devonshire Street
London W1N 2AU

    Fuel Abstracts and Current Titles
    Journal of the Institute of Fuel

1312 INSTITUTE OF GROCERY DISTRIBUTION
Grange Lane
Letchmore Heath
Watford WD2 8DQ

    Grocery Distribution

1313 INSTITUTE OF HEALTH EDUCATION
35, Victoria Road
Sheffield S10 2DJ

    Journal of the Institute of Health Education

1314 INSTITUTE OF HEALTH SERVICE ADMINISTRA-
TORS
75, Portland Place
London W1N 4AN

    Hospital and Health Services Purchasing
    Hospital and Health Services Review

1315 INSTITUTE OF HERALDIC AND GENEALOGICAL
STUDIES
Northgate
Canterbury
Kent

    Family History

1316 INSTITUTE OF HISTORICAL RESEARCH
Senate House
London WC1E 7HU

    Bulletin of the Institute of Historical Research

1317 INSTITUTE OF HOME HELP ORGANISERS
15, Blackheath Road
Greenwich
London SE10

    Journal of the Institute of Home Help Organiser

1318 INSTITUTE OF HOUSING MANAGERS
Victoria House
Southampton Row
London WC1B 4EB

    Housing

1319 INSTITUTE OF INDUSTRIAL RESEARCH
Ballymun Road
Dublin 9

Food Progress

1320 INSTITUTE OF JEWISH AFFAIRS
13-16, Jacob's Well Mews
George Street
London W1H 5PD

Christian Attitudes on Jews and Judaism
Patterns of Prejudice
Soviet Jewish Affairs

1321 INSTITUTE OF LANDSCAPE ARCHITECTS
12, Carlton House Terrace
London SW1

Landscape Design

1322 INSTITUTE OF LEGAL EXECUTIVES
Ilex House
Barrhill Road
London SW2 4RW

Legal Executive

1323 INSTITUTE OF LINGUISTS
Lloyds Bank Chambers
91, Newington Causeway
London SE1 6BN

Incorporated Linquist

1324 INSTITUTE OF MEASUREMENT AND CONTROL
20, Peel Street
London W8

Measurement and Control

1325 INSTITUTE OF MANAGEMENT IN PRINTING
55, Temple Chambers
London EC4

Management in Printing

1326 INSTITUTE OF MARINE ENGINEERS
76, Mark Lane
London EC3R 7JN

Marine Engineering and Shipbuilding Abstracts
Marine Engineers Review
Transactions: Institute of Marine Engineers

1327 INSTITUTE OF MEDICAL LABORATORY TECH-
NOLOGY
12, Queen Anne Street
London W1M OAV

Gazette of the Institute of Medical Laboratory
Technology

1328 INSTITUTE OF METAL FINISHING
178, Goswell Road
London EC1

Transactions of the Institute of Metal Finishing

1329 INSTITUTE OF METALS
17, Belgrave Square
London SW1

Metals Abstracts
Metals and Materials
Powder Metallurgy

1330 INSTITUTE OF MINING AND METALLURGY
44, Portland Place
London W1N 4BR

IMM Abstracts

1331 INSTITUTE OF MUNICIPAL TREASURERS AND
ACCOUNTANTS
1, Buckingham Place
London SW1

Local Government Finance

1332 INSTITUTE OF NAVAL MEDICINE
Alverstoke
Hants

Journal of the Royal Naval Medical Service

1333 INSTITUTE OF PACKAGING
Malcolm House
Empire Way
Wembley
Middx

Packaging Technology

1334 INSTITUTE OF PATENTEES AND INVENTORS
207-208, Abbey House
2, Victoria Street
London SWLH OLD

Inventor

1335 INSTITUTE OF PERSONNEL MANAGEMENT
5, Winsley Street
London WIN 7AQ

IPM Digest

1336 INSTITUTE OF PETROLEUM
61, New Cavendish Street
London W2M 8AN

Gas and Liquid Chromatography Abstracts
Institute of Petroleum Abstracts
Journal of the Institute of Petroleum
Petroleum Review

1337 INSTITUTE OF PHYSICS
Netherton House
Marsh Street
Bristol BS1 4BT

Journal of Physics
Metal Physics
Physics Bulletin
Physics Education
Physics in Medicine and Biology
Reports in Progress in Physics
Review of Physics in Technology

1338 INSTITUTE OF PLUMBING
North Street
Hornchurch
Essex

Plumbing

1339 INSTITUTE OF POPULATION REGISTRATION
11, Selborne Road
Littlehampton
Sussex

Population Registration

1340 INSTITUTE OF PRINTING
10/11, Bedford Row
London WC1R 4D2

Professional Printer

1341 INSTITUTE OF PSYCHOLOGY
Roebuck Park House
Dundrum
Dublin 14

Man

1342   INSTITUTE OF PSYCHOPHYSICAL RESEARCH
        118, Banbury Road
        Oxford OX2 6JU

            Proceedings of the Institute of Psychophysical
            Research

1343   INSTITUTE OF PURCHASING AND SUPPLY
        York House
        Westminster Bridge Road
        London SE1

            Purchasing Journal

1344   INSTITUTE OF PYRAMIDOLOGY
        31, Station Road
        Harpenden
        Hertfordshire

            Pyramidology Magazine

1345   INSTITUTE OF QUANTITY SURVEYORS
        98, Gloucester Place
        London W1H 4AT

            Quantity Surveyor

1346   INSTITUTE OF RACE RELATIONS
        36, Jermyn Street
        London SW1

            Race Relations Abstracts
            Race Today

1347   INSTITUTE OF REFRIGERATION
        272, London Road
        Wallington
        Surrey

            Proceedings of the Institute of Refrigeration

1348   INSTITUTE OF ROAD TRANSPORT ENGINEERS
        1, Cromwell Place
        London SW7

            Transport Engineer

1349   INSTITUTE OF RURAL LIFE AT HOME AND OVER-
        SEAS
        27, Northumberland Road
        New Barnet
        Herts

            Rural Life

1350   INSTITUTE OF SCIENCE TECHNOLOGY
        66, Seggart Terrace
        Aberdeen AB1 5UD

            Bulletin of the Institute of Science Technology

1351   INSTITUTE OF SHOPS ACTS ADMINISTRATION
        Shops and other Acts Dept.
        Guildhall
        London EC2

            Inspector

1352   INSTITUTE OF SOCIAL ANTHROPOLOGY
        51, Banbury Road
        Oxford

            Journal of the Anthrapological Society of
            Oxford

1353   INSTITUTE OF SUPERVISORY MANAGEMENT
        22, Bore Street
        Lichfield
        Staffs

            Supervisory Management

1354   INSTITUTE OF TECHNICAL PUBLICITY AND PUB-
        LICATIONS LTD.
        c/o 17, Bluebridge Avenue
        Brookmans Park
        Hatfield
        Herts

            Communicator of Technical Information

1355   INSTITUTE OF THE MOTOR INDUSTRY
        'Fanshaws'
        Brickendon
        Hertford

            Motor Management

1356   INSTITUTE OF TIBETAN STUDIES
        36, King Street
        Tring
        Herts

            Shambala

1357   INSTITUTE OF TRICHOLOGISTS
        228, Stockwell Road
        Brixton
        London SW9

            Trichologist

1358   INSTITUTE OF WATER POLLUTION CONTROL
        49/55, Victoria Street
        London SW1

            Water Pollution Control

1359   INSTITUTE OF WEIGHTS AND MEASURES AD-
        MINISTRATION
        Tredegar Street
        Cardiff CF1 2FB

            Monthly Review of the Institute of Weights and
            Measures Administration

1360   INSTITUTE OF WELFARE OFFICERS
        Red Cross House
        73, Penrhyn Road
        Kingston upon Thames
        Surrey KT1 2EQ

            Welfare Officer

1361   INSTITUTE OF WOOD SCIENCE
        62, Oxford Street
        London W1

            Journal of the Institute of Wood Science

1362   INSTITUTE OF WORK STUDY PRACTITIONERS
        9/10, River Front
        Enfield
        Middlesex

            Work Study and Management Service

1363   INSTITUTION OF CHEMICAL ENGINEERS
        16, Belgrave Square
        London SW1

            Chemical Engineer and Transactions of the
            Institution of Chemical Engineers

1364   INSTITUTION OF CIVIL ENGINEERS
        1-7, Great George Street
        London SW1P 3AA

            British Nuclear Energy Society Journal
            Geotechnique
            Institution of Civil Engineers Proceedings
            New Civil Engineer

1365 INSTITUTION OF COMPUTER SCIENCES
37-39 London End
Beaconsfield
Bucks

Journal of the Institution of Computer
Sciences

1366 INSTITUTION OF ELECTRICAL AND ELECTRO-
NICS TECHNICIAN ENGINEERS
2 Savoy Hill
London WC2

Electrical and Electronics Technician
Engineer
Electro Technology

1367 INSTITUTION OF ELECTRICAL ENGINEERS
Savoy Place
London WC2R OBL

IEE News
Control and Science Record
Electronics and Power
Electronics Letters
Electronics Record
Power Record
Proceedings of the Institution of Electrical
Engineers

1368 INSTITUTION OF ELECTRONIC AND RADIO
ENGINEERS
8-9, Bedford Square
London WC1B 5RG

Radio and Electronic Engineer

1369 INSTITUTION OF ENGINEERING INSPECTION
616, Grand Buildings
London WC2

Quality Engineer

1370 INSTITUTION OF ENGINEERS AND SHIPBUILDERS
IN SCOTLAND
183, Bath Street
Glasgow C2

Transactions of the Institution of Engineers and
Shipbuilders in Scotland

1371 INSTITUTION OF FIRE ENGINEERS
148, New Walk
Leicester LE1 7QB

Institution of Fire Engineers Quarterly

1372 INSTITUTION OF GAS ENGINEERS
17, Grosvenor Crescent
London SW1

Journal of the Institution of Gas Engineers

1373 INSTITUTION OF MECHANICAL ENGINEERS
1, Birdcage Walk
London SW1H 9JJ

Automotive Engineering
Chartered Mechanical Engineer
Heat and Fluid Flow
Journal of Automotive Engineering
Journal of Mechanical Engineering Science
Journal of Strain Analysis
Mechanical Engineering News
Railway Engineering Journal

1374 INSTITUTION OF MINING AND METALLURGY
44, Portland Place
London W1N 4BR

Transactions of the Institution of Mining and
Metallurgy

1375 INSTITUTION OF MINING ENGINEERS
3, Grosvenor Crescent
London SW1X 7EG

Mining Engineer

1376 INSTITUTION OF MUNICIPAL ENGINEERS
25, Eccleston Square
London SW1V 1NX

Journal of the Institution of Municipal
Engineers

1377 INSTITUTION OF NUCLEAR ENGINEERS
24, Holwood Road
Bromley
Kent

Journal of the Institution of Nuclear
Engineers

1378 INSTITUTION OF POST OFFICE ELECTRICAL
ENGINEERS
CT/ETW15
Post Office Tower
Howland Street
London WC1

New Quarterly Journal

1379 INSTITUTION OF PRODUCTION ENGINEERS
10, Chesterfield Street
London W1X 8DE

Production Engineer

1380 INSTITUTION OF PROFESSIONAL CIVIL SERVANTS
3-7, Northumberland Street
London WC2N 5BS

State Service

1381 INSTITUTION OF RAILWAY SIGNAL ENGINEERS
21, Avalon Road
Earley
Reading

Proceedings of the Institution of Railway Signal
Engineers

1382 INSTITUTION OF STRUCTURAL ENGINEERS
203-9, North Gower Street
London NW1

Structural Engineer

1383 INSTITUTION OF WATER ENGINEERS
6-8, Sackville Street
London W1X 1DD

Journal of the Institution of Water Engineers

1384 INSTITUTION OF WORKS MANAGERS
34, Bloomsbury Way
London WC1A 2SB

Works Management

1385 INSURANCE INSTITUTE OF LONDON
20, Aldermanbury
London EC2

Journal of the Insurance Institute of London

1386 INSURANCE PUBLISHING AND PRINTING CO.
9, Market Street
Starbridge
Worcs

Insurance Broker's Monthly

1387 INTER-VARSITY FELLOWSHIP
39, Bedford Square
London WC1B 3GY

Christian Graduate
Voice

1388 INTERNATIONAL AFRICAN INSTITUTE
10-11, Fetter Lane
London EC4A 1BJ

International African Bibliography

1389 INTERNATIONAL ASSOCIATION OF HYDROLOGICAL
SCIENCE
Wallingford
Berks

Hydrological Sciences Bulletin

1390 INTERNATIONAL ASSOCIATION OF INDIVIDUAL
PSYCHOLOGY
6, Vale Rise
London NW11 8SD

Individual Psychology News Letter

1391 INTERNATIONAL ASSOCIATION OF MUSIC
LIBRARIES

c/o Haldane Library
Imperial College
London SW7 2A2

Brio

1392 INTERNATIONAL BANK NOTE SOCIETY
19/21, Great Tower Street
London EC3

International Bank Note Society

1393 INTERNATIONAL BAR ASSOCIATION
14, Waterloo Place
London SW1Y 4AR

International Bar Journal

1394 INTERNATIONAL CAMELLIA SOCIETY
Bodnant Garden
Tal-y-cafn
Colwyn Bay
Denbighshire
N. Wales

International Camellia Journal

1395 INTERNATIONAL COMMISSION OF AGRICULTURAL
ENGINEERING
53, Upper Ground
London SE1

International Journal of Farm Building Research

1396 INTERNATIONAL COMPUTERS LTD.
ICL House
Putney
London SW15

Computer International

1397 INTERNATIONAL CO-OPERATIVE ALLIANCE
11 Upper Grosvenor Street
London W1X 9PA

Agricultural Co-operative Bulletin
Consumer Affairs Bulletin
Co-operative News Services
Review of International Co-operation

1398 INTERNATIONAL COUNCIL FOR EDUCATIONAL
MEDIA
Modino Press Ltd.
68, Queen Street
London EC4 1SL

Educational Media International

1399 INTERNATIONAL DANCE TEACHERS ASSOCIATION
76, Bennett Road
Brighton BN2 5JL

Dance Teacher

1400 INTERNATIONAL DEMOCRATIC ACTION
143a, Croydon Road
Beckenham
Kent BR3 3RB

International Democratic Review

1401 INTERNATIONAL ECONOMIC SERVICES
Foremarke House
Thorpe Green
Egham
Surrey TW20 8QL

International Financial Bulletin

1402 INTERNATIONAL EGG COMMISSION
Room 434
Agriculture House
Knightsbridge
London SW1

Market Review
Six-Monthly Statistical Bulletin

1403 INTERNATIONAL FEDERATION OF LIBRARY
ASSOCIATIONS
Dept. of Printed Books
British Museum
London WC1B 3DG

International Cataloguing

1404 INTERNATIONAL FOOD INFORMATION SERVICE
Farnham Royal
Slough
Bucks SL2 3BN

Food Science and Technology Abstracts

1405 INTERNATIONAL GLACIOLOGICAL SOCIETY
Lensfield Road
Cambridge CB2 1ER

Ice
Journal of Glaciology

1406 INTERNATIONAL HARVESTER COMPANY OF
GREAT BRITAIN LTD.
PO Box 25
259, City Road
London EC1P 1AD

International Harvester Review

1407 INTERNATIONAL HISTORY MAGAZINE
73-79, Farringdon Street
London EC4A 4BJ

International History Magazine

1408 INTERNATIONAL INSTITUTE FOR CONSERVATION
608, Grand Buildings
Trafalgar Square
London WC2N 5HN

Studies in Conservation

1409 INTERNATIONAL INSTITUTE FOR CONSERVATION
OF HISTORIC AND ARTISTIC WORKS
176, Old Brompton Road
London SW5

Studies in Conservation

1410 INTERNATIONAL INSTITUTE OF WELDING
54, Princes Gate
Exhibition Road
London SW7

Welding in the World

1411   INTERNATIONAL LANGUAGE CENTRE
    40, Shaftesbury Avenue
    London W1V 8HJ

      Modern English
      Modern English Teacher

1412   INTERNATIONAL LANGUAGE (IDO) SOCIETY OF
    GREAT BRITIAN
    1, Hillside Road
    Darlington
    Co. Durham DL3 8HB

      Ido-Letro

1413   INTERNATIONAL LICENSING LTD.
    92, Cannon Lane
    Pinner
    Middx HA5 1HT

      International Licensing

1414   INTERNATIONAL ORDER OF GOOD TEMPLARS
    11, Warstone Lane
    Birmingham B18 6JE

      English Templar Youth
      Good Templar Watchwood
      Juvenile Templar

1415   INTERNATIONAL PERFUMER
    12A, KC
    East Molesey
    Surrey KT8 9HL

      International Perfumer

1416   INTERNATIONAL PHONETIC ASSOCIATION
    University College
    Gower Street
    London WC1E 6BT

      Journal of the International Phonetic Associa-
      tion

1417   INTERNATIONAL PLANNED PARENTHOOD
    FEDERATION
    18-20, Lower Regent Street
    London SW1Y 4PW

      IPPF Medical Bulletin
      International Planned Parenthood News
      Research in Reproduction

1418   INTERNATIONAL POSTCARD MARKET
    96, Idmiston Road
    West Norwood
    London SE27 9HL

      International Postcard Market

1419   INTERNATIONAL RUBBER STUDY GROUP
    Brettenham House
    5/6, Lancaster Place
    London WC2E 7ET

      International Rubber Digest
      Quarterly Rubber Statistical News Sheet
      Rubber Statistical Bulletin

1420   INTERNATIONAL SEISMOLOGICAL CENTRE
    6, South Oswald Road
    Edinburgh EH9 2HX

      Bibliography of Seismology
      Bulletin of the International Seismological
        Centre
      Regional Catalogue of Earthquakes

1421   INTERNATIONAL SOCIALISTS
    6, Cottons Gardens
    London E2 8DN

      Socialist Worker

1422   INTERNATIONAL SOCIETY FOR KRISHNA CON-
    SCIOUSNESS
    7, Bury Place
    Bloomsbury
    London WC1

      Back to Godhead

1423   INTERNATIONAL SOCIETY FOR THE EVANGELIZA-
    TION OF THE JEWS
    45, Gildredge Road
    Eastbourne
    Sussex

      Herald

1424   INTERNATIONAL SOCIETY FOR THE PROTECTION
    OF ANIMALS
    106, Jermyn Street
    London SW1

      ISPA News

1425   INTERNATIONAL SUGAR JOURNALS LTD.
    23A, Easton Street
    High Wycombe
    Bucks

      International Sugar Journal

1426   INTERNATIONAL TELEPHONE AND TELEGRAPH
    CORP.
    190, Strand
    London WC2R 1DU

      Electrical Communication

1427   INTERNATIONAL TEMPERANCE ASSOCIATION
    119, St. Peter's Street
    St. Albans
    Herts

      African Mims
      Alert

1428   INTERNATIONAL TIN COUNCIL
    28, Haymarket
    London SW1

      Monthly Statistical Bulletin

1429   INTERNATIONAL TRADE PUBLICATIONS LTD
    John Adam House
    17/19, John Adam St
    London WC2

      International Tax-Free Trader Duty-Free
        World
      Tableware International
      Tobacco
      World Tobacco

1430   INTERNATIONAL TRANSPORT WORKERS
    FEDERATION
    Maritime House
    Old Town
    Clapham
    London SW4 0JR

      ITF Journal
      ITF Newsletter

1431   INTERNATIONAL TRUST FOR ZOOLOGICAL
    NOMENCLATURE
    14, Belgrave Square
    London SW1X 8PS

      Bulletin of Zoological Nomenclature

1432   INTERNATIONAL UNION OF PURE AND APPLIED
       CHEMISTRY
          Bank Court Chambers
          2-3, Pound Way
          Cowley Centre
          Oxford OX4 3YF

             IUPAC Information Bulletin

1433   INTERNATIONAL WATERFOWL RESEARCH
       BUREAU
          Slimbridge
          Glos GL2 7BX

             International Wildfowl Research Bureau
             Bulletin

1434   INTERNATIONAL WOOL SECRETARIAT
          Carlton Gardens
          London SW1Y 5AE

             Wool Science Review

1435   INTERNATIONALIST
          Britwell Salome
          Oxford OX9 5BR

             Internationalist

1436   INTERSTATS LIMITED
          Brockhill House
          Pinemount Road
          Camberley
          Surrey

             Vital Economic Trends in the United Kingdom

1437   INVESTORS BULLETIN
          Suite 491
          Park West
          Marble Arch
          London W2

             Investors Bulletin

1438   IRISH ANCESTOR
          Pirton House
          Sydenham Villas
          Dundrum
          Dublin 14

             Irish Ancestor

1439   IRISH COMPUTER SOCIETY
          c/o St. Stephen's Green
          Dublin 2

             Irish Computer Society Bulletin

1440   IRISH CONTRACTS WEEKLY
          6, Berkeley Street
          Dublin 7

             Irish Contracts Weekly

1441   IRISH CREAMERY MILK SUPPLIERS ASSOCIATION
          John Feely House
          15, Upper Mallow Street
          Limerick
          Ireland

             Irish Farming News

1442   IRISH DENTAL ASSOCIATION
          29, Kenilworth Square
          Dublin 6

             Journal of the Irish Dental Association

1443   IRISH GENEALOGICAL RESEARCH SOCIETY
          82, Eaton Square
          London SW1

             Irish Genealogist

1444   IRISH GROCERY WORLD
          114, Somerton Road
          Belfast BT 15 4DG

             Irish Grocery World

1445   IRISH LEAGUE OF CREDIT UNIONS
          9, Appion Way
          Dublin 6

             Newsletter: Irish League of Credit Unions

1446   IRISH MARITIME PRESS LTD.
          7, Crampton Quay
          Dublin 2

             Irish Skipper

1447   IRISH MEDICAL ASSOCIATION
          10 Fitzwilliam Place
          Dublin 2

             Journal of the Irish Medical Association

1448   IRISH MESSENGER OFFICE
          37, Lower Leeson Street
          Dublin 2
          Ireland

             Irish Messenger
             Madonna

1449   IRISH POST LTD.
          2/4, The Broadway
          Southall
          Middx

             Irish Post

1450   IRISH PUBLISHING CO.
          39, Lower Leeson Street
          Dublin 2

             Building and Contract Journal
             Transport and Materials Handling

1451   IRISH SOCIETY FOR ARCHIVES
          University College
          Dublin

             Irish Archives Bulletin

1452   IRISH UNIVERSITY PRESS
          81, Merrion Square
          Dublin 2

             International Journal of Early Childhood

1453   IRON AND STEEL INSTITUTE
          4, Grosvenor Gardens
          London SW1

             Journal of the Iron and Steel Instutute
             Steel in the USSR

1454   IRON AND STEEL TRADES CONFEDERATION
          Swinton House
          324, Grays Inn Road
          London WC1X 8DD

             Man and Metal

1455   IRONBRIDGE GORGE MUSEUM TRUST
          Church Hill,
          Ironbridge
          Telford
          Shropshire

             Ironbridge Quarterly

1456   JH FENNER & CO. LTD.
          Marfleet
          Hull

             Conveyor Journal

1457 JJ BLACK (PUBLISHERS) LTD.
Somerset Farm
Cranleigh
Surrey

Accordion Times and Modern Musician
Southern Farmer

1458 J. LYONS & Co. LTD.
Cadby Hall
London W14 OPA

Lyons Mail

1459 JMP SERVICES LTD.
Amberley House
Norfolk Street
London WC2

Beauty Counter
Era

1460 J. WALTER THOMPSON CO. LTD.
40 Berkeley Square
London W1X 6AD

Scrip

1461 J. W. WARDEN & CO.
12, Panmure Street
Dundee

Prices Current

1462 J. WHITAKER & SONS LTD.
13, Bedford Square
London WC1B 3JE

Bookseller
Current Literature
Paperbacks in Print
Whitaker's Books of the Month and Books to
Come

1463 BRYAN JACKSON
Maple Cottage
Ashburnham Avenue
Harrow-on-the-Hill

Railway Enthusiasts and Historians Guide
to their Literature

1464 F. S. JAFRI
391, Kingston Road
London SW20

Bangladesh Newsletter

1465 D. R. JAMES
118, Windham Road
Bournemouth
Hants

Insight Magazine

1466 JAMES PATON J & J COOK LTD.
18/20, Gordon Street
Paisley

Scan

1467 JAMES PIKE LTD.
St Ives
Cornwall

Import

1468 JAPAN EVANGELISTIC BAND
26, Woodside Park Road
London N12 8RR

Japan News

1469 JAS SMITH & SONS LTD.
Dewsbury
Yorks

Smith Express

1470 JEMMA PUBLICATIONS
Richardson House
Main Street
Blackrock
Co. Dublin

Furnishing Ireland
Irish Catering Review
Irish Licensing World

1471 A. JENNINGS
186a, Clapham High Street
London SW4

Keep Left

1472 JERSEY CATTLE SOCIETY OF THE U. K.
154, Castle Hill
Reading
Berks

The Jersey

1473 JERSEY LIFE LTD.
Grosvenor Street
St. Helier
Jersey
C. I.

Jersey Life

1474 JETLINE SCHEDULES LTD.
Golden House
29, Gt. Putteney Street
London W1

Jetline Schedules

1475 JEWISH GAZETTE LTD.
18, Cheetham Parade
Manchester M8 6DJ

Jewish Gazette

1476 JEWISH LITERARY PUBLICATIONS LTD.
68, Worcester Crescent
London NW7 4NA

Jewish Quarterly

1477 JEWISH TELEGRAPH LTD.
Levi House
Bury Old Road
Manchester 8

Jewish Telegraph

1478 JEWISH VEGETARIAN & NATURAL HEALTH
SOCIETY
'Bet Teva'
855, Finchley Road
London NW11

Jewish Vegetarian

1479 C. E. JOEL
39, West Street
Great Gransden
Sandy
Beds

New Diffusionist

1480 JOHANN STRAUSS SOCIETY OF GREAT BRITAIN
301A, Harrow Road
Wembley
Middx

Tritsch-Tratsch

1481 **JOHN BALL PUBLICATIONS LTD.**
Topic House
389, Alfred Street North
Nottingham NG3 1AA

Leeds & West Riding Topic
Leicester & Rutland Topic
Nottingham Topic

1482 **JOHN CATT LTD.**
114, High Street
Billericay
Essex

Church building

1483 **JOHN DICKINSON & CO. LTD.**
Apsley
Hemel Hempstead
Herts

Dickinson News

1484 **JOHN MURRAY (PUBLISHERS) LTD.**
50, Albemarle Street
London W1X 4BD

Cornhill Magazine
Journal of Navigation
Proceedings of the Classical Association
Quarterly Review
School Science Review

1485 **JOHN RYLANDS LIBRARY**
Deansgate
Manchester M3 3EH

Bulletin of the John Rylands Library

1486 **JOHN SHERRATT & SON LTD.**
St. Ann's Press
Park Road
Altrineham

Journal of the Chester Archaeological Society

1487 **JOHN WADDINTON LTD**
Wakefield Road
Leeds 10

Bridge Magazine

1488 **JOHN WILEY & SONS LTD.**
Baffins Lane
Chichester
Sussex PO 19 1UD

International Journal of Circuit Theory and
Applications
International Journal for Numerical Methods
in Engineering
International Journal of Earthquake
Engineering and Structural Dynamics
International Journal of Mathematical
Education in Science and Technology
Software Practice and Experience

1489 **JOHN WRIGHT & SONS LTD.**
44, Triangle West
Bristol 8

British Journal of Mathematical and
Statistical Psychology
British Journal of Surgery
Community Health
Dental Practitioner and Dental Record
Injury
Journal of Dentistry
Medicine Science and the Law

1490 **JOHNSON SOCIETY OF LONDON**
Broadmeed
Eynsford Road
Farningham
Kent DA4 0BQ

New Rambler

1491 **JOINT FIRE RESEARCH ORGANISATION**
Fire Research Station
Borehamwood
Herts

JOFRO

1492 **JOINT UNIVERSITY COUNCIL FOR SOCIAL &
PUBLIC ADMINISTRATION**
Royal Institute of Public Administration
Hamilton House
Mabledon Place
London WC1H 9BD

Public Administration Bulletin

1493 **C. M. JONES**
'Lowlands'
Wenhaston
Halesworth
Suffolk IP19 9DY

World Bowls

1494 **JORDAN & SONS LTD.**
Wilec House
82, City Road
London EC1Y 2BX

Company Information

1495 **JOSEPH LUCAS LTD.**
Reflections Office J. 2,
Great King Street
Birmingham B19 2XF

Lucas Reflections

1496 **L. V. JOSEPHI**
National Mutual House
South Park
Sevenoaks
Kent

Her Majestys Consuls List

1497 **JOSEPHINE BUTLER SOCIETY**
'Candida'
49, Hawkshead Lane
North Mimms
Hatfield
Herts

Shield

1498 **JOSIAH WEDGWOOD & SONS LTD.**
Barlaston
Stoke-on-Trent

Wedgwood Review

1499 **JOURNAL OF COMMERCE AND SHIPPING
TELEGRAPH LTD.**
19, James Street
Liverpool L2 7PE

Journal of Commerce
Sea Breezes

1500 **JOURNAL OF CONTEMPORARY ASIA**
c/o 37, Macaulay Court
London SW4 0QU

Journal of Contemporary Asia

1501 JOURNAL OF PARK ADMINISTRATION LTD.
      The Adelphi
      John Adam Street
      London WC2N 6AY

          Parks and Recreation

1502 JOURNAL OF REFRIGERATION LTD.
      19, Harcourt Street
      London W1

          Journal of Refrigeration

1503 JUDO LTD.
      91, Wellesley Road
      Croydon
      Surrey

          Judo

1504 JUNIOR ASTRONOMICAL SOCIETY
      58, Vaughan Gardens
      Ilford
      Essex

          Hermes

1505 JUNIOR BOOKSHELF
      Marsh Hall
      Thurstonland
      Huddersfield HD4 6XB

          Junior Bookshelf

1506 JUNIOR CHAMBER DUBLIN
      34, Upper Gardiner St
      Dublin

          Flashpoint

1507 JUNIOR CLUB PUBLICATIONS LTD.
      36, Craven Street
      London WC2N 5NG

          Science Teacher

1508 JUNIOR HOSPITAL DOCTORS ASSOCIATION LTD.
      136-139, Temple Chambers
      Temple Avenue
      London EC4

          On-Call

1509 JUNIOR INSTITUTION OF ENGINEERS
      33, Ovington Square
      London SW3

          Journal of the Junior Institution of Engineers

1510 JUNIPER JOURNALS LTD.
      49-50, Hatton Garden
      London EC1N 8XS

          New Electronics

1511 JUSTICE OF THE PEACE LTD.
      Little London
      Chichester
      Sussex

          Anglo-American Law Review
          Family Law
          Justice of the Peace Reports
          Justice of the Peace
          J. P. Weekly Law Digest
          Local Government Review

1512 JUSTICES' CLERKS' SOCIETY
      P. J. Halnan
      County Hall
      Cambridge

          Justices' Clerk

1513 KALAMAZOO LTD.
      Mill Lane
      Northfield
      Birmingham B31 2RW

          Insight
          KWA News

1514 KALERGHI PUBLICATIONS
      51, Welbeck Street
      London W1

          Hovering Craft and Hydrofoil

1515 KARTING MAGAZINE LTD.
      Bank House
      Summerhill
      Chislehurst
      Kent

          Karting

1516 KAYSER BONDOR LTD.
      Baldock
      Herts

          Kayser News

1517 KAZIMIERZ OBTULOWICZ
      76, Cleveland Street
      London W1P 5DS

          Chowanna

1518 KEIGHLEY & WORTH VALLEY RAILWAY
      PRESERVATION SOCIETY
      Haworth Station
      Haworth
      Keighley
      Yorks

          Push and Pull

1519 KEMP'S PRINTING & PUBLISHING CO. LTD.
      299, Grays Inn Road
      London WC1

          Dog News

1520 KENNEDY & DONKIN CONSULTING ENGINEERS
      Premier House
      Percy Street
      Woking
      Surrey

          House Journal of Kennedy and Donkin

1521 KENNEDY PRESS LTD.
      31 King Street
      Manchester 3

          Metallurgia

1522 KENNEL CLUB
      1-4 Clarges Street
      Piccadilly
      London W1Y 8AB

          Kennel Gazette

1523 F. P. KENNETT
      1, Earl's Lane
      South Mimms
      Potters Bar
      Herts

          Engineering Designer
          Engineering Fracture Mechanics

1524 KENT ARCHAEOLOGICAL SOCIETY
      The Museum
      Maidstone
      Kent

          Archaeologia Cantiana

1525 KENT EDUCATION COMMITTEE
Springfield
Maidstone
Kent

Kent Education Gazette

1526 KENT MESSENGER GROUP
123, Week Street
Maidstone
Kent

Kent Life
Sussex Life

1527 KERNOW BRANCH OF THE CELTIC LEAGUE
c/o Lodener Press
14/16 Market Street
Padstow
Cornwall

Omma

1528 KERSHAW PUBLICATIONS
46, The Albany
Liverpool L3 9EG

Merseyside Business News

1529 KINGDOM REVIVAL CRUSADE
Riverside Cottage
Bridgend
Harpforth
Sidmouth
Devon EX10 0NG

Kingdom Voice

1530 KINGFISHER
6, Gombards
St. Albans
Herts

Kingfisher

1531 KINGS CROSS PUBLISHING CO. LTD.
205, Euston Road
London NW1

Railway Review

1532 KIPLING SOCIETY
18, Northumberland Avenue
London WC2

Kipling Journal

1533 KNIGHTON PUBLICATIONS
5, Knighton Close
South Croydon CR2 6DP

Pet Product Marketing and Garden Supplies

1534 C. C. KOHLER
141, High Street
Dorking
Surrey

Gissing Newsletter

1535 KRAFT FOODS LTD.
Regina House
259/269, Old Marylebone Rd.
London NW1 5RB

Kraftsman

1536 G. KRAUS
39, West Street
Great Gransden
Sandy
Beds

New Diffusionist

1537 KRIKOS LTD
33, Mapesbury Road
London NW2

Krikos

1538 L. S. DIXON & CO. LTD.
Sir Thomas Street
Liverpool L16 BR

Dixon's Paper Circular

1539 L. V. A. CENTRE
Anglesea Road
Ballsbridge
Dublin 4

Licensed Vintner

1540 LABAN ART OF MOVEMENT GUILD
3, Beech Grove
Burton-on-Stather
Scunthorpe DN1S 9DB

Laban Art of Movement Guild Magazine

1541 LABORATORY ANIMALS LTD.
7, Warwick Court
London WC1R 5DP

Laboratory Animals

1542 LABOUR PARTY
Transport House
Smith Square
London SW1P 3JA

Labour Weekly

1543 LABOUR PARTY YOUNG SOCIALISTS NATIONAL
COMMITTEE
Transport House
Smith Square
London SW1

Left

1544 LACE SOCIETY OF WALES
57, Annefield Park
Gresford
Wrexham
Denbighshire LL12 8NR

Lacemaking

1545 LADIES' ALPINE CLUB
c/o Bishop's Lodge
10, Springfield Road
Leicester LE 2 3BD

Journal of the Ladies' Alpine Club

1546 LAMBEG INDUSTRIAL RESEARCH ASSOCIATION
Lambeg
Lisburn
Co. Antrim

Lambeg Research Review

1548 LANCASHIRE AND CHESHIRE ANTIQUARIAN
SOCIETY
c/o The Portico Library
57, Mosley Street
Manchester 2

Transactions of the Lancashire and Cheshire
Antiquarian Society

1549 LANCASHIRE AND CHESHIRE ENTOMOLOGICAL
SOCIETY
Royal Institution
Colquitt Street
Liverpool

Annual Report and Proceedings of the
Lancashire and Cheshire Entomological
Society

1550 LANCASHIRE AND CHESHIRE FAUNA SOCIETY
11, Ashmore Avenue
Stockport SK3 0QY

Proceedings of the Lancashire and Cheshire
Fauna Society

1551 LANCASHIRE DIALECT SOCIETY
c/o Professor G. L. Brook
Department of English
The University
Manchester M13 9PL

Journal of the Lancashire Dialect Society

1552 LANCET LTD.
7, Adam Street
London WC2N 6AD

Lancet

1553 LAND AND LIBERTY PRESS LTD.
177, Vauxhall Bridge Road
London SW1

Land and Liberty

1554 LANGHAMS HERALD PRESS
Farnham
Surrey

Carthusian
Lacrosse

1555 LANGUAGE PRESS LTD.
161, Fleet Street
London EC4

Music Business Weekly

1556 LANSBURY HOUSE TRUST FUND
3, Caledonian Road
London N1

Compulsory Military Service and the Objector

1557 LAPIDARY PUBLICATIONS
29, Ludgate Hill
London EC4

Gems

1558 LASER
26, Selwood Road
Addiscombe
Croydon
Surrey

Laser

1559 LAVENDER PUBLICATIONS LTD.
Borough Green
Kent

Strad

1560 LAW & LOCAL GOVERNMENT PUBLICATIONS
LTD.
27-29, Furnival Street
London EC4

British Hospital Journal

1561 LAW NOTES
25/26, Chancery Lane
London WC2

Law Notes

1562 LAW SOCIETY
113, Chancery Lane
London WC2

Law Society's Gazette

1563 LAW SOCIETY OF SCOTLAND
Law Society's Hall
26 Drumsheugh Gardens
Edinburgh EH3 7YR

Journal of the Law Society of Scotland

1564 LAURENCE FRENCH PUBLICATIONS LTD.
3, Belsize Crescent
London NW3 5QZ

Far East Trade and Development

1565 LEAD DEVELOPMENT ASSOCIATION
34, Berkeley Square
London W1X 6A5

Lead Abstracts

1566 LEADER PRESS LTD.
Thomas Street
Hull

Bristol Ports Journal
Port of Hull and Humber Ports Journal
Southampton and Solent Ports Journal

1567 LEAGUE AGAINST CRUEL SPORTS LTD.
1, Reform Row
London N17 9TW

Cruel Sports

1568 LEAGUE OF ANGLICAL LOYALISTS
11, Cumberland Mansions
West Hampstead
London NW6 1LL

Loyalist Links

1569 LEATHER INSTITUTE
9, St. Thomas Street
London SE1

Wear

1570 LEATHERGOODS ASSOCIATION OF BUYERS &
RETAILERS
9 St. Thomas Street
London SE1

International Leathergoods Buyer

1571 LEEDS CHAMBER OF COMMERCE & INDUSTRY
9, Quebec Street
Leeds LS1 2HD

Leeds Journal

1572 LEEDS GEOLOGICAL ASSOCIATION
c/o Dept of Earth Sciences
University
Leeds LS2 9JT

Journal of Earth Sciences

1573 LEEDS LOCAL
10, Burkett Terrace
Leeds 6

Leeds Local

1574 LEEDS PERMANENT BUILDING SOCIETY
The Headrow
Leeds 1

Permanent Light

1575 LEGAL ACTION GROUP
Nuffield Lodge
Regents Park
London NW1

LAG Bulletin

1576 LEGAL & GENERAL ASSURANCE SOCIETY LTD.
Temple Court
11, Queen Victoria Street
London EC4

Legal and General Gazette

1577 LEGION PUBLISHING CO. LTD.
25, Breams Buildings
London EC4

Advertising Statistical Review

1578 LEICESTER AND COUNTY CHAMBER OF COM-
MERCE AND INDUSTRY
4, Horsefair Street
Leicester LE1 6EA

Journal of the Leicester and County Chamber
of Commerce and Industry

1579 LEICESTER GRAPHIC
58, Granby Street
Leicester

Leicester Graphic

1580 LEICESTER UNIVERSITY PRESS
2, University Road
Leicester LE1 7RB

Journal of Commonwealth Political Studies

1581 LEICESTERSHIRE & RUTLAND TRUST FOR NATURE
CONSERVATION
68 Outwoods Road
Loughborough

Newsletter: Leicestershire & Rutland Trust
for Nature Conservation

1582 LEICESTERSHIRE ARCHAEOLOGICAL & HISTORI-
CAL SOCIETY
Guildhall
Leicester

Transactions of the Leicestershire Archaeological & Historical Society

1583 LEICESTERSHIRE LOCAL HISTORY COUNCIL
c/o County Record Office
57, New Walk
Leicester

Leicestershire Historian

1584 LENSBURY CLUB
Shell Centre
London SE17 NA

Lensbury Club News

1585 LEPROSY MISSION
50, Portland Place
London W1N 3DG

Project

1586 LETCHWORTH PRINTERS LTD.
Norton Way North
Letchworth
Herts

Bucks Life and Thames Valley Countryside
Essex Countryside
Hertfordshire Countryside

1587 LEWIS CARROLL SOCIETY
Room 16
South Block
County Hall
London SE1 7PB

Jabberwocky

1588 LEYDEN PUBLISHING CO. LTD.
5-7, Carnaby Street
London W1A 4XT

Travelling

1589 LEYDEN PUBLISHING CO. LTD.
Sheraton House
14, Great Chapel Street
London W1

Giroscope
You and Your Health

1590 LIBERTARIAN EDUCATION GROUP
180, Melbourne Road
Leicester

Libertarian Teacher

1591 LIBRARY ACTION GROUP
21, Bainbrigge Road
Leeds LS6 3AD

Library Action

1592 LIBRARY ASSOCIATION
7, Ridgmount Street
Store Street
London WC1E 7AE

Bibliotheck
British Humanities Index
British Technology Index
Catalogue and Index
East Midlands Bibliography
Focus on International and Comparative Lib-
rarianship
Journal of Librarianship
Library and Information Bulletin
Library and Information Science Abstracts
Library Association Record
Medical Section of the Library Association
Bulletin

1593 LIBRARY ASSOCIATION
Eastern Branch
County Library
Rope Walk
Ipswich
Suffolk IP4 1LX

Easterner

1594 LIBRARY ASSOCIATION
Kent Sub-Branch
c/o County Library
Maidstone
Kent

Kent Newsletter

1595 LIBRARY ASSOCIATION
  Library History Group
  54, George Lane
  Marlborough
  Wilts SN8 4BY

   Library History

1596 LIBRARY ASSOCIATION
  North Western Branch
  County Branch Library
  Cross Street
  Standish
  Wigan, Lancs.

   North Western Newsletter

1597 LIBRARY ASSOCIATION
  Library Education Group
  School of Librarianship
  Polytechnic of North London
  Essex Street
  London NW1

   LEG News

1598 LIBRARY ASSOCIATION
  West Midland Branch
  Reference Library
  Birmingham B3 3HQ

   Open Access

1599 LIBRARY ASSOCIATION
  Yorkshire Branch
  c/o Dept of Librarianship
  Polytechnic
  Leeds

   Stress

1600 LIBRARY ASSOCIATION
  Yorkshire Branch
  Regional College of Art
  Anlaby Road
  Hull

   Yorkshire Librarian

1601 LIBRARY ASSOCIATION
  Youth Libraries Group
  c/o Comprehensive School
  Hattersley
  Cheshire

   YLG News

1602 LIBRARY ASSOCIATION OF IRELAND
  The Library
  Queen's University
  Belfast

   An Leabharlaun
   Northern Ireland Libraries

1603 LIGHT RAILWAY TRANSPORT LEAGUE
  14, Cudlow Avenue
  Rustington
  Littlehampton
  Sussex

   Tramway Review

1604 LIGHT STEAM POWER
  Kirk Michael
  Isle of Man

   Light Steam Power

1605 LIGUE DES BIBLIOTHEQUES EUROPEENNES DE RECHERCHE
  Main Library
  University
  P.O. Box 363
  Birmingham B15 2TT

   Liber Bulletin

1606 LINCOLNSHIRE LIFE LTD.
  Barclay's Bank Chambers
  Victoria Street
  Grimsby

   Lincolnshire Life

1607 LINCOLNSHIRE LOCAL HISTORY SOCIETY
  86, Newland
  Lincoln

   Lincolnshire History and Archaeology

1608 LINCOLNSHIRE NATURALISTS UNION
  City & County Museum
  Lincoln

   Transactions of the Lincolnshire Naturalists
    Union

1609 LINCOLNSHIRE STANDARD GROUP LTD.
  Chronicle Building
  Waterside North
  Lincoln

   Architecture East Midlands

1610 LINK HOUSE PUBLICATIONS LTD.
  Link House
  Dingwall Avenue
  Croydon
  Surrey CR9 2TA

   Camping
   Caravan
   Cars and Car Conversions
   Coins
   Custom Car
   Do it Yourself
   Hi-Fi News and Record Review
   Modern Caravan
   Prediction
   Small Boat
   Stamp Magazine
   Stamp Weekly
   Studio Sound

1611 LINK HOUSE PUBLICATIONS LTD.
  45, Moray Place
  Edinburgh EH3 6DD

   Opportunities

1612 LITTLE JOHN PUBLICATIONS
  15-21, Wilton Way
  Hackney
  London E8

   Screen 'n' Heard

1613 LIVERPOOL COTTON SERVICES LTD.
  Cotton Exchange Building
  Liverpool 3

   Cotton Outlook

1614 LIVERPOOL GEOLOGICAL SOCIETY
  c/o Geology Dept.
  University
  Liverpool

   Amateur Geologist

1615   LIVERPOOL UNIVERSITY PRESS
        123 Grove Street
        Liverpool L7 7AF

          Annals of Tropical Medicine and Parasitology
          Bulletin of Hispanic Studies
          International Review of Applied Psychology
          Journal of Comparative Pathology
          Journal of Small Animal Practice
          Research in Veterinary Science
          Town Planning Review

1616   E & S LIVINGSTONE LTD.
        15-17, Teviot Place
        Edinburgh 1

          Paraplegia
          Transactions of the Society of Occupational
            Medicine

1617   LLOYDS BANK LTD.
        71, Lombard Street
        London EC3

          Lloyds Bank Review

1618   LLOYDS BANK
        Elizabeth House
        9-11, Bush Lane
        London EC4R OAR

          Dark Horse

1619   LOCKWOOD PRESS LTD.
        6-7, Gough Square
        Fleet Street
        London EC4 A3DL

          Eurofruit

1620   LODGEMARK PRESS LTD.
        Bank House
        Summerhill
        Chislehurst
        Kent

          RAC Motor Sport News

1621   LOMAX, ERSKINE & CO. LTD.
        8, Buckingham Street
        London WC2

          Civil Engineering & Public Works Review
          Insulation

1622   LONDON & MIDDLESEX ARCHAEOLOGICAL SOCI-
    ETY
        Bishopsgate Institute
        230, Bishopsgate
        London EC2

          Transactions of the London & Middlesex Ar-
            chaeological Society

1623   LONDON & SHEFFIELD PUBLISHING CO.
        65-66, Turnmill Street
        London EC1

          Clay Crafts & Structural Ceramics
          Refractories Journal

1624   LONDON ARCHAEOLOGIST PUBLISHING COM-
    MITTEE
        7, Coalecroft Road
        London SW15

          London Archaeologist

1625   LONDON ASSOCIATION OF ENGINEERS
        12, St. Martin's Drive
        Eynsford
        Dartford
        Kent

          Journal of the London Association of Engineers

1626   LONDON BOROUGH OF CAMDEN
        St. Pancras Library
        100, Euston Road
        London NW1 2AJ

          Camden Journal

1627   LONDON BOROUGH OF LAMBETH
        Town Hall
        Brixton Hill
        London SW2 1RW

          Lambeth Local

1628   LONDON BOROUGH of NEWHAM EDUCATION
    OFFICES
        Broadway
        Stratford
        London E15

          Forum

1629   LONDON BOROUGH OF REDBRIDGE
        Health & Welfare Dept.
        17/23, Clements Road
        Ilford
        Essex

          Redbridge Medical Journal

1630   LONDON BRICK CO. LTD.
        Stewartby,
        Bedford

          L.B.C. Review

1631   LONDON BUREAU
        266-272, Kirkdale
        Sydenham
        London SE26 4R2

          Exhibition Bulletin

1632   LONDON CHAMBER OF COMMERCE & INDUSTRY
        69, Cannon Street
        London EC4N 5AB

          Eastern Europe
          Home & Economic Affairs Newsletter

1633   LONDON COLLEGE OF MUSIC
        47, Great Marlborough Street
        London W1

          London College of Music Magazine

1634   LONDON CORN CIRCULAR LTD.
        52, Mark Lane
        London EC3

          London Corn Circular

1635   LONDON DIARY PUBLICATIONS LTD.
        39, Hertford Street
        London W1Y 8HR

          London Weekly Diary of Social Events

1636   LONDON MAGAZINE
        30, Thurloe Place
        London SW7

          London Magazine

1637   LONDON MOSQUE
        16, Gressenhall Road
        London SW18 5Q1

          Muslim Herald

1638   LONDON PUBS
        8, Charing Cross Road
        London WC2

          London Pubs

1639 LONDON RECUSANT SOCIETY
21, Merryhills Drive
Enfield
Middlesex EN2 7N5

London Recusant

1640 LONDON REGION FREE RADIO CAMPAIGN
35, Glenmore Road
London NW3

Script

1641 LONDON REVIEW
60, The Priory
Priory Park
London SE3 9U2

London Review

1642 LONDON SCHOOL OF ECONOMICS & POLITICAL
SCIENCE
St. Clement's Building
Clare Market
London WC2A 2AE

Clare Market Review

1643 LONDON SCHOOL OF ECONOMICS
Houghton Street
Aldwych
London WC2A 2AE

British Journal of Industrial Relations
Economica
Journal of Transport Economics and Policy
L.S.E.

1644 LONDON SCHOOL OF ECONOMICS
Population Investigation Committee
Houghton Street
Aldwych
London WC2A 2AE

Population Studies

1645 LONDON SCHOOL OF HYGIENE AND TROPICAL
MEDICINE
Keppel Street
London WC1

Journal of Helminthology

1646 LONDON SOCIETY
4, Carmelite Street
London EC4

Journal of the London Society

1647 LONDON SOCIETY
3, Dean's Yard
London SW1

London Society Journal

1648 LONGACRE PRESS LTD
161-166, Fleet Street
London EC4

Cycling
Football Monthly
Rugby World

1649 LONGMAC LTD.
Research Publications Services
Victoria Hall
East Greenwich
London SE10 0RF

Recall

1650 LONGMAN GROUP LTD.
33, Montgomery Street
Edinburgh EH7 5JX

British Journal of Disorders of Communica-
tion
British Journal of Oral Surgery
British Journal of Plastic Surgery
British Journal of Urology
Clinical Radiology
Hand
Journal of Bone and Joint Surgery
Journal of the Royal College of General Prac-
titioners
Paraplegia
Quarterly Journal of Experimental Physiology
Practitioner
Scottish Medical Journal
Transactions of the Society of Occupational
Medicine
Tropical Animal Health and Production
Tubercle

1651 LONGMAN'S GROUP LTD.
5, Bentinck Street
London W1M 5RN

Animal Production
B.T.T.A. Review
British Poultry Science
English Historical Review
General Education
Mathematics in School
Remedial Education
Statistician
Teaching Politics
Urban Studies

1652 LONGMAN GROUP LTD.
43/9, Annandale Street
Edinburgh EH7 4AT

Heredity
Journal of Medical Microbiology
Journal of Pathology
Review of Economic Studies
Scottish Journal of Political Economy
Tissue and Cell

1653 LONGMANS GREEN & CO. LTD.
48, Grosvenor Street
London W1

Review of English Literature

1654 LONGRIDGE HOUSE
Manchester M60 4DT

British Engine Technical Report

1655 LONSDALE PUBLICATIONS LTD.
120, Lower Ham Road
Kingston on Thames
Surrey

Florist

1656 LORD BEAUMONT OF WHITLEY
59, West Heath Road
London NW3

New Outlook

1657 LORD'S DAY OBSERVANCE SOCIETY
55, Fleet Street
London EC4Y 1LQ

Joy and Light

1658 LOVERSEED PRESS
Woolacombe House
141, Woolacombe Road
Blackheath
London SE3

Day by Day

1659 LUCIS PRESS LTD.
128, Finchley Road
Hampstead
London NW3

Beacon

1660 LUDD'S MILL POETRY PUBLISHING CO-OPERA-
TIVE
4, Novell Place
Almondbury
Huddersfield
Yorks

Ludd's Mill

1661 LUTE SOCIETY
5, Wilton Square
London N1

Journal of the Lute Society

1662 LYONS MAID LTD.
Glacier House
Hammersmith Grove
London W6 0NG

Salemaker

1663 M.C.B. EUROPEAN TRAINING LTD.
200, Keighley Road
Bradford BD9 4JZ

European Training
International Journal of Physical Distribution
Management Decision

M.I.A. PUBLISHING LTD.
9, Victoria Road
Coulsdon
Surrey CR3 2NN

Management in Action

1665 M.P.U. PUBLICATIONS LTD.
55-56, Russell Square
London WC1

Medical World

1666 M.R.A. INFORMATION SERVICE
45, Hays Mews
London W1X 7RT

M.R.A. Information Service

1667 M.S.O.R. LTD.
288, High Street
Croydon
Surrey CRO 1NG

Computer Executive

1668 M & W PUBLICATIONS LTD.
42, Stanley Street
Liverpool L1 6AW

Police College Magazine
Police World

1669 M.A.C.
c/o 42, Ladyland Road
Maybole
Ayr

Mac

1670 M.A.C. FISHERIES LTD.
Ocean House
Bracknell
Berks

Mac Matters

1671 MACE MARKETING SERVICES
113, Upper Richmond Road
London SW15 2TL

Mace Forum

1672 McEVOY PRESS LTD.
58, Middle Abbey Street
Dublin 1

Irish Industry

1673 McGRAW HILL INTERNATIONAL PUBLICATIONS
McGraw-Hill House
Maidenhead SL6 QL
Berks

International Management (English Language
Edition)
International Management (Spanish
Language Edition)
Metalworking Production

1674 MACHINE TOOL INDUSTRY RESEARCH ASSO-
CIATION
Hulley Road
Hurdsfield
Macclesfield
Cheshire

Machine Tool Research
Production Technology

1675 MACHINERY MARKET LTD.
146A, Queen Victoria Street
London EC4V 5AR

Machinery Market

1676 MACHINERY PUBLISHING CO. LTD.
New England House
New England Street
Brighton BN1 4HN

Machinery and Production Engineering

1677 MACLAREN PUBLISHERS LTD.
P.O. Box 109
69/77, Davis House
High Street
Croydon CR9 1QH

Audio Visual
Baking Industries Journal
British Baker
Food and Drink Weekly
Incentive Marketing
Index
Industrial and Commercial Photographer
Materials Reclamation Weekly
Mintel
Plastics and Rubber Weekly
Refrigeration and Air Conditioning
Rubber Journal

1678 MACLEAN-HUNTER LTD.
30, Old Burlington Street
London W1X 2AE

British Printer
British Rate & Data
Business Systems and Equipment
Modern Purchasing
Packaging News
Small Offset Printing

1679 T. McMAHON
31, Marlborough Park Centre
Belfast BT9 6HN

Caret

1680 MACMILLAN & CO. LTD.
Houndmills
Basingstoke
Hants.

Theoria to Theory

1681 MACMILLAN (JOURNALS) LTD.
Brunel Road
Basingstoke
Hants.

Brain
British Journal of Pharmacology
Economic Journal
Education and Training
Nature
Occupational Health
Philosophy
Policy and Politics

1682 R. MADLEY
54, Grafton Way
London W1

University College Hospital Magazine

1683 MAGAZINES FOR INDUSTRY INC.
59, Fleet Street
London EC4Y 1JU

European Board Markets

1684 DEREK MAGGS
36, Sherand Road
London SE9 6EP

Poet

1685 MAGNUM PUBLICATIONS LTD.
157, Station Road East
Oxted
Surrey RH8 0QE

Furniture and Bedding Production

1686 MANAGEMENT PUBLICATIONS LTD.
Gillow House
5, Winsley Street
London W1A 2HG

Management Today

1687 MAGAZINES FOR INDUSTRY INC.
59, Fleet Street
London EC4

Agricultural Supply Industry
International Container Directory
Packaging Week
Paperboard Packaging International

1688 MAGIC CIRCLE
84, Chenies Mews
London WC1

Magic Circular

1689 J. KENNETH MAJOR
2, Eldon Road
Reading RG1 4DH

Millnotes

1690 MALLARD PUBLISHING CO. LTD.
167, High Holborn
London WC1

Glass Age

1691 MAMMILLARIA SOCIETY
c/o 26, Glenfield Road
Banstead
Surrey

Journal of the Mammillaria Society

1692 MANCHESTER ASSOCIATION OF ENGINEERS
MTA Office
UMIST
Sackville Street
Manchester

Manchester Engineer

1693 MANCHESTER BUSINESS SCHOOL LIBRARY
Booth Street West
Manchester

Current Contents in Management

1694 MANCHESTER CHAMBER OF COMMERCE & IN-
DUSTRY
P.O. Box 559
Ship Canal House
King Street
Manchester M60 2HB

Monthly Record

1695 MANCHESTER CULTURAL COMMITTEE
Central Library
St Peter's Square
Manchester M2 5PD

Manchester Review

1696 MANCHESTER LITERARY AND PHILOSOPHICAL
SOCIETY
36, George Street
Manchester M1 4HA

Memoirs and Proceedings: Manchester Literary and Philosophical Society

1697 MANCHESTER MENSA
Sear House
Sear Square
212, Buxton Road
Stockport

Sear

1698 MANCHESTER TRANSPORT MUSEUM SOCIETY
1020, Manchester Road
Castleton
Rochdale
Lancs

765 Journal

1699 MANCHESTER UNIVERSITY PRESS
316-324, Oxford Road
Manchester M13 9NR

African Social Research
Research in Education

1700 MANIFOLD PUBLICATIONS
Mathematics Institute
University of Warwick
Coventry CV4 7AL

Manifold

1701 MANUFACTURERS AGENTS ASSOCIATION
P.O. Box 8
Majestic House
Staines
Middx.

Manufacturer's Agent

1702 MANX MUSEUM AND NATIONAL TRUST
Douglas
I.O.M.

Journal of the Manx Museum

1703 MARCHAM MANOR PRESS
c/o Department of Religious Studies
University of Aberdeen
Aberdeen AB9 2UB

Bulletin of the Society For African Church
History

1704 MARCONI-ELLIOTT AVIONIC SYSTEMS LTD.
Airadio Division
Christopher Martin Road
Basildon
Essex

Airadio News

1705 MARCONI COMMUNICATION SYSTEMS LTD.
Marconi House
Chelmsford
Essex

Marconi Communication Systems
Point to Point Communications
Sound and Vision Broadcasting

1706 MARCONI INSTRUMENTS LTD.
Longacres
St.Albans
Herts

Contact
Marconi Instrumentation

1707 MARCONI INTERNATIONAL MARINE CO.LTD.
Elettra House
Westway
Chelmsford
Essex

Mariner

1708 MARCONI RADAR SYSTEMS LTD.
Crompton Works
Chelmsford
Essex

Radar Systems International

1709 MARDON SON & HALL LTD.
Caxton Printers
Temple Street
Bristol BS99 7PB

The Caxtonian

1710 MARINE PUBLICATIONS
55, High West Street
Dorchester
Dorset

Marine Product Guide
Multihull

1711 MARITIME WORLD LTD.
24, Petworth Road
Haslemere
Surrey

Navy International

1712 MARJAN PRESS
Bedwell Community Centre
Bedwell Crescent
Stevenage
Herts.

PSI: Popular and Amateur Science Index
Photography Index For Amateurs

1713 MARKET RESEARCH SOCIETY
51, Charles Street
London W1X 7PA

Journal of the Market Research Society
Market Research Abstracts

1714 MARKHAM HOUSE PRESS LTD.
58, West Street
Brighton

New World Antiquity

1715 MARLAND LEE LTD.
2, Arundel Street
London WC2

Art and Antiques Weekly
Coins, Medals and Currency Digest
Coins, Medals and Currency Weekly
Silver Bulletin

1716 MARLEY LTD.
Riverhead
Sevenoaks
Kent

Marley News

1717 MARLOWE SOCIETY
193, White Horse Hill
Chislehurst
Kent

Marlovian Chronicle

1718 MARRIED WOMENS ASSOCIATION
87, Redington Road
London NW3 7RR

Married Women's Association Bulletin

1719 MARTEC PUBLISHING GROUP LTD.
61, Berners Street
London W1P 3AE

Monthly Soccer
Spacewise

1720 MARXIST-LENINIST ORGANISATION OF BRITAIN
18, Camberwell Church Street
London SE5

Red Front
Red Vanguard

1721 MARY GLASGOW PUBLICATIONS LTD.
140, Kensington Church Street
London W8

Current
Schuss

1722 MARYLEBONE PRESS LTD.
276/282, Corn Exchange
Fennel Street
Manchester M4 3HF

Barnsley
Training Officer

1723 H.A.MASON
Newhayes
Huntingdon Road
Cambridge

Cambridge Quarterly

1724 MASONIC RECORD CO. LTD.
38, Great Queen Street
London WC2

Masonic Record

1725 MASS SPECTROMETRY DATA CENTRE
Aldermaston
Reading RG7 4PR

Mass Spectrometry Bulletin

1726 MASTER BAKER
114, Somerton Road
Belfast BT15 4DG

Master Baker

1727 MASTER PHOTOGRAPHER'S ASSOCIATION
80, Rochester Row
London SW1

Master Photographer

1728 MATHEMATICAL PIE LTD.
Alpha House
The Avenue
Rowington
Warks

Mathematical Pie

1729 MATHEMATICAL SPECTRUM
c/o Hicks Building
University
Sheffield S3 7RH

Mathematical Spectrum

1730 MAXWELL PUBLICITY LTD.
49, Wainsfort Park
Dublin 6

World of Irish Nursing

1731 MEAT AND LIVESTOCK COMMISSION
Economic Information Service
Queensway House
Bletchley
Bucks

International Market Survey
Market Survey

1732 MEAT TRADES JOURNAL
5, Charterhouse Square
London EC1

Meat Trades Journal

1733 MEDIA EXPENDITURE ANALYSIS LTD.
66, Dean Street
London W1

MEAL Monthly Digest

1734 MEDIA PROMOTION LTD.
1, Chester Close
Chester Street
London SW1X 7BG

Time Sale

1735 MEDICAL AND ALLIED PUBLICATIONS
24, Merchants Quay
Dublin 8

Irish Medical Times
MIMS Ireland

1736 MEDICAL AND TECHNICAL PUBLISHING CO. LTD.
PO Box 55
St. Leonards House
Lancaster

Environment this Month

1737 MEDICAL ENGINEERING WORKING PARTY
The Institution of Mechanical Engineers
1, Birdcage Walk
London SW1H 9JJ

Engineering in Medicine

1738 MEDICAL TRIBUNE LTD.
37 New Bond Street
London W1

Medical News-Tribune

1739 MEDICAL WOMEN'S FEDERATION
Tavistock House North
Tavistock Square
London WC1

Journal of the Medical Women's Federation

1740 MEDIUM
20, Morningside Place
Norris Green
Liverpool 11

Medium

1741 MEDWAY CHAMBER OF COMMERCE
21, Railway Street
Chatham
Kent

Medway

1742 MEN OF THE TREES
Crawley Down
Crawley
Sussex

Trees

1743 MENDIP PUBLICATIONS LTD.
7, Swans Lane
Draycott
Somerset BS27 3SS

Moneymaker

1744 MENSA JOURNAL
1, Carlingford Road
Hampstead
London NW3

Mensa Journal

1745 MENTAL HEALTH ASSOCIATION OF IRELAND
7, Upper Pembroke Street
Dublin 2

Newsletter: Mental Health Association of
Ireland

1746 MERCHANT NAVY & AIRLINE OFFICERS' ASSOCIA-
TION
133-137, Whitechapel High Street
London E1 7PU

Telegraph

1747 MERCURY HOUSE CONSUMER PUBLICATIONS LTD.
109, Waterloo Road
London SE1

Motor Cycle Mechanics
Motorcycle, Scooter and 3-Wheeler Mechanics

1748 MERCURY HOUSE PUBLICATIONS LTD.
Waterloo Road
London SE1

Car Mechanics
Football Pictorial
Hot Car
Popular Motoring

1749 MERCURY HOUSE BUSINESS PUBLICATIONS LTD.
Waterloo Road
London SE1 8UL

Automotive Design Engineering
Cricketer
Journal of Environmental Planning and Pollu-
tion Control

1750 MERIDIAN LTD.
   Haydn Road
   Nottingham

   Meridian News

1751 METAL BULLETIN LTD.
   46, Wigmore Street
   London W1H 0BJ

   Industrial Minerals
   Metal Bulletin

1752 METALS AND METALLURGY TRUST
   17, Belgrave Square
   London SW1

   Journal of the Institute of Metals

1753 METEOROLOGICAL OFFICE
   MET 08
   London Road
   Bracknell
   Berks RG12 2SZ

   Estimated Soil Moisture Deficit and Potential
   Evapotranspiration over Great Britain

1754 METHODIST BOOK CENTRE
   Caernarvon
   St. David's Rd
   Caernarvon

   Y Traethodydd

1755 METHODIST CHURCH MUSIC SOCIETY
   5, Leyton Villas
   Redland
   Bristol BS6 6JF

   Methodist Church Music Society Bulletin

1756 METHODIST MISSIONARY SOCIETY
   25, Marylebone Road
   London NW1 5JR

   Now

1757 METRIC INFORMATION SERVICE
   Triumph House
   189, Regent Street
   London W1R 7WF

   Metric Information Service Bulletin
   Metrication News

1758 METRICATION BOARD
   22, Kingsway
   London WC2B 6LE

   Going Metric

1759 METROPRESS LTD.
   1, Newport House
   15/18, Great Newport Street
   London WC2

   Antiques Trade Gazette

1760 MICROFILM ASSOCIATION OF GREAT BRITAIN
   c/o Science Library
   Queen's University of Belfast
   Chlorine Gardens
   Belfast 9

   Microdoc

1761 MICROINFO LTD.
   4, High Street
   Alton
   Hants

   FT Abstracts in Science and Technology
   Microinfo
   Pollution

1762 MICROSCOPE PUBLICATIONS LTD.
   2, McGrove Mews
   Belsize Lane
   London NW3

   Microscope

1763 MIDDLE EAST INTERNATIONAL PUBLISHERS LTD
   4, Vincent Square
   London SW1

   Middle East International

1764 MIDDLESEX PUBLISHING CO. LTD.
   21, New Street
   London EC2M 4NT

   Resuscitation
   Timber and Plywood

1765 MIDLAND BANK LTD.
   Economics Dept.
   Poultry
   London EC2P 2BX

   Midland Bank

1766 MIDLAND BANK LTD.
   Bucklersbury House
   83, Cannon Street
   London EC4N 8DS

   Midbank Chronicle

1767 MIDLAND SOCIETY FOR THE STUDY OF MENTAL
   SUBNORMALITY
   Monyhull Hospital
   Birmingham 30

   Journal of Mental Subnormality

1768 MIGRAINE TRUST
   23, Queen Square
   London WC1N 3AY

   Hemicrania
   Migraine News

1769 MILES MEDIA LTD.
   High Street
   Gillingham
   Dorset

   Market Report

1770 MILK MARKETING BOARD
   Thames Ditton
   Surrey

   Milk Producer

1771 B. MILLS
   3, Ilford Road
   High West
   Jesmond
   Newcastle-on-Tyne 3

   Dreamer

1772 MILTON PUBLISHING CO. LTD.
   28, Craven Street
   London WC2N 5PD

   Electro Optics
   Lab
   Medical Equipment
   Science Teaching Equipment

1773 MINERALOGICAL SOCIETY
   41, Queen's Gate
   London SW7 5HR

   Mineralogical Abstracts
   Mineralogical Magazine

1774 MINING JOURNAL LTD.
      15, Wilson Street
      London EC2

          Mining Journal
          Mining Magazine

1775 MINISTRY OF DEFENCE
      Navy Dept.
      H.M. Dockyard
      Rosyth
      Inverkeithing

          Spotlight

1776 MISSIONS TO SEAMEN
      St Michael's Paternoster Royal
      College Hill
      London EC4R 2RL

          Flying Angel News

1777 MITCHELL COTTS GROUP LTD.
      Cotts House
      Camomile Street
      London EC3P 3AJ

          Cottsman

1778 MODEL & ALLIED PUBLICATIONS LTD.
      13-35, Bridge Street
      Hemel Hempstead
      Herts

          Aeromodeller
          Military Modelling Magazine
          Model Cars
          Model Engineer
          Model Maker and Model Boats
          Radio Control Models and Electronics

1779 MODERN CHURCHMEN'S UNION
      Caynham Vicarage
      Ludlow
      Salop

          The Modern Churchman

1780 MODERN HUMANITIES RESEARCH ASSOCIATION
      c/o Bedford College
      Regent's Park
      London NW1

          Modern Language Review

1781 MODERN LANGUAGE ASSOCIATION
      2, Manchester Square
      London W1M 5RF

          Modern Languages

1782 MODERN MEDICINE OF GREAT BRITAIN LTD.
      414, High Road
      London W4

          Modern Geriatrics
          Modern Medicine

1783 MODINO PRESS LTD.
      6, Conduit Street
      London W1R 9TG

          Oxford Magazine

1784 MOLE EXPRESS
      7, Summer Terrace
      Manchester 14

          Mole Express

1785 MOLE EXPRESS
      19, New Brown Street
      Manchester 4

          Mole Express

1786 MONARCHIST LEAGUE
      29, York Street
      London W1

          Monarchist

1787 MONDAY CLUB OF SCOTLAND
      59, Ravelston Road
      Bearsden
      Glasgow

          Monday Scot

1788 MONEYSAVERS ASSOCIATION
      Tower Suite
      1, Whitehall Place
      London SW1

          Money Savers

1789 MONITOR CONSULTANTS
      35, John Street
      London WC1N 2AT

          China Trade and Economic Newsletter

1790 MONITOR NAVAL PUBLICATIONS LTD.
      4, Vicarage Road
      Eastbourne
      Sussex

          Naval Record

1791 MONOGRAM PUBLICATIONS
      63, Old Compton Street
      London W1V 5PN

          Monogram

1792 MONOTYPE CORPORATION LTD.
      43, Fetter Lane
      London EC4

          Monotype Bulletin
          Monotype Recorder

1793 MONTH PUBLICATIONS
      114, Mount Street
      London W1Y 6AH

          Month

1794 MOODIES SERVICES
      6-8, Bonhill Street
      London EC2A 4BU

          Moodies Information Services
          Moodies Japanese Review

1795 S. MOORE
      7, Hillend
      Shooters Hill
      London SE18 3NH

          Doomlore
          Orpheus

1796 MORGAN CRUCIBLE CO. LTD.
      98, Petty France
      London SW1H 9EG

          Morgan's World

1797 MORGAN GRAMPIAN LTD.
      Commercial Exhibitions & Publications Ltd.
      Riverside House
      Hough Street
      Woolwich
      London SE18 6LR

          Business Administration
          World Fishing

1798 MORGAN GRAMPIAN (PUBLISHERS) LTD.
Morgan Grampian House
Calderwood Street
London SE18 6QH

Building Design
Construction Plant and Equipment
Control and Instrumentation
Design Engineering
Design Engineering—Product Information
Electronic Engineering
Engineer
Factory
Fluid Power International
Food Manufacture
Freight Transport Equipment
Freight Transport—Services
Hardware Merchandiser
Manufacturing Chemist & Aerosol News
Metalworking Production International
Paint Manufacture
Process Engineering
World Crops

1799 MORNING ADVERTISER
18-20, St Andrew Street
London EC4

Licensee

1800 MORGAN-SUTTON AND ASSOCIATES LTD.
8, North Street
Guildford
Surrey

Doctor

1801 MORRIS INTERNATIONAL
4, Vincent Square
Westminster
London SW1

Voice

1802 MORTON NEWSPAPER GROUP
Windsor Avenue
Lurgan

Farm Week

1803 MOTHER'S UNION
St. Mary's House
125, Herne Hill
London SE24

Home & Family

1804 MOTOR AGENTS ASSOCIATION
201, Great Portland Street
London W1N 6AB

Motor Track Executive

1805 MOTOR INDUSTRY RESEARCH ASSOCIATION
Lindley
Nuneaton
Warwicks

MIRA Abstracts
Automobile Abstracts

1806 MOTOR SCHOOLS ASSOCIATION OF GREAT BRITAIN
Atherton House
12, Tilton Street
London SW6 7LR

MSA News

1807 MOTORING LIFE
39, Lower Ormond Quay
Dublin 1

Motoring Life

1808 MOUNTAIN MAGAZINES LTD.
102A, Westbourne Grove
London W2

Mountain

1809 MOVEMENT
14, Hanley Road
London N4

Movement

1810 JOSEPH MULHOLLAND
43, Westbourne Gardens
Glasgow G12 9XQ

Glasgow Review

1811 MULTI-SCIENCE PUBLISHING CO. LTD.
28, Greville Street
London EC1

Acoustics Abstracts
Electronics and Communications Abstracts
Medical Electronics and Communications
Abstracts
Noise and Vibration Bulletin
Russian Ultrasonics
Surface Wave Abstracts

1812 MUNICIPAL JOURNAL LTD.
178-202, Great Portland Street
London W1N 6NH

Municipal and Public Services Journal
Municipal Engineering

1813 MUNICIPAL PUBLICATIONS
3, Clements Inn,
London WC2

Rural District Review

1814 MUNRO BARR PUBLICATIONS
94, Hope Street
Glasgow C2

Golf Monthly
National Guardian

1815 MUSCULAR DYSTROPHY GROUP OF GREAT
BRITAIN
26, Borough High Street
London SE1 9QG

Muscular Dystrophy Journal

1816 MUSEUMS ASSOCIATION
87, Charlotte Street
London W1P 2BX

Museums Association Monthly Bulletin
Museums Calendar
Museums Journal

1817 MUSHROOM GROWERS' ASSOCIATION
Agriculture House
Knightsbridge
London SW1X 7 NJ

MGA Bulletin

1818 MUSIC BOX SOCIETY OF GREAT BRITAIN
Bylands
Crockham Hill
Edenbridge
Kent

Music Box

1819 MUSICAL INSTRUMENT PROMOTION ASSOCIATION
44, Berners Street
London W1P 3AB

Living Music

1820 MUSICAL OPINION LTD.
87, Wellington Street
Luton

Musical Opinion
Organ

1821 MUZZLE LOADERS ASSOCIATION OF GREAT
BRITAIN
Old Manor House
Radcliffe-on-Trent
Notts

Black Powder

1822 NC MAGAZINES LTD.
172-174, Kingston Road
Ewell
Surrey

Index of Veterinary Specialists
Modern Photographer
Vending
Veterinary News

1823 NEDO
Millbank Tower
Millbank
London SW1P 4QX

Neddy in print

1824 NAAFI
Public Relations Dept.
London SE11 5QX

Naafi News

1825 NALGO ACTION NEWS
42, Southwood Avenue
London N6

Nalgo Action News

1826 NALGO
8, Harwood Row
London NW1

Public Service

1827 NAMES SOCIETY
7, Aragon Avenue
Thames Ditton
Surrey KT7 0PY

Viz

1828 NARROW GAUGE RAILWAY SOCIETY
47, Birchington Avenue
Birchencliffe,
Huddersfield HD3 3RD

Narrow Gauge
Narrow Gauge News

1829 NATIONAL ADULT SCHOOL UNION
Drayton House
Gordon Street
London WC1H 0BE

One and All

1830 NATIONAL AND COMMERCIAL BANKING GROUP
LTD.
3, Bishopsgate
London EC2N 3AA

Three Banks Review

1831 NATIONAL ANTI-VIVISECTION SOCIETY LTD.
51, Harley Street
London W1

Animals Defender and Anti-Vivisection News

1832 NATIONAL ASSOCIATION FOR THE CARE AND RE-
SETTLEMENT OF OFFENDERS
125, Kennington Park Road
London SE11

NACRO Information Bulletin

1833 NATIONAL ASSOCIATION FOR MENTAL HEALTH
39, Queen Anne Street
London W1 0AJ

British Journal of Ophthalmology
British Journal of Venereal Diseases
Mental Health
Mind
Ophthalmic Literature
Psychological Medicine

1834 NATIONAL ASSOCIATION OF ALMSHOUSES
Billingbear Lodge
Wokingham
Berks

Almshouses Gazette

1835 NATIONAL ASSOCIATION OF BOOKMAKERS LTD.
Sabian House
26-27, Cowcross Street
London EC1

British Bookmaker

1836 NATIONAL ASSOCIATION OF CLINICAL TUTORS
General Infirmary
Salisbury
Wilts

Bulletin of the National Association of Clinical
Tutors

1837 NATIONAL ASSOCIATION OF DROP FORGERS AND
STAMPERS
245, Grove Lane
Handsworth
Birmingham 20

Drop Forging Bulletin

1838 NATIONAL ASSOCIATION OF FLOWER ARRANGE-
MENT SOCIETIES
Lye End Link
St John's
Woking
Surrey

Flower Arranger

1839 NATIONAL ASSOCIATION OF LADIES CIRCLES
Provincial House
Cooke Street
Keighley
Yorks BD21 3NN

Ladies Circle Magazine

1840 NATIONAL ASSOCIATION OF MASTER BAKERS
Queen's House
Holly Road
Twickenham
Middx

Bakers' Review

1841 NATIONAL SOCIETY OF MASTER PATTERN-
MAKERS
12, Cherry Street
Birmingham 2

British Master Patternmaker

1842 NATIONAL ASSOCIATION OF PARISH COUNCILS
100, Great Russell Street
London WC1

Parish Council's Review

1843 NATIONAL ASSOCIATION OF POULTRY PACKERS
LTD.
High Holborn House
52/54, High Holborn
London WC1

National Association of Poultry Packers Ltd.
Weekly Industry
National Association of Poultry Packers Ltd.
Market Price Report

1844 NATIONAL ASSOCIATION OF PROBATION
OFFICERS
6, Endsleigh Street
London WC1H 0D2

Probation

1845 NATIONAL ASSOCIATION OF PROPERTY OWNERS
14-16, Bressenden Place
London SW1

Property Journal

1846 NATIONAL ASSOCIATION OF ROUND TABLES OF
GREAT BRITAIN & IRELAND
78, Old Broad Street
London EC3

News and Views

1847 NATIONAL ASSOCIATION OF SEED POTATO
MERCHANTS
11A, High Street
Chippenham
Wilts

Seed Potato

1848 NATIONAL ASSOCIATION OF SOFT DRINKS
MANUFACTURERS LTD.
The Gatehouse
2, Holly Road
Twickenham TW1 4EF

Soft Drinks Trade Journal

1849 NATIONAL ASSOCIATION OF TEACHERS OF THE
MENTALLY HANDICAPPED
1, Beechfield Avenue
Urmston
Manchester 31 3RT

Teaching and Training

1850 NATIONAL ASSOCIATION OF THEATRE NURSES
6, Gordon Road
Windsor
Berks

Natnews

1851 NATIONAL AURICULA & PRIMULA SOCIETY
67, Warnham Court Road
Carshalton Beeches
Surrey

Offsets

1852 NATIONAL BEGONIA SOCIETY
c/o 50, Woodlands Farm Road
Erdington
Birmingham 24

National Begonia Society Bulletin

1853 NATIONAL BOOK LEAGUE
7, Albemarle Street
London W1X 4BB

Books

1854 NATIONAL CACTUS AND SUCCULENT SOCIETY
19, Crabtree Road
Bottey
Oxford OX2 9DU

National Cactus and Succulent Society Journal

1855 NATIONAL CAMPAIGN FOR THE HOMELESS &
ROOTLESS
7, Sole Street
Crundale
Canterbury

Cyrenian

1856 NATIONAL CASH REGISTER CO. LTD.
206/216, Marylebone Road
London NW1

NCR Post

1857 NATIONAL CENTRAL LIBRARY
Store Street
London WC1E 7DG

Solanus

1858 NATIONAL CENTRE FOR SCHOOL TECHNOLOGY
Trent Polytechnic
Burton Street
Nottingham

Satis
School Technology

1859 NATIONAL CHAMBER OF TRADE
Enterprise House
Henley-on-Thames
Oxon

National Chamber of Trade Journal

1860 NATIONAL CHILDBIRTH TRUST
9, Queensborough Terrace
Bayswater
London W2 3TB

National Childbirth Trust Newsletter

1861 NATIONAL CHILDREN'S BUREAU
85, Highbury Park
London N5

Concern

1862 NATIONAL COAL BOARD
Mining Research and Development Establishment
Ashby Road
Stanhope Bretby
Burton-on-Trent DE15 0QD

Mining Research and Development Review

1863 NATIONAL COAL BOARD
Hobart House
Grosvenor Place
London SW1X 7AE

Coal News

1864 NATIONAL COLLEGE OF TEACHERS OF THE DEAF
32, Merston Drive,
Manchester M20 0WT

Teacher of the Deaf

1865 NATIONAL COMMITTEE FOR AUDIO VISUAL AIDS
IN EDUCATION
33, Queen Anne Street
London W1M 0AL

Visual Education

1866   NATIONAL COUNCIL FOR ANIMALS WELFARE
         126, Royal College Street
         London NW1

         Animals' Friend Magazine

1867   NATIONAL COUNCIL FOR CIVIL LIBERTIES
         152, Camden High Street
         London NW1

         NCCL Bulletin
         Speak-out

1868   NATIONAL COUNCIL FOR EDUCATIONAL TECH-
       NOLOGY
         160, Great Portland Street
         London W1N 5TB

         NCET News

1869   NATIONAL COUNCIL FOR QUALITY AND RELIA-
       BILITY
         1, Birdcage Walk
         London SW1H 9JY

         Quality Matters

1870   NATIONAL COUNCIL OF SOCIAL SERVICE
         26, Bedford Square
         London WC1B 3HU

         Social Service Quarterly
         Village

1871   NATIONAL COUNCIL OF SOCIAL SERVICE FOR
       THE STANDING CONFERENCE FOR LOCAL
       HISTORY
         26, Bedford Square
         London

         Local Historian

1872   NATIONAL COUNCIL OF SOCIAL SERVICE FOR
       WOMEN'S GROUP ON PUBLIC WELFARE
         26, Bedford Square
         London WC1B 3HU

         Newsletter of the Women's Group on Public
           Welfare and the Standing Conferences of
           Women's Organisations

1873   NATIONAL COUNCIL OF YOUNG MEN'S CHRISTIAN
       ASSOCIATIONS
         112, Great Russell Street
         London WC1

         YMCA World

1874   NATIONAL DEAF CHILDREN'S SOCIETY
         31, Gloucester Place
         London W1H 4EA

         Talk

1875   NATIONAL ECONOMIC DEVELOPMENT OFFICE
         Millbank
         London SW1P 4OX

         Newsletter: Economic Development Committee
           for Electrical Engineering

1876   NATIONAL ELECTRONICS COUNCIL
         Abell House
         John Islip Street
         London SW1P 4CN

         National Electronics Review

1877   NATIONAL EXTENSION COLLEGE
         Shaftesbury Road
         Cambridge

         Home Study

1878   NATIONAL FARMERS UNION
         Agriculture House
         Knightsbridge
         London SW1

         British Farmer

1879   NATIONAL FARMERS UNION
         Springfield
         Spalding
         Lincs

         South Lincolnshire Farmer

1880   NATIONAL FARMERS UNION OF SCOTLAND
         17, Grosvenor Crescent
         Edinburgh EN12 5EN

         Farming Leader

1881   NATIONAL FEDERATION OF BUSINESS AND
       PROFESSIONAL WOMEN'S CLUBS OF GREAT
       BRITAIN & N. IRELAND
         54, Bloomsbury Street
         London WC1

         Business and Professional Woman

1882   NATIONAL FEDERATION OF CLAIMANTS UNIONS
         74A, Stratford Road
         Sparkbrook
         Birmingham B11 1AN

         NFCU Journal

1883   NATIONAL FEDERATION OF MASTER PAINTERS
       & DECORATORS
         6, Haywra Street
         Harrogate
         Yorks HG1 5BC

         Master painter and Decorator

1884   NATIONAL FEDERATION OF MASTER WINDOW
       CLEANERS
         104, Hathersage Road
         Charlton-on-Medlock
         Manchester M13 0XH

         Window Talk

1885   NATIONAL FEDERATION OF MEAT TRADERS
       ASSOCIATIONS
         29, Linkfield Lane
         Redhill
         Surrey

         Meat Trader

1886   NATIONAL FEDERATION OF OLD AGE PENSIONS
       ASSOCIATIONS
         91, Preston New Road
         Blackburn
         Lancs

         Pensioner's Voice

1887   NATIONAL FEDERATION OF PARENT-TEACHER
       ASSOCIATIONS
         5, Ransley Green
         Ruckinge
         Ashford
         Kent

         Parent-Teacher

1888   NATIONAL FEDERATION OF ROOFING
       CONTRACTORS
         West Bar Chambers
         38, Boar Lane
         Leeds LS1 5DE

         Roofing Contractor

1889 NATIONAL FEDERATION OF SUB-POSTMASTERS
22, Windlesham Gardens
Shoreham-by-Sea
Sussex

Sub-Postmaster

1890 NATIONAL FEDERATION OF VILLAGE PRODUCE
ASSOCIATIONS
Northam
North Road
Berkhamsted
Herts

Village Life

1891 NATIONAL FEDERATION OF WHOLESALE
GROCERS & PROVISION MERCHANTS
18, Fleet Street
London EC4

Wholesale Grocer

1892 NATIONAL FEDERATION OF WOMEN'S INSTITUTES
11a, King's Road
Sloane Square
London SW3

Home & Country

1893 NATIONAL FOUNDATION FOR EDUCATIONAL
RESEARCH IN ENGLAND & WALES
The Mere
Upton Park
Slough
Bucks

Educational Research

1894 NATIONAL FREIGHT CORPORATION
Argosy House
215, Great Portland Street
London W1N 6BD

Freightway

1895 NATIONAL FROEBEL FOUNDATION
Froebel Institute
Grove House
Roehampton Lane
London SW15

Froebel Journal

1896 NATIONAL GRAPHICAL ASSOCIATION
63/67, Bromham Road
Bedford

Print

1897 NATIONAL HAMSTER COUNCIL
c/o Crantock
Goatacre Lane
Medstead
Alton
Hants

National Hamster Council Journal

1898 NATIONAL HOUSING & TOWN PLANNING COUNCIL
11, Green Street
London W1Y 4ES

Housing & Planning Review

1899 NATIONAL INDUSTRIAL MATERIALS RECOVERY
ASSOCIATION
Carolyn House
Dingwall Road
Croydon CR9 2YU

Industrial Recovery

1900 NATIONAL INDUSTRIAL SAFETY ORGANIZATION
Ansley House
Mespil Road
Dublin 4

Sciath

1901 NATIONAL INSTITUTE FOR ADULT EDUCATION
35, Queen Anne Street
London W1M 0BL

Adult Education
Teaching Adults

1902 NATIONAL INSTITUTE OF AGRICULTURAL
BOTANY
Huntingdon Road
Cambridge

Journal of the National Institute of Agricultural
Botany

1903 NATIONAL INSTITUTE OF ECONOMIC & SOCIAL
RESEARCH
2, Dean Trench Street,
Smith Square
London SW1P 3NE

National Institute Economic Review

1904 NATIONAL INSTITUTE OF INDUSTRIAL
PSYCHOLOGY
14, Welbeck Street
London W1M 8DR

NIIP Bulletin
Occupational Psychology

1905 NATIONAL INSTITUTE OF MEDICAL HERBALISTS
LTD.
169, Norfolk Street
Sheffield

Herbal Practitioner

1906 NATIONAL LENDING LIBRARY FOR SCIENCE &
TECHNOLOGY
Boston Spa
Yorks

NLL Announcements Bulletin
NLL Review

1907 NATIONAL LIBRARY OF WALES
Aberystwyth
Cardigan SW23 3BU

National Library of Wales Journal

1908 NATIONAL MAGAZINE CO. LTD.
Chestergate House
Vauxhall Bridge Road
London SW1V 2HF

Connoisseur
Good Housekeeping

1909 NATIONAL MAGAZINE CO. LTD.
680, Garrett Lane
London SW17

Bike
Car
Containerisation International
Cosmopolitan
Environmental Pollution Management
Harpers Bazaar and Queen
She

1910 NATIONAL MARRIAGE GUIDANCE COUNCIL
3, Gower Street
London WC1E 6HA

Marriage Guidance

1911	NATIONAL MILK PUBLICITY COUNCIL INC. John Princes Street London W1M 0AP Dairy Education	1924	NATIONAL SOCIETY FOR THE PREVENTION OF CRUELTY TO CHILDREN 1, Riding House Street London W1 Child's Guardian
1912	NATIONAL MUSEUM OF WALES Cathays Park Cardiff CF1 3NP Amgueddfa	1925	NATIONAL SOCIETY OF CHILDREN'S NURSERIES 45, Russell Square London WC1 Nursery Journal
1913	NATIONAL OPERATIC & DRAMATIC ASSOCIATION 1, Crestfield Street London WC1N 8AV NODA Bulletin	1926	NATIONAL SOCIETY OF OPERATIVE PRINTERS GRAPHICAL AND MEDIA PERSONNEL 13-16, Borough Road London SE1 0AL Journal and Graphical Review
1914	NATIONAL OPINION POLLS LTD. 76/86, Strand London WC2R 0DZ NOP Bulletin	1927	NATIONAL SWEET PEA SOCIETY 33, Priory Road Rustington, Littlehampton Sussex Bulletin of the National Sweet Pea Society
1915	NATIONAL PHILATELIC SOCIETY 44, Fleet Street London EC4 Stamp Lover	1928	NATIONAL TROLLEY BUS ASSOCIATION 12, Coltsfoot Drive Burpham Guildford Surrey Trolley bus Magazine
1916	NATIONAL PIG BREEDERS ASSOCATION 51A, Clarendon Road Watford Herts WD1 1HT Pig Breeders Gazette	1929	NATIONAL TRUST 42, Queen Annes Gate London SW1 National Trust News
1917	NATIONAL PLAYING FIELDS ASSOCIATION 57B, Catherine Place London SW1 Playing Fields	1930	NATIONAL UNION OF SEAMEN Maritime House Old Town Clapham London SW4 Seaman
1918	NATIONAL PORTS COUNCIL 1-19, New Oxford Street London WC1A 1DZ National Ports Council Bulletin	1931	NATIONAL UNION OF TAILORS AND GARMENT WORKERS 14, Kensington Square London W8 Garment Worker
1919	NATIONAL RADIOLOGICAL PROTECTION BOARD Clifton Avenue Belmont Sutton Surrey Radiological Protection Bulletin	1932	NATIONAL UNION OF TEACHERS Hamilton House Mabledon Place London WC1 Higher Education Journal Secondary Education
1920	NATIONAL RIFLE ASSOCIATION Bisley Camp Brookwood Woking Surrey National Rifle Assocation Journal	1933	NATIONAL VULCAN ENGINEERING INSURANCE GROUP LTD. St. Mary's Parsonage Manchester M60 9AP Vigilance
1921	NATIONAL SCHOOL BRASS BAND ASSOCIATION c/o 2, Gray's Close Barton-le-Clay Bedford Trumpeter	1934	NATIONAL WESTMINSTER BANK LTD. 41, Lothbury London EC2 National Westminster Bank Quarterly Review
1922	NATIONAL SOCIETY FOR CLEAN AIR 136, North Street Brighton Sussex BN1 1RQ Clean Air	1935	NATIONAL WESTMINSTER BANK 75, Shaftesbury Avenue London W1V 8AT National Westminster
1923	NATIONAL SOCIETY FOR MENTALLY HANDI-CAPPED CHILDREN 86, Newman Street London W1 Journal of Mental Deficiency Research		

1936 NATIONWIDE BUILDING SOCIETY
New Oxford House
Holborn
London WC1V 6PW

Occasional Bulletin

1937 NATIONAL DAIRYMEN'S ASSOCIATION
37, Queen's Gate
London SW7

Milk Industry

1938 NATURAL ENVIRONMENT RESEARCH COUNCIL
Alhambra House
27-33, Charing Cross Road
London WC2H 0AX

NERC News Journal

1939 NATURAL HISTORY AND ANTIQUARIAN SOCIETY
OF MID ARGYLL
Harbour House
Crinan
Lochgilphead
Argyll

Kist

1940 NATURAL HISTORY SOCIETY OF NORTHUMBER-
LAND, DURHAM & NEWCASTLE-ON-TYNE
Hancock Museum
Newcastle-on-Tyne NE2 4PT

Transactions of the Natural History Society of
Northumberland, Durham and Newcastle-
on-Tyne

1941 NATURAL RUBBER PRODUCERS RESEARCH
ASSOCIATION
56, Tewin Road
Welwyn Garden City
Herts

NR Technology
Quarterly List of Publications
Rubber Developments

1942 NAVAL REVIEW
Hell Cross
Swanmore
Southampton

Naval Review

1943 NEEDLE
27, Pearman Street
London SE1

Needle

1944 NEEDLE INDUSTRIES
Stationery Office
Studley
Warwickshire

Ensign

1945 NEEDLECRAFT LTD.
School Street
Bromley Cross
Bolton
Lancs

Needlewoman and Needlecraft

1946 NESTLÉ CO. LTD.
St. George's House
Park Lane
Croydon
Surrey CR9 1NR

Nestlé Group News

1947 NEW BELLS PRESS
Walnut Tree Manor
Haughley
Stowmarket
Suffolk IP14 3RS

SPAN (Soil-Plant-Animal-Man)
Soil Biology and Biochemistry
Journal of the Soil Association

1948 NEW BLACKFRIARS
St Dominics Priory
Southampton Road
London NW5

New Blackfriars

1949 NEW CENTURY PUBLISHING CO. LTD.
84-88, Great Eastern Street
London EC2

Shoe and Leather News

1950 NEW DEPARTURES
Pidmont
Bisley
Stroud
Glos

New Departures

1951 NEW EDUCATIONAL PRESS
Pekes
Hellingley
Hailsham
Sussex

Debate
European Parliament Digest
Problems of Society
Westminster Summary

1952 NEW LEFT REVIEW
7, Carlisle Street
London W1

New Left Review

1953 NEW MEDIA LTD.
5/6, Argyll Street
London W1

Motor Trade Equipment Monitor

1954 NEW MEDICAL JOURNALS LTD.
26/27, Oxandon Street
London SW1Y 4EL

World Medicine

1955 NEW PROPERTY PRESS
5, St. Peters' Street
London N1

Building and Heating Products Guide

1956 NEW SCIENCE PUBLICATIONS
128, Long Acre
London WC2E 9QH

New Scientist and Science Journal
New Society

1957 NEW TOWNS ASSOCIATION
Glen House
Stag Place
London SW1E 5AJ

New Towns Bulletin

1958 NEW WRITERS' PRESS
19, Warrenmount Place
Dublin 8

Lace Curtain

1959   NEWCASTLE REGIONAL HOSPITAL BOARD
        Editorial Office
        Shotley Bridge General Hospital
        Consett
        Co. Durham

        Adverse Drug Reaction Bulletin

1960   NEWCOMEN SOCIETY
        Science Museum
        London SW7

        Transactions of the Newcomen Society

1961   NEWMAN BOOKS LTD.
        48, Poland Street
        London W1V 4PP

        Nutrition
        Property and Investment Review
        Shop Property

1962   NEWS & BOOK TRADE REVIEW & STATIONER'S
        GAZETTE LTD.
        15, Charterhouse Street
        London EC1N 6RL

        Retail Newsagent

1963   NEWS & MEDIA LTD.
        33, Stroud Green Road
        London N4 3EF

        Impact

1964   NEWSLETTERS FOR BUSINESS
        139, Northolt Road
        South Harrow
        Middx HA2 0LX

        VAT Newsletter

1965   NEWSPAPER SOCIETY
        6, Carmelite Street
        London EC4Y 0BL

        Production Journal

1966   NEWTON CHAMBERS GROUP
        Chapeltown
        Sheffield S3O 4YP

        NC News

1967   NICHOLSON & BASS LTD.
        34, Alfred Street
        Belfast

        Short Story

1968   NIGEL SITWELL LTD.
        21-22, Great Castle Street
        London W1

        Animals

1969   NON-DESTRUCTIVE TESTING SOCIETY OF GREAT
        BRITAIN
        700, London Road
        Westcliff-on-Sea
        Essex

        British Journal of Non-Destructive Testing

1970   NORFOLK & NORWICH ARCHAEOLOGICAL
        SOCIETY
        Garrert House
        St Andrews Hall Plain
        Norwich NOR 16J

        Norfolk Archaeology

1971   NORFOLK NAUTICAL SOCIETY
        Opie House
        Castle Meadow
        Norwich NOR O3D

        East Coast Mariner

1972   NORTH EAST COAST INSTITUTION OF ENGINEERS
        & SHIPBUILDERS
        Bolbec Hall
        Newcastle-upon-Tyne NE1 1TB

        Transactions of the North East Coast Institution
        of Engineers & Shipbuilders

1973   NORTH EAST GROUP FOR THE STUDY OF LABOUR
        HISTORY
        c/o Department of Humanities
        Newcastle upon Tyne Polytechnic
        NE1 8ST

        Bulletin of North East Group for the Study of
        Labour History

1974   NORTH EAST PUBLICITY ASSOCIATION
        c/o Repro Services Ltd.
        17, Portland Terrace
        Newcastle-upon-Tyne NE2 1SJ

        Periscope

1975   NORTH EAST SCOTLAND DEVELOPMENT
        AUTHORITY
        15, Union Terrace
        Aberdeen AB1 1NJ

        North Light

1976   NORTH EASTERN ELECTRICITY BOARD
        Carliol House
        Newcastle-on-Tyne NE99 1SE

        Nor'-Easter

1977   NORTH MAGAZINE
        49, Stonegate
        York

        North Magazine

1978   NORTH OF ENGLAND ZOOLOGICAL SOCIETY
        Zoological Gardens
        Upton-by-Chester
        Cheshire

        Cheshire Zoo News

1979   NORTH OF SCOTLAND COLLEGE OF AGRICUL-
        TURE
        School of Agriculture
        Aberdeen

        Farm Management Review

1980   NORTH OF SCOTLAND GRASSLAND SOCIETY
        c/o 581, King Street
        Aberdeen

        Norgrass

1981   NORTH STAFFORDSHIRE CHAMBER OF
        COMMERCE & INDUSTRY
        Winton House
        Stoke Road
        Stoke-on-Trent

        Focus on Industry and Commerce

1982   NORTH STAFFORDSHIRE FIELD CLUB
        c/o University of Keele
        Keele
        Staffs ST5 5BG

        North Staffordshire Journal of Field Studies

1983 NORTH SURREY DYSLEXIA SOCIETY
c/o Mrs V. M. Fisher
Cambridge Cottage
Broadway
Laleham
Staines
Middx TW18 1SB

Dyslexia Review

1984 NORTH THAMES GAS BOARD
30, Kensington Church Street
London W8 4HB

Modern Living
Thames Gas

1985 NORTH WALES ASSOCIATION FOR THE ARTS
9-11 Wellfield House
Bangor
Sir Gaernarfon

Mabon

1986 NORTH WALES NEWSPAPERS LTD
Caxton Press
Oswestry
Salop

Country Quest

1987 NORTH WEST LANCASHIRE CHAMBER OF
COMMERCE
1, Garstang Road
Preston

Forum

1988 NORTH WESTERN ELECTRICITY BOARD
Cheetwood Road
Manchester

Norweb News

1989 NORTHAMPTON INDEPENDENT LTD.
The Parade
Northampton

Northampton and Country Independent

1990 NORTHAMPTONSHIRE FEDERATION OF
ARCHAEOLOGICAL SOCIETIES
c/o Department of Adult Education
The University
Leicester

Northamptonshire Archaeology

1991 NORTHAMPTONSHIRE RECORD SOCIETY
Delapré Abbey
Northampton

Northamptonshire Past and Present

1992 NORTHERN ARTS
31, New Bridge Street
Newcastle-upon-Tyne NE1 8JY

Arts North

1993 NORTHERN HORTICULTURAL SOCIETY
Harlow Car Gardens
Harrogate
Yorks

Northern Gardner

1994 NORTHERN HOUSE
58, Queen's Road
Newcastle-upon-Tyne NE2 2PR

Northern House Pamphlet Poets

1995 NORTHERN IRELAND ASSOCIATION FOR MENTAL
HEALTH
Beacon House
84, University Street
Belfast BT7 1HE

Beacon House News

1996 NORTHERN IRELAND COMMUNITY RELATIONS
COMMISSION
Bedford House
Bedford Street
Belfast BT2 7FD

Community Forum

1997 N. IRELAND INFORMATION SERVICE
Stormont Castle
Belfast 4

Ulster Commentary

1998 NORTHERN NOTES
2, Whinway
Washington
Co. Durham

Northern Notes

1999 NORTHUMBRIAN PUBLISHING CO.
36, St Mary's Place
Newcastle-upon-Tyne 1

Northumbrian

2000 NORTHWOOD PUBLICATIONS LTD.
Elm House
Elm Street
London WC1

Catering Times
Factory Management
Farm and Country
Furnishing Review
Industrial Management
Business Publications Ltd
Print Room
Printing Equipment and Materials

2001 NORTHWOOD PUBLICATIONS LTD.
(Thomson Organisation Ltd.)
Northwood House
93-99, Goswell Road
London EC1V 7QA

Big Farm Management
Brewer's Guardian
Paper Facts and Figures
Retail Jeweller
TAB-Tyres Accessories Batteries

2002 NORWICH UNION INSURANCE GROUP
Surrey Street
Norwich NOR 88A

NU Norwich Newsletter
Norwich Union Group Magazine

2003 NOTTINGHAM & NOTTINGHAMSHIRE TECHNICAL
INFORMATION SERVICE
Central Library
South Sherwood Street
Nottingham NG1 4DA

Nantis News

2004 NOTTINGHAM CHAMBER OF COMMERCE &
INDUSTRY
395, Mansfield Road
Nottingham NG5 2DL

Industrial Nottingham

2005 NOTTINGHAM CORPORATION
Publicity & Information Dept.
54, Milton Street
Nottingham

Nottingham City News and Calendar

2006 NOTTINGHAM FRENCH STUDIES
The University
Nottingham

Nottingham French Studies

2007 NOTTINGHAM MEDIAEVAL STUDIES
The University
Nottingham

Nottingham Mediaeval Studies

2008 NOTTINGHAMSHIRE NATIONAL FARMERS' UNION
7, The Ropewalk
Nottingham NG1 1BR

Nottinghamshire Farmers' Journal

2009 NOVEL PUBLISHERS LTD.
132, Wardour Street
London W1

Embassy

2010 NOVELLO & CO. LTD.
27, Soho Square
London W1V 6BR

Music in Education
Musical Times
Sounding Brass

2011 NOVELLO & CO. LTD.
Borough Green
Kent

Jazz Journal

2012 JOHN NOYCE
67, Vere Road
Brighton

Librarians for Social Change

2013 NUMISMATIC PUBLISHING CO.
Sovereign House
High Street
Brentwood
Essex

Coin Monthly

2014 NU-SWIFT INTERNATIONAL LTD.
Elland
Yorks HX5 9DS

Nu-Swift Fire Fighting News

2015 NURSING NOTES LTD.
98, Belsize Lane
London NW3 5BB

Midwives Chronicle

2016 O.S. & S. LTD.
14, Peterborough Road
Harrow
Middx

Contact Lens

2017 OASIS BOOKS
12, Stevenage Road
London SW6 6ES

Oasis

2018 OFF-LICENCE JOURNAL
1, Dorset Buildings
London EC4

Off-Licence Journal

2019 OFFICE FOR SCIENTIFIC AND TECHNICAL
INFORMATION
Elizabeth House
39, York Road
London SE1 7PH

OSTI Newsletter

2020 OSTI LIBRARY AUTOMATION PROJECT
University Library
Southampton

Vine

2021 OFFICE PUBLICATIONS LTD.
Mercury House
Waterloo Road
London SE1

Surface Coatings

2022 OIL AND COLOUR CHEMISTS ASSOCIATION
Wax Chandlers Hall
Gresham Street
London EC2V 7AB

Journal of the Oil and Colour Chemists
Association

2023 OIL FIRING PUBLICATIONS LTD.
The Fernery
Market Place
Midhurst
Sussex

Oil and Gas Firing

2024 OLD ATHLONE SOCIETY
Athlone County
Westmeath
Ireland

Journal of the Old Athlone Society

2025 OLD CATHOLIC CHURCH IN BRITAIN
267, Beechings Way
Rainham
Kent

Old Catholic Church Herald

2026 OLD TIME MUSIC
33, Brunswick Gardens
London W8

Old Time Music

2027 OLIVER & BOYD LTD.
Tweeddale Court
14 High Street
Edinburgh 1

Proceedings of the Edinburgh Mathematical
Society
Transactions of the Glasgow Archaeological
Society

2028 OPEN UNIVERSITY
Walton Hall
Milton Keynes
Bucks

Sesame

2029 OPENINGS PRESS
Rooksmoor House
Woodchester
Glos.

Openings

2030 OPTICAL WORLD LTD.
65, Brook Street
London W1Y 2DT

Optical World

2031 ORE PUBLICATIONS
11, High Plash
Cutty's Lane
Stevenage
Herts.

Ore

2032 ORGAN CLUB
c/o Graham & Bramber
93, Lynton Road
Acton
London W3 9HL

Organ Club Journal

2033 ORIEL PRESS LTD.
32, Ridley Place
Newcastle-upon-Tyne
NE1 8LH

Glass Circle
Religion
Transactions of the Architectural & Archaeological Society of Durham and Northumberland
Vernacular Architective

2034 ORIENTAL ART MAGAZINE LTD.
12, Ennerdale Road
Richmond
Surrey
Oriental Art

2035 ORION PRESS
81, Marlborough Road
Salford
Manchester M8 7DT

L'Incroyable Cinema

2036 OUTPOSTS PUBLICATIONS
72, Burwood Road
Walton-on-Thames
Surrey

Outposts

2037 OUR DOGS PUBLISHING CO. LTD.
5, Oxford Road
Station Approach
Manchester M60 1SY

Our Dogs

2038 OUR LADY OF ENGLAND PRIORY
Storrington
Pulborough
Sussex

White Canons

2039 OVE ARUP PARTNERSHIP
13 Fitzroy Street
London W1P 6BQ

Arup Journal

2040 OVERSEAS DEVELOPMENT ADMINISTRATION
Foreign & Commonwealth Office
Eland House
Stag Place
London SW1

Overseas Development

2041 OXFAM
74A, High Street
Wallingford
Berks

New Internationalist

2042 OXFORD CONSUMERS GROUP
11, Cooper Place
Headington Quarry
Oxford OX3 8JW

Oxford Consumer

2043 OXFORD SOCIETY FOR SOCIAL RESPONSIBILITY IN SCIENCE
27, Wytham Street
Oxford

Fulcrum

2044 OXFORD UNIVERSITY FOREST SOCIETY
Department of Forestry
South Parks Road
Oxford OX1 3RB

Oxford University Forest Society Journal

2045 OXFORD UNIVERSITY PRESS
Press Road
Neasden
London NW10

African Affairs
Annals of Botany
Antiquaries Journal
British Economy Survey
Classical Quarterly
Classical Review
Community Development Journal
Critical Quarterly
English
English in Education
English Language Teaching
Forestry
Greece and Rome
International Affairs
International Journal of Agrarian Affairs
International Journal of Epidemiology
International Review of Applied Linguistics in Language Teaching
Journal of Commonwealth Literature
Journal of Experimental Botany
Journal of Petrology
Journal of Soil Science
Journal of Theological Studies
Library
Multiracial School
Music and Letters
Notes and Queries
Oxford Economic Papers
Oxford German Studies
Political Studies
Proceedings of the London Mathematical Socie
Quarterly Journal of Mathematics
Quarterly Journal of Mechanics and Applied Mathematics
Quarterly Journal of Medicine
Race
Review of English Studies
Round Table
Sociology
World Today

2046 OZ PUBLICATIONS INK LTD.
19, Gt. Newport Street,
London WC2

Oz

2047 PF PUBLICATIONS
554, Garratt Lane
London SW17 0NY

Petfish Monthly

2048 PH PRESS LTD.
231, Strand
London WC2R 1DA

Policy Holder Insurance Journal

2049 PIRA
Randalls Road
Leatherhead
Surrey

PIRA Marketing Abstracts
PIRA News
PIRA Packaging Journal
Packaging Abstracts
Paper and Board Abstracts
Printing Abstracts
Printing Journal

2050 P S L PUBLICATIONS LTD.
9, Ely Place
London EC1N 6SQ

Airfix Magazine
Autoworld

2051 P S W PUBLICATIONS
11, Pendene Road
Leicester LE2 3DQ

Forum For the Discussion of New Trends in
Education

2052 PAGAN MOVEMENT IN BRITAIN AND IRELAND
Cymdeithas Selene,
Cân y Lloer,
Ffarmers,
Llanwrda,
Sir Gaer Fyrddin
South Wales

Waxing Moon

2053 PAINT RESEARCH ASSOCIATION
Woldegrave Road
Teddington
Middx TW11 8LD

World Surface Coatings Abstracts

2054 PALAEONTOLOGICAL ASSOCIATION
c/o Hunterian Museum University
Glasgow G12 8QQ

Palaeontology
Special Papers in Palaeontology

2055 PALESTINE EXPLORATION FUND
2, Hinde Mews
Marlebone Lane
London W1

Palestine Exploration Quarterly

2056 PALL MALL LTD.
South Bank House
Black Prince Road
Lambeth
London SE11

Bartender

2057 PAN AFRICANIST CONGRESS OF AZANIA
(SOUTH AFRICA)
22a, Hillview Gardens
London NW4 2JH

Azania Combat

2058 PAPER & PAPER PRODUCTS INDUSTRY
TRAINING BOARD
Star House
Potters Bar
Herts.

Paper Training News

2059 PARCHMENT (OXFORD) LTD.
100 Bullingdon Road
Oxford

Carcanet

2060 PARK LANE PUBLICATIONS LTD.
70, Chiswick High Road
London W4

Stone Industries

2061 PARK LANE PUBLICATIONS LTD.
54/55 Wilton Road
London SW1

Hair and Beauty
Light Aviation

2062 PARK STREET PUBLISHING CO.
Kennington Oval
London SE11

Golf International

2063 B W PARKER
30 George Square
Glasgow C2

Scottish Plumbers Journal

2064 S. E. PARKER
2, Orsett Terrace
London W2 6AH

Minus One

2065 PARKER PEN CO. LTD.
15, Grosvenor Gardens
London SW1W 0BL

Pen & Ink

2066 PARKERS PRICE GUIDES
52, Parker Street
London WC2B 5QB

Parkers Car Price Guide

2067 PARLIAMENTARY DIGEST
171, Queen Victoria Street
London EC4

Review of Parliament
Review of Parliament and Parliamentary Digest

2068 PARTICLE SCIENCE AND TECHNOLOGY
INFORMATION SERVICE
University of Technology
Loughborough
LE11 3TV

Particulate Information

2069 PATENT OFFICE
St. Mary Cray
Orpington
Kent BR5 3RD

Official Journal (Patents)
Trade Marks Journal

2070 PATERNOSTER PRESS
Paternoster House
3 Mount Radford Crescent
Exeter EX2 4JW

Emergency Post
Evangelical Quarterly
Harvester

2071 PAULL & GOODE PUBLISHING LTD.
Midland Bank Chambers
St Thomas Street
Sunderland

Northern Industry
Northern Perspective
Yorkshire Architect

2072 PAUL CAVE PUBLICATIONS LTD.
39, Above Bar
Southampton
Hampshire

Hampshire

2073 PEARL & DEAN LTD.
33, Dover Street
London W1X 4AJ

Cunard Trafalgar

2074 PECO PUBLICATIONS & PUBLICITY LTD.
Pecoway House
7/9, Harbour Road
Seaton
Devon Ex12 2LV

Railway Modeller

2075 PEDESTRIANS' ASSOCIATION FOR ROAD SAFETY
Suite 4
166, Shaftesbury Avenue
London WC2H 8JH

Arrive

2076 PEGLERS LTD.
Belmont Works
St. Catherine's Avenue
Doncaster

Belmont Standard

2077 R. PEMBERTON
76, Rosedale Avenue
Great Crosby
Liverpool L23 0UA

Contrasts

2078 PEMBERTON PUBLISHING CO. LTD.
88, Islington High Street
London N1 8EL

Journal of Moral Education
New Humanist
Question

2079 PEMBROKESHIRE LOCAL HISTORY SOCIETY
4, Victoria Place
Haverfordwest

Pembrokeshire Historian

2080 PENGELLY CAVE STUDIES TRUST LTD.
British Museum (Natural History)
Cromwell Road
London SW7 5BD

Studies in Speleology

2081 PENGUIN BOOKS LTD.
Harmondsworth
Middx

Penguins in Print
Penguin News
Puffin Post

2082 PENSION PUBLICATIONS LTD.
Management Office
14, Finsbury Circus
London EC2

Benefits International

2083 PENTECOSTAL HOLINESS CHURCH
35, Dongola Road
Bristol BS7 0HW

Proclaimer

2084 PENTHOUSE PUBLICATIONS LTD.
2 Bramber Road
London W14 9PB

Penthouse

2085 PENTON PUBLISHING CO. LTD.
26/28, Addiscombe Road
Croydon CR9 5BW

Service Station

2086 PEOPLE'S DISPENSARY FOR SICK ANIMALS
PDSA House
South Street
Dorking
Surrey

Animals Magazine

2087 PERCY LUND HUMPHRIES & CO. LTD.
Bradford

Asia Major

2088 PERENNIAL BOOKS LTD.
Pates Manor
Bedfont
Middx TW14 8JP

Studies in Comparative Religion

2089 PERGAMON PRESS LTD.
Headington Hill Hall
Oxford OX3 0BW

Accident Analysis and Prevention
Acta Metallurgica
Annals of Occupational Hygiene
Annals of the C I R P
Archives of Oral Biology
Art Psychotherapy
Astronautica Acta
Atmospheric Environment
Automatica
Behaviour Research and Therapy
Biochemical Pharmacology
Biochemical Systematics
Biophysics
Biorheology
British Journal of Addiction
Building Science
Bulletin of Mechanical Engineering Education
Carbon
Cement and Concrete Research
Chemical Engineering Science
Chemosphere
Chromatographia
Clays and Clay Minerals
Comparative Biochemistry and Physiology
Computers and Algorithms
Computers and Electrical Engineering
Computers and Fluids

Computers and Graphics
Computers and Mathematics
Computers and Structures
Computers in Biology and Medicine
Contributions to Atmospheric Physics
Corrosion Science
Deep-Sea Research and Oceonographic Abstracts
    Abstracts
Direct Current
Electric Technology USSR
Electrochemica Acta
Energy Conversion
European Journal of Cancer
European Polymer Journal
Experimental Gerontology
Food and Cosmetics Toxicology
Forma et Functio
Geochimica et Cosmochimica Acta
Geoforum
Group Analysis
Health Physics
Immunochemistry
Information Storage and Retrieval
Infrared Physics
Inorganic and Nuclear Chemistry Letters
International Abstracts of Biological Sciences
International Journal of Engineering Science
International Journal for Parasitology
International Journal for Radiation Physics and
    Chemistry
International Journal of Applied Radiation and
    Isotopes
International Journal of Electrical Engineering
    Education
International Journal of Heat and Mass Transfer
International Journal of Insect Morphology
    and Embryology
International Journal of Machine Tool Design
    and Research
International Journal of Mechanical Sciences
International Journal of Non-Linear Mechanics
International Journal of Nuclear Medicine
    and Biology
International Journal of Nursing Studies
International Journal of Rock Mechanics and
    Mining Sciences
International Journal of Solids and Structures
Isis
Journal of Aerosol Science
Journal of Applied Mathematics and Mechanics
Journal of Atmospheric and Terrestrial
    Physics
Journal of Behaviour Therapy and Experi-
    mental Psychiatry
Journal of Biomechanics
Journal of Child Psychology and Psychiatry
    and Allied Disciplines
Journal of Criminal Justice
Journal of Inorganic and Nuclear Chemistry
Journal of Insect Physiology
Journal of Mechanisms
Journal of Neurochemistry
Journal of Nuclear Energy
Journal of Physics and Chemistry of Solids
Journal of Psychiatric Research
Journal of Psychosomatic Research
Journal of Stored Products Research
Journal of the Franklin Institute
Journal of the Mechanics and Physics of
    Solids
Journal of Quantitative Spectroscopy and
    Radioactive Transfer
Journal of Steroid Biochemistry
Journal of Terramechanics
Journal of Ultrasound in Medicine and
    Biology
Leonardo
Letters in Applied and Engineering Sciences
Life Sciences
Long Range Planning

Materials and Research Bulletin
Meccanica
Mechanical Sciences Research Communications
Medical Officer
Microelectronics and Reliability
Neuropharmacology
Neuropsychologia
New Schoolmaster
Ocean Engineering
Omega
Operational Research Quarterly
Pattern Recognition
Photochemistry and Photobiology
Physics of Metals and Metallography
Physiology and Behaviour
Phytochemistry
Planetary and Space Science
Plasma Physics
Polymer Science USSR
Radiation Botany
Regional Studies
Rheology Abstracts
Science, Medicine and Man
Scottish Educational Journal
Scripta Metallurgica
Social Science and Medicine
Socio-Economic Planning Sciences
Sociology of Education Abstracts
Solar Energy
Solid State Communications
Solid-State Electronics
Supervisor
Talanta
Tetrahedron
Tetrahedron Letters
Thermal Engineering
Topology
Toxicon
Transportation Research
USSR Computational Mathematics &
    Mathematical Physics
Vacuum
Vision Research
Water Research

2090   PERIVALE BIRD SANCTUARY
    c/o 3, Cambalt Road
    London SW15 6EL

        Newsletter of the Perivale Bird Sanctuary

2091   PERKIN-ELMER LTD.
    Post Office Lane
    Beaconsfield
    Bucks HP9 1QA

        Perkin-Elmer Analytical News (PELAN)
        Perkin-Elmer Electron Microscopy News
        Perkin-Elmer Instrument News
        Perkin-Elmer NMR Quarterly

2092   PERSONAL RIGHTS ASSOCIATION
    31, Parkside Gardens
    London SW19

        Individualist

2093   PETER DOMINIC LTD
    12, York Gate
    London NW1

        Wine Mine

2094   PETER WAY LTD.
    28, James Street
    Covent Garden
    London WC2E 8PA

        Great Newspapers Reprinted
        Then

2095　PETERSON PUBLISHING CO. LTD.
　　　Peterson House
　　　Livery Street
　　　Birmingham 3

　　　　British Food Journal
　　　　Midland Industrialist
　　　　Plumbing Equipment News and Heating
　　　　　Engineer
　　　　Warm Air Heating and Environmental
　　　　　Engineering

2096　PHARMACEUTICAL BUSINESS ANALYSIS
　　　SERVICE
　　　27, Park View
　　　Hatch End
　　　Pinner
　　　Middx HA5 4LL

　　　　Pharmacy Management

2097　PHARMACEUTICAL PROMOTION LTD.
　　　41, Parker Street
　　　London WC2B 5NX

　　　　Folio Pharmaceutica

2098　PHARMACEUTICAL SOCIETY OF GREAT BRITAIN
　　　17, Bloomsbury Square
　　　London WC1

　　　　Journal of Pharmacy and Pharmacology
　　　　Pharmaceutical Journal

2099　PHAROS PRESS
　　　47, Nottingham Place
　　　London W1M 4BN

　　　　Pharos

2100　PHILATELIC EXPORTER LTD.
　　　PO Box 4
　　　Edgware
　　　Middx

　　　　Philatelic Exporter

2101　PHILATELIC TRADERS SOCIETY LTD.
　　　27, John Adam Street
　　　London WC2

　　　　P.T.S. Journal

2102　PHILIP KING LTD.
　　　54/55, Wilton Road
　　　London SW1

　　　　British Hospital Equipment Directory

2103　PHILLIMORE AND CO. LTD.
　　　Shopwyke Hall
　　　Chichester, Sussex

　　　　Cantium
　　　　Essex Journal
　　　　Genealogists' Magazine
　　　　Midland History
　　　　Severn and Wye Review
　　　　Sussex Industrial History

2104　PHOTOGRAMMETRIC SOCIETY
　　　5, Ashbourne Grove
　　　London NW7
　　　　Photogrammetric Record

2105　PHYSICAL EDUCATION ASSOCIATION OF GREAT
　　　BRITAIN AND NORTHERN IRELAND
　　　Ling House
　　　10, Nottingham Place
　　　London W1M 4AX

　　　　British Journal of Physical Education
　　　　Outdoors

2106　BILL PICKARD
　　　Director of Literature Bristol Arts Centre
　　　King Square
　　　Bristol 2

　　　　Poetry of the Circle in the Square

2107　C. M. PICKLES
　　　The Red House
　　　Whitehill Road
　　　Hitchin
　　　Herts.

　　　　Vole

2108　PION LTD.
　　　207, Brondesbury Park
　　　London NW2 5JN

　　　　High Temperatures—High Pressures
　　　　Perception

2109　PIPELINE INDUSTRIES GUILD
　　　7, Iddesleigh House
　　　Caston Street
　　　London SW1

　　　　Pipeline Industries Guild Bulletin

2110　PITMAN MEDICAL AND SCIENTIFIC PUBLISHING
　　　CO. LTD.
　　　31, Fitzroy Square
　　　London W1P 6BH

　　　　Journal of the Royal College of Physicians of
　　　　London

2111　PITMAN PERIODICALS LTD.
　　　33, Warwick Square
　　　London SW1U 2AN

　　　　Memo
　　　　Office Skills

2112　PLAID CYMRU
　　　Heol y Dŵr
　　　Caerfyrddin

　　　　Y Ddraig Goch

2113　PLAID CYMRU
　　　8, Heol y Frenhines
　　　Cardiff

　　　　Welsh Nation

2114　PLANET
　　　Llangeitho
　　　Tregaron
　　　Cardiganshire
　　　Wales

　　　　Planet

2115　PLANT AND EQUIPMENT PUBLICATIONS LTD.
　　　The Adelphi
　　　John Adam Street
　　　London WC2N 6AY

　　　　Construction Plant Hire

2116　PLANT PROTECTION LTD./I.C.I.
　　　Jealott's Hill Research Station
　　　Bracknell
　　　Berkshire RG12 6EY

　　　　Outlook on Agriculture

2117　PLASTICS INSTITUTE
　　　11, Hobart Place
　　　London SW1W 0HL

　　　　Plastics and Polymers

2118 PLENUM PUBLISHING CO. LTD.
Davis House
8, Scrubs Lan
Harlesden
London NW10 6SF

Behaviour Genetics

2119 PLENUM PUBLISHING CO. LTD.
Antvar House
London Road
Wembley
Middx.

Automatic Monitoring and Measuring
Electrochemistry in Industrial Processing and
Biology
Human Relations

2120 PLESSEY CO. LTD
Ilford
Essex

Systems Technology

2121 PLUMBING TRADE JOURNAL CO. LTD.
30, Princes Street
Southport
Lancs.

Plumbing and Heating Journal

2122 POETRY BOOK SOCIETY
105, Piccadilly
London W1U 0AU

Poetry Supplement

2123 POETRY SOCIETY
21, Earls Court Square
London SW5

Poetry Review

2124 POLICE FEDERATION
15-17, Langley Road
Surbiton
Surrey KT6 6LP

Police

2125 POLICE JOURNAL
Little London
Chichester
Sussex

Police Journal

2126 POLICE REVIEW PUBLISHING CO. LTD
67, Clerkenwell Road
London ECLR 5BJ

Police Review

2127 POLICY JOURNALS LTD.
13-14, Homewell
Havant
Hants

Environmental Engineering

2128 POLITICAL QUARTERLY PUBLISHING CO. LTD.
49, Park Lane
London W1

Political Quarterly

2129 POLITICAL REFERENCE PUBLICATION
18, Lincoln Green
Chichester
Sussex.

Political Companion

2130 POLITICS AND MONEY PUBLISHING CO.
14, South Hill Park Gardens
London NW3

Politics and Money

2131 POLYSTYLE PUBLICATIONS
382-386, Edgware Road
London W2 1EP

TV Action

2132 POLYTECHNIC OF CENTRAL LONDON
Dept. of Communication Studies
Regent Street
London W1

Images

2133 POPULAR ARTS REVIEW
8, Laneside Avenue
Rutherglen
Glasgow

Popular Arts Review

2134 POPULAR FLYING ASSOCIATION
2, Waldens Park Road
Horsell
Woking
Surrey

Popular Flying

2135 PORT OF LONDON AUTHORITY
World Trade Centre
London E1

Polanews
Port of London

2136 PORTAL PRESS LTD.
72, London Road
Croydon CRO 2TB

Construction Steelwork

2137 POST OFFICE
St Martin's-le-Grand
London EC1

Courier
Philatelic Bulletin

2138 POST OFFICE
23, Howland Street
London W1P 6HQ

Post Office Telecommunications Journal

2139 POST OFFICE
Camelford House
Albert Embankment
London SE1 7TS

News and Views

2140 POST OFFICE ELECTRICAL ENGINEERS
JOURNAL
2-12, Gresham Street
London EC2U 7AG

Post Office Electrical Engineers Journal

2141 POST OFFICE ENGINEERING UNION
Greystoke House
Hanger Lane
London W5

Post Office Engineering Union Journal

2142 POTATO MARKETING BOARD
50, Hans Crescent
Knightsbridge
London SW1X 0NB

Potato Quarterly

2143　POWYSLAND NEWSPAPERS
　　　　Albion Street
　　　　Hanley
　　　　Stoke-on-Trent

　　　　　Six Towns Magazine
　　　　　Staffordshire Magazine

2144　PRACTICAL PRESS LTD.
　　　　1, Dorset Buildings
　　　　London EC4

　　　　　Power Laundry and Cleaning News

2145　PREHISTORIC SOCIETY
　　　　Dept. of Archaeology
　　　　Cambridge

　　　　　Proceedings of the Prehistoric Society

2146　PRENBOURNE PUBLISHING CO. LTD.
　　　　3, Heathcock Court
　　　　Strand
　　　　London WC2

　　　　　Dinghy Sailing

2147　PRESBYTERIAN CHURCH IN IRELAND
　　　　Church House
　　　　Belfast BT1 6DW

　　　　　Presbyterian Herald

2148　PRESBYTERIAN HISTORICAL SOCIETY OF
　　　　ENGLAND
　　　　86, Tavistock Place
　　　　London WC1H 9RT

　　　　　Journal of the Presbyterian Historical Society
　　　　　of England

2149　PRESS ASSOCIATION LTD.
　　　　85, Fleet Street
　　　　London EC4P 4BE

　　　　　Press Association Link

2150　PRESS FEATURES INTERNATIONAL
　　　　For British Car Auctions (Publications) Ltd
　　　　187, Wollaton Street
　　　　Nottingham

　　　　　Motor Market News

2151　PRESS MEDIA LTD.
　　　　Ivy Hatch
　　　　Sevenoaks
　　　　Kent

　　　　　Board Manufacture

2152　PRESS SERVICES
　　　　184, Corporation Street
　　　　Birmingham 4

　　　　　MEB News

2153　PRESSDRAM LTD.
　　　　34, Greek Street
　　　　London W1

　　　　　Private Eye

2154　PREVIEW MAGAZINE LTD.
　　　　77, Park Street
　　　　Bristol 1

　　　　　Preview

2155　PRINT BUYER MAGAZINE LTD.
　　　　58, Parker Street
　　　　London WC2

　　　　　Print Buyer

2156　PRINTERHALL LTD.
　　　　34/40, Ludgate Hill
　　　　London EC4

　　　　　Traffic Engineering and Control

2157　PRINTING HISTORICAL SOCIETY
　　　　St Bride Institute
　　　　Bride Lane
　　　　Fleet Street
　　　　London EC4

　　　　　Journal of the Printing Historical Society

2158　PRINTING MANAGEMENT ASSOCIATION
　　　　55, Temple Chambers
　　　　London EC4

　　　　　Managing Printer

2159　PRINTING SERVICES PARTNERSHIP
　　　　82, High Road
　　　　East Finchley
　　　　London N2

　　　　　Community

2160　PRIORY PRESS LTD.
　　　　Priory House
　　　　Royston
　　　　Herts.

　　　　　Shopping and Homes Gazette

2161　PRISON OFFICERS ASSOCIATION
　　　　245, Church Street
　　　　Edmonton
　　　　London N9

　　　　　Prison Officers Magazine

2162　PRIVATE LIBRARIES ASSOCIATION
　　　　41, Cuckoo Hill Road
　　　　Pinner
　　　　Middx.

　　　　　Private Library

2163　PRODUCTION ENGINEERING RESEARCH
　　　　ASSOCIATION
　　　　Melton Mowbray
　　　　Leics.

　　　　　P.E.R.A. Bulletin
　　　　　Machines and Tooling
　　　　　Russian Engineering Journal

2164　PROFESSIONAL PROJECTS LTD.
　　　　Ryde House
　　　　Chobham Road
　　　　Woking
　　　　Surrey

　　　　　Pulse

2165　PROFILE PUBLICATIONS LTD.
　　　　Coberg House
　　　　Sheet Street
　　　　Windsor
　　　　Berks.

　　　　　AFV/Weapons Profile
　　　　　Aircraft in Profile
　　　　　Cars in Profile
　　　　　Locomotives in Profile
　　　　　Small Arms in Profile
　　　　　Warship Profile

2166　PROJECT SCOTLAND
　　　　62, Virginia Street
　　　　Glasgow G1 1PX

　　　　　Project Scotland

2167 PROPHETIC WITNESS PUBLISHING CO.
2, Upperton Gardens
Eastbourne
Sussex

Prophetic Witness

2168 PROUD-BAILEY CO. LTD.
96, Queen's Road
Brighton

Postal History International

2169 PROVINCIAL INSURANCE CO. LTD.
Stramongate
Kendal
Westmorland

Cover
White and Red

2170 PROVINCIAL TRADE PRESS LTD.
320, Higher Lane
Lymm
Cheshire

Club Committee

2171 PSIONIC MEDICAL SOCIETY
c/o Sandy Balls Estate
Godshill
Fordingbridge
Hants

Psionic Medicine

2172 PSYCHOLOGICAL SOCIETY OF IRELAND
Woodlands
Renmore
Galway
Ireland

Irish Journal of Psychology

2173 PSYCHOLOGIST MAGAZINE
Manfield House
1, Southampton Street
London WC2

Psychologist Magazine

2174 PUBLIC ENTERPRISE GROUP
13A, Sanderstead Hill
South Croydon
Surrey

Public Enterprise

2175 PUBLIC LIBRARY
Mare Street
Hackney
London E8 1HG

Profile

2176 PUBLIC LIBRARY
Swindon
Wilts.

In Print

2177 PUBLIC ROAD TRANSPORT ASSOCIATION
172, Buckingham Palace Road
London SW1

Public Road Transport Association Journal

2178 PUBLIC SCHOOLS APPOINTMENTS BUREAU
17, Queen Street
London W1X 8BL

PSAB News Bulletin

2179 PUBLISHERS CIRCULAR LTD.
79, Limpsfield Road
South Croydon
Surrey CR2 97E

Publisher

2180 PUNCH PUBLICATIONS LTD.
Watling Street
Bletchley
Bucks.

Punch

2181 PURITAN PRESS LTD.
353, Great Horton Road
Bradford
Yorks. BD7 3BZ

Apostolic Herald

2182 PUZZLER
16, Ellerdale Road
London NW3

Puzzler

2183 QUAINTANCE & CO. LTD.
24a, Chertsey Street
Guildford

Business Credit

2184 QUARRY MANAGERS JOURNAL LTD.
62-64, Baker Street
London W1M 2BN

Cement, Lime and Gravel
Quarry Managers Journal

2185 QUEEN'S INSTITUTE OF DISTRICT NURSING
57, Lower Belgrave Street
London SW1W 0LR

District Nursing

2186 THE QUEENS REGIMENT
Howe Barracks
Canterbury
Kent

Journal of the Queen's Regiment

2187 QUEKETT MICROSCOPICAL CLUB
c/o Royal Society
Burlington House
London W1

Journal of the Quekett Microscopical Club

2188 QUEST
209, Abbey House
Victoria Street
London SW1H 0LP

Quest

2189 R. A. SLINN LTD.
52, Kettering Road
Northampton

Remedial Gymnastics and Recreational
Therapy

2190 RAF ORNITHOLOGICAL SOCIETY
110, Edinburgh Drive
Ickenham
Uxbridge
Middx.

Journal of the RAF Ornithological Society

2191 RFWW PUBLICATIONS LTD.
Lloyds Bank Chambers
Cirencester
Glos.

Safer Motoring

2192 R. MAXWELL LTD.
Headington Hall
Oxford OX3 0PJ

Current Advances in Plant Science

2193 RACAL GROUP SERVICES LTD.
26, Broad Street
Wokingham
Berks.

Racal Grapevine
Racal Review

2194 RACE RELATIONS BOARD
5, Lower Belgrave Street
London SW1W 0NR

Race Relations

2195 RADAR AND ELECTRONICS ASSOCIATION
43, Grove Park Road
Chiswick
London W4

Radar and Electronics

2196 RADICAL PHILOSOPHY GROUP
c/o Darwin College
University of Kent
Canterbury

Radical Philosophy

2197 RADIO AND ELECTRONIC OFFICERS UNION
4-6, Branfill Road
Upminster
Essex RM14 2XX

Signal

2198 RADIO SOCIETY OF GREAT BRITAIN
35, Doughty Street
London WC1

Radio Communication

2199 RADIOCHEMICAL CENTRE
Amersham
Bucks.

Carrier Free
Technical Bulletin

2200 RADIONIC-MAGNETIC CENTRE
Raleigh Park Road
Oxford OX2 9BE

Radionic-Magnetic Centre Newsletter

2201 RADNORSHIRE SOCIETY
c/o, Radnorshire County Library H.Q.
Cefnllys Road
Llandrindod Wells
Radnorshire
Wales

Transactions of the Radnorshire Society

2202 RAILWAY AND CANAL HISTORICAL SOCIETY
34, Manor Avenue
Caterham
Surrey CR3 6AN

Journal of the Railway and Canal Historical
Society

2203 RAILWAY CORRESPONDENCE & TRAVEL SOCIET
82, Natal Road
London N11

Railway Observer

2204 RAILWAY DEVELOPMENT ASSOCIATION
3, Hall Way
Purley
Surrey

Development Report

2205 RAILWAY INDUSTRY ASSOCIATION
30/34, Buckingham Gate
London SW1E 6LH

Railpower

2206 RAILWAY INVIGORATION SOCIETY
BM-RIS
London WC1

Railway Invigoration Society Progress Report

2207 RAILWAY PHILATELIC GROUP
59A, Hartley Road
Kirkby-in-Ashfield
Nottingham NG17 8DG

Railway Philately

2208 RAILWAY PRESERVATION SOCIETY OF IRELAND
416, Lisburn Road
Belfast 9

Five Foot Three

2209 RAMBLERS ASSOCIATION
1/4, Crawford Mews
London W1H 1PT

Rucksack

2210 RAMBLERS ASSOCIATION (LAKE DISTRICT AREA
62, Loop Road North
Whitehaven

Lakeland Rambler

2211 RAMBLERS ASSOCIATION (SCOTTISH AREA)
173, Braidcroft Road
Glasgow SW3

Heel and Toe

2212 RAMSAY SOCIETY OF CHEMICAL ENGINEERS
University College
Gower Street
London WC1

Journal of the Ramsay Society of Chemical
Engineers

2213 RAMSBURY BUILDING SOCIETY
The Square
Ramsbury
Marlborough
Wilts.

Ramsbury Tree

2214 RANK AND FILE
17, Dingle Road
Ashford
Middx.

Rank and File

2215 RANK & FILE TEACHERS
28, Manor Road
London N16

Rank and File

2216   RATING PUBLISHERS LTD
        2, Paper Buildings
        Temple
        London EC4

        Rating and Valuation Reporter

2217   RAVENHILL PUBLISHING CO. LTD.
        Standard House
        Bonhill Street
        London EC2

        Guns Review

2218   READER'S DIGEST ASSOCIATION LTD.
        25, Berkeley Square
        London W1X 6AB

        Reader's Digest

2219   READERS UNION GROUP OF BOOK CLUBS
        P.O.Box 6
        Newton Abbot
        Devon TQ12 1XD

        Readers News

2220   READY MIXED CONCRETE LTD.
        RMC House
        High Street
        Feltham
        Middx.

        Strata
        Substrata

2221   REALITÉS
        195, Sloane Street
        London SW1X 9RE

        Realités

2222   RECORD SPECIALITIES
        9, Dean Street
        London W1

        New Consensus and Review

2223   RECORDER PRESS LTD.
        Church Street
        London N16

        Midwife and Health Visitor

2224   RED CANDLE PUBLICATIONS
        19, South Hill Park
        London NW3

        Candelabrum

2225   RED MACHINERY GUIDE LTD.
        13, North Audley Street
        London W1

        Red Machinery Guide

2226   RED RAG
        c/o 6, Grove Road
        London N12

        Red Rag

2227   RED RAT
        42, Essendive Mansions
        Essendine Road
        London W9

        Red Rat

2228   RED RAT
        197, Goldhurst Terrace
        London NW6

        Red Rat

2229   REDEMPTORIST PUBLICATIONS
        Alphonsus House
        Chawton
        Alton
        Hants

        Novena

2230   REDEMPTORIST PUBLICATIONS
        75, Orwell Road
        Rathgar
        Dublin 6

        Reality

2231   REEVES & SONS LTD.
        Lincoln Road
        Enfield
        Middx.

        Leisure Painter

2232   E. R. REID-SMITH
        34, Norfolk Street
        Werneth
        Oldham
        Lancs.

        Research in Librarianship

2233   RELAY SERVICES ASSOCIATION OF GREAT
        BRITAIN
        75, Cannon Street
        London EC4

        Royal Association Journal

2234   RELGOCREST LTD.
        182, Pentonville Road
        London N1

        Red Mole

2235   RELIGION IN COMMUNIST COUNTRIES

        Religion in Communist Countries

2236   RELIGIOUS SOCIETY OF FRIENDS
        6, Eustace Street
        Dublin 2

        Irish Young Friend

2237   RENOLD LTD.
        Renold House
        Wythenshawe
        Manchester M22 5WL

        Newsletter

2238   REPORT ON WORLD AFFAIRS LTD.
        32, St. James Street
        London SW1A 1HR

        Report on World Affairs

2239   REPRINT REVIEW
        47, Museum Street
        London WC1

        Reprint Review

2240   RESEARCH DEFENCE SOCIETY
        11, Chandos Street
        London W1M 9DE

        Conquest

2241   RESURGENCE
        24, Abercorn Place
        London NW8

        Resurgence

2242   RETAIL CONFECTIONER'S ASSOCIATION
        PUBLICATIONS & EXHIBITIONS LTD.
           53, Christchurch Avenue
           London N12

              Retail Confectioner
              Triple Trader

2243   RETAIL FRUIT TRADE FEDERATION LTD.
           Russell Chambers
           Covent Garden
           London WC2

              Retail Fruit Trade Review

2244   RETAIL JOURNALS LTD.
           17/19, John Adam Street
           London WC2

              Bakery Management
              Fish Trades Gazette
              Frozen Foods

2245   REVOLUTIONARY MARXIST TENDENCY OF THE
        4th INTERNATIONAL
           IMR Publications
           16a, Holmdale Road
           London NW6

              International Marxist

2246   REVOLUTIONARY WORKERS PARTY
           24, Cranbourn Street
           London WC2

              Red Flag

2247   REX COLLINGS LTD.
           6, Paddington Street
           London W1

              Africa Contemporary Record

2248   RHODES INDUSTRIAL SERVICES LTD.
           54/55, Wilton Road
           London SW1

              International Mining Equipment

2249   RHODES MARINE PUBLICATIONS LTD.
           54/5, Wilton Road
           London SW1

              Safety at Sea International

2250   M.A.RICH
           Laceys
           Berry Lane
           Chorleywood
           Herts.

              Journal of the Confederate Historical Society
              Newsletter: Confederate Historical Society

2251   RICHARD GAINSBOROUGH PERIODICALS LTD.
           8, Wyndham Place
           London W1H 2AY

              Arts Review

2252   RICHARD III SOCIETY
           72, Heathfield Road
           Croydon
           Surrey

              Ricardian

2253   CLIVE RICHARDSON
           46, Slades Drive
           Chislehurst
           Kent BR7 6JX

              Short

2254   RICKMANSWORTH HISTORICAL SOCIETY
           c/o 18, Pheasants Way
           Rickmansworth
           Herts.

              Rickmansworth Historian

2255   RIDGWAY PUBLICATIONS
           62, Doughty Street
           London WC1

              Garage

2256   RIDING SCHOOL & STABLE MANAGEMENT LTD.
           1, Tahoma Lodge
           Lubbock Road
           Chislehurst
           Kent

              Stable Management

2257   THE RIDINGS PUBLISHING COMPANY
           33, Beverley Road
           Driffield
           Yorkshire

              Yorkshire Ridings Magazine

2258   RIDLEYS LTD.
           Wheatsheaf House
           Carmelite Street
           London EC4

              Ridleys Wine & Spirit Trade Circular

2259   RINGSPORT PUBLICATIONS
           5, Stockland Street
           Caerphilly
           Glam. CF8 1GD

              Ringsport

2260   RION LTD.
           207, Brondesbury Park
           London NW2 5JN

              Environment & Planning

2261   ROAD HAULAGE ASSOCIATION
           22, Upper Woburn Place
           London WC1

              Roadway

2262   ROAD TRANSPORT INDUSTRY TRAINING BOARD
           Capital House
           Empire Way
           Wembley
           Middx.

              Transport Training

2263   ROBERT DRAPER LTD.
           85, Udney Park Road
           Teddington
           Middx.

              Language & Speech
              Language in Society

2264   ROBERT FLETCHER & SON LTD.
           Kearsley Paper Works
           Stoneclough
           Radcliffe
           Manchester M26 9EH

              Archer

2265   ROCKSPORT
           14, Warser Gate
           Nottingham

              Rocksport

2266 **RODALE PRESS**
Berkhamsted
Herts.

Prevention

2267 **ROMFORD & DISTRICT HISTORICAL SOCIETY**
Central Library
St. Edward's Way
Romford
Essex RM1 3AR

Romford Record

2268 **ROTARY INTERNATIONAL IN GREAT BRITAIN & IRELAND**
Sheen Lane House
Sheen Lane
London SW14 8AF

Rotary

2269 **ROUTLEDGE AND KEGAN PAUL LTD.**
68-74, Carter Lane
London EC4V 5EL

British Journal of Sociology
Economy and Society
Religion
World Archaeology

2270 **ROWNTREE MACKINTOSH LTD.**
York

Rowntree Mackintosh News

2271 **ROY FAIERS LTD.**
8A, St. David's Hill
Exeter

Cotswold Life
Devon Life
Norfolk Fair
Wessex Life

2272 **ROYAL AERONAUTICAL SOCIETY**
251, Regent Street
London W1

Journal of the Guild of Air Pilots and Air Navigators

2273 **ROYAL AERONAUTICAL SOCIETY**
4, Hamilton Place
London W1V 0BQ

Aeronautical Journal
Aeronautical Quarterly
Aerospace

2274 **ROYAL ARCHAEOLOGICAL INSTITUTE**
c/o London Museum
Kensington Palace
London W8

Archaeological Journal

2275 **ROYAL ARMY EDUCATIONAL CORPS**
Eltham Palace
Eltham
London SE9 5QE

RAEL Gazette

2276 **ROYAL ASIATIC SOCIETY**
56, Queen Anne Street
London W1M 9LA

Journal of the Royal Asiatic Society of Great Britain & Ireland

2277 **ROYAL ASSOCIATION OF BRITISH DAIRY FARMERS**
17, Devonshire Street
London W1N 2BQ

Dairying
Journal of Dairy Research

2278 **ROYAL BANK OF SCOTLAND LTD.**
42, St. Andrew Square
Edinburgh EH2 27E

Countertalk

2279 **ROYAL CENTRAL ASIAN SOCIETY**
42, Devonshire Street
London W1N 1LN

Asian Affairs

2280 **ROYAL COLLEGE OF ART**
Exhibition Road
London SW7 2RJ

Ark

2281 **ROYAL COLLEGE OF MUSIC**
Prince Consort Road
London SW7

Royal College of Music Magazine

2282 **ROYAL COLLEGE OF NURSING**
Henrietta Place
Cavendish Square
London W1M 0AB

Nursing Bibliography

2283 **ROYAL COLLEGE OF OBSTETRICIANS AND GYNAECOLOGISTS**
27, Sussex Place
Regent's Park
London NW1

Journal of Obstetrics and Gynaecology of the British Commonwealth

2284 **ROYAL COLLEGE OF SURGEONS**
18, Nicolson Street
Edinburgh EH8 9DW

Journal of the Royal College of Surgeons of Edinburgh

2285 **ROYAL COLLEGE OF SURGEONS OF ENGLAND**
35/43, Lincoln's Inn Fields
London WC2A 3PN

Annals of The Royal College of Surgeons of England

2286 **ROYAL COMMONWEALTH SOCIETY**
Northumberland Avenue
London WC2N 5BJ

Library Notes

2287 **ROYAL DOULTON TABLEWARE LTD.**
Mile Street
Burslem
Stoke-on-Trent
Staffs.

Tableware Times

2288 **ROYAL ENTOMOLOGICAL SOCIETY**
41, Queen's Gate
London SW7

Journal of Entomology
Proceedings of the Royal Entomological Society
Transactions of the Royal Entomological Society

2289 ROYAL FORESTRY SOCIETY OF ENGLAND, WALES
     AND NORTHERN IRELAND
     102, High Street
     Tring
     Herts.

     Quarterly Journal of Forestry

2290 ROYAL GEOGRAPHICAL SOCIETY
     1, Kensington Gore
     London SW7 2AR

     Geographical Journal
     New Geographical Literature and Maps

2291 ROYAL GEOLOGICAL SOCIETY OF CORNWALL
     Penzance

     Transactions of the Royal Geological Society of
     Cornwall

2292 ROYAL GREENWICH OBSERVATORY
     Herstmonceux Castle
     Hailsham
     Sussex

     Greenwich Time Report
     Observatory
     Royal Observatory Annals
     Royal Observatory Bulletins

2293 ROYAL HISTORICAL SOCIETY
     96, Cheyne Walk
     London SW10

     Transactions of the Royal Historical Society

2294 ROYAL HORTICULTURAL SOCIETY
     Vincent Square
     London SW1P 2PE

     Journal of the Royal Horticultural Society

2295 ROYAL INSTITUTE OF BRITISH ARCHITECTS
     66, Portland Place
     London W1N 4AD

     RIBA Annual Review of Periodical Articles
     RIBA Journal
     RIBA Library Bulletin

2296 ROYAL INSTITUTE OF PUBLIC ADMINISTRATION
     Hamilton House
     Mabledon Place
     London WC1H 9BD

     Public Administration

2297 ROYAL INSTITUTION OF CHARTERED SURVEYORS
     12, Great George Street
     London SW1P 3AD

     Chartered Surveyor

2298 ROYAL INSTITUTION OF NAVAL ARCHITECTS
     10, Upper Belgrave Street
     London SW1X 8BQ

     Naval Architect

2299 ROYAL JERSEY AGRICULTURAL & HORTICUL-
     TURAL SOCIETY
     Springfield
     St. Helier
     Jersey C.I.

     Jersey at Home

2300 ROYAL METEOROLOGICAL SOCIETY
     49, Cromwell Road
     London SW7

     Quarterly Journal of the Royal Meteorological
     Society
     Weather

2301 ROYAL MICROSCOPICAL SOCIETY
     Tavistock House South
     London WC1

     Journal of the Royal Microscopical Society

2302 ROYAL MICROSCOPICAL SOCIETY
     Clarendon House
     Cornmarket Street
     Oxford OX1 3HA

     Royal Microscopical Society Proceedings

2303 ROYAL MILITARY SCHOOL OF MUSIC
     Kneller Hall
     Twickenham
     Middx. TW2 7DU

     Fan Fare

2304 ROYAL MUSICAL ASSOCIATION
     44, Philip Victor Road
     Handsworth
     Birmingham 21

     RMA Research Chronicle

2305 ROYAL NATIONAL INSTITUTE FOR THE BLIND
     224, Great Portland Street
     London W1N 6AA

     New Beacon

2306 ROYAL NATIONAL INSTITUTE FOR THE DEAF
     105, Gower Street
     London WC1E 6AH

     British Journal of Audiology
     Hearing
     Progress

2307 ROYAL NATIONAL LIFEBOAT INSTITUTION
     42, Grosvenor Gardens
     London SW1

     Life-boat

2308 ROYAL NATIONAL MISSION TO DEEP SEA FISHER-
     MEN
     43, Nottingham Place
     London W1M 4BX

     Toilers of the Deep

2309 ROYAL NATIONAL ROSE SOCIETY
     Bore Hill
     Chiswell Green Lane
     St Albans
     Herts.

     Rose Bulletin

2310 ROYAL NAVAL SAILING ASSOCIATION
     c/o R.N. Club
     Pembroke Road
     Portsmouth
     Hants

     Royal Naval Sailing Association Journal

2311 ROYAL PHOTOGRAPHIC SOCIETY
     14, South Audley Street
     London W1Y 5DP

     Journal of Photographic Science
     Photographic Journal

2312 ROYAL RADAR ESTABLISHMENT
     Malvern
     Worcs.

     RRE Journal

2313   ROYAL SCHOOL FOR THE DEAF
       50, Topsham Road
       Exeter EX2 4NF

         Teacher of the Deaf

2314   ROYAL SCOTTISH FORESTY SOCIETY
       26, Rutland Square
       Edinburgh
       EH1 2B4

         Scottish Forestry

2315   ROYAL SCOTTISH GEOGRAPHICAL SOCIETY
       10, Randolph Crescent
       Edinburgh 3

         Scottish Geographical Magazine

2316   ROYAL SOCIETY
       6, Carlton House Terrace
       London SW1Y 5AG

         Biographical Memoirs of Fellows of the Royal
          Society
         Notes and Records of the Royal Society
         Philosphical Transactions of the Royal Society
         Proceedings of the Royal Society

2317   ROYAL SOCIETY FOR INDIA, PAKISTAN & CEYLON
       3, Temple Chambers
       Temple Avenue
       London EC4Y OHB

         South Asian Review

2318   ROYAL SOCIETY FOR THE PREVENTION OF
       ACCIDENTS
       52, Grosvenor Gardens
       London SW1

         British Journal of Occupational Safety

2319   ROYAL SOCIETY FOR THE PREVENTION OF
       CRUELTY TO ANIMALS
       105, Jermyn Street
       London SW1

         Animal World

2320   ROYAL SOCIETY FOR THE PROMOTION OF HEALTH
       c/o Buckingham Palace Road
       London SW1W 0SX

         Royal Society of Health Journal

2321   ROYAL SOCIETY FOR THE PROTECTION OF BIRDS
       The Lodge
       Sandy
       Beds.

         Bird Life
         Birds

2322   ROYAL SOCIETY OF EDINBURGH
       22/24, George Street
       Edinburgh EH2 2PQ

         Proceedings of the Royal Society of Edinburgh
         Transactions of the Royal Society of Edinburgh

2323   ROYAL SOCIETY OF MEDICINE
       Chandos House
       2, Queen Anne Street
       London W1M 0BR

         Tropical Doctor

2324   ROYAL SOCIETY OF MEDICINE
       1, Wimpole Street
       London W1

         Proceedings of the Royal Society of Medicine

2325   ROYAL STATISTICAL SOCIETY
       21, Bentinck Street
       London W1M 6AR

         Journal of the Royal Statistical Society

2326   ROYAL STUART SOCIETY
       8, Lakeside Avenue
       Redbridge
       Ilford
       Essex

         Royal Stuart Papers
         Royalist Viewpoint

2327   ROYAL TELEVISION SOCIETY
       166, Shaftesbury Avenue
       London WC2

         Bulletin of the Royal Television Society

2328   ROYAL TOWN PLANNING INSTITUTE
       26, Portland Place
       London W1N 4BE

         Journal of the Royal Town Planning Institute

2329   ROYAL YACHTING ASSOCIATION
       5, Buckingham Gate
       London SW1

         RYA Magazine

2330   RUBBER & PLASTICS RESEARCH ASSOCIATION OF
       GREAT BRITAIN
       Shawbury
       Shrewsbury SY4 4NR

         RAPRA Abstracts
         New Trade Names in the Rubber and Plastics
          Industries
         Soviet Plastics
         Soviet Rubber Technology

2331   RUBBER & TECHNICAL PRESS LTD.
       25, Lloyd Baker Street
       London WC1

         Plastics, Rubbers, Textiles

2332   RUBBER & TECHNICAL PRESS LTD.
       Tenterden
       Kent

         Journal of the British Boot and Shoe Institution
         Journal of the IRI
         PRT—Polymer Age

2334   RUBERY OWEN HOLDINGS LTD.
       P.O. Box 10
       Darlaston
       Wednesbury
       Staffs. WS10 8JD

         Goodwill
         Rubery Owen News

2335   RUDGE & CO. LTD
       Sardinia House
       Sardinia Street
       London WC2A 3NW

         Genealogical Quarterly

2336   RUNNYMEDE TRUST
       Stuart House
       1, Tudor Street
       London EC4Y 0AD

         Race Relations Bulletin

2337 RURAL ENVIRONMENT PUBLICATIONS LTD.
Francis House
King's Head Yard
Borough High Street
London SE1 1NA

Rural Medicine

2338 RURAL MUSIC SCHOOLS ASSOCIATION
Little Benslow Hills
Hitchin
Herts. SG4 9RD

Making Music

2339 RUSKIN COLLEGE
Students Association
Ruskin College
Oxford

New Epoch

2340 S.C. PHILLIPS & CO. LTD.
50, Fetter Lane
London EC4

Converting Industry

2341 SCM PRESS LTD.
63, Bloomsbury Street
London WC1B 3QX

Learning for Living

2342 SIRA
Chislehurst
Kent

Metron

2343 SP TECHNICAL PUBLICATIONS LTD.
2, Walker Street
Edinburgh

Scottish Plumbing and Heating Monthly

2344 S.P.C.K
Holy Trinity Church
Marylebone Road
London NW1

Theology

2345 S. REDMAYNE & SONS LTD.
Station Road
Wigton
Cumberland

John Peel Jottings

2346 SAD TRAFFIC
12, Regent Street South
Barnsley
Yorks.

Sad Traffic

2347 RALPH SADGROVE
33, Gamage Building
Holborn
London EC1N 2NA

Gift Buyer International

2348 SAFETY IN MINES RESEARCH ESTABLISHMENT
Red Hill
Off Broad Lane
Sheffield S3 7HQ

Safety in Mines Abstracts

2349 SAGE PUBLICATIONS LTD.
St. George's House
44, Hatton Garden
London EC1N 8ER

American Behavioural Scientist

Comparative Group Studies
Comparative Political Studies
Criminology
Education and Urban Society
Environment and Behavior
International Studies Quarterly
Journal of Black Studies
Journal of Comparative Administration
Journal of Contemporary History
Journal of InterAmerican Studies and World
Affairs
Journal of Management Studies
Pacific Sociological Review
Poverty and Human Resources Abstracts
Simulation and Games
Urban Affairs Quarterly
Urban Education
Youth and Society

2350 SAIL TRAINING ASSOCIATION
Bosham
Chichester
Sussex

Sail

2351 ST. ALBAN'S PRESS
Drayton House
30, Gordon Street
London WC1H 0BE

Liberal Catholic

2352 ST. ANN'S PRESS
Park Road
Altrincham
Cheshire WA14 5QQ

British Journal of Anaesthesia

2353 ST. GEORGE'S HOSPITAL MEDICAL SCHOOL
Hyde Park Corner
London SW1X 7NA

St. George's Hospital Gazette

2354 ST. JAMES PRESS LTD.
19, Montagu Mews North
London W1

Research in Progress in English and Historica
Studies in the Universities of the British
Isles

2355 ST. JOAN'S ALLIANCE
Newman House
15, Carlisle Street
London W1

Catholic Citizen

2356 ST. JOHN AMBULANCE
1, Grosvenor Crescent
London SW1

St. John Review

2357 ST. JOHN'S HOSPITAL DERMATOLOGICAL SOCIET
5, Lisle Street
London WC2H 7BJ

Transactions of the St. John's Hospital Dermatological Society

2358 ST. LUKE'S COLLEGE OF EDUCATION
Institute of Education
University
Exeter

Studies in Education

2359 ST. MARTIN'S PRESS
18, Queen's Road
Brighton
Sussex

Club Mirror

2360 ST. MARY'S COLLEGE
Strawberry Hill
Twickenham
Middx.

Catholic Education Today

2361 ST. PATRICK'S COLLEGE
Maynooth
Co. Kildare
Ireland

Social Studies

2362 ST. SYMEON'S FELLOWSHIP
St. Symeon's House
Oswaldkirk
York

Aion

2363 ST. THOMAS' HOSPITAL MEDICAL SCHOOL
London SE1

St. Thomas' Hospital Gazette

2364 SALISBURY & SOUTH WILTS INDUSTRIAL
ARCHAEOLOGICAL SOCIETY
The Secretary
34, Countess Road
Amesbury
Wilts.

Wiltshire Industrial Archaeology

2365 SALMON AND TROUT ASSOCIATION
Fishmongers' Hall
London EC4R 9EL

Salmon and Trout Magazine

2366 SATIPS LTD.
Kilvington
Ringley Avenue
Horsley
Surrey

News and Views

2367 SAVE THE CHILDREN FUND
29, Queen Anne's Gate
London SW1

Third World
Today's Children
World's Children

2368 SAWELL PUBLICATIONS LTD.
4, Ludgate Circus
London EC4

Anti-Corrosion Methods and Materials
Garden Supplies Retailer
Mass Production
Paint Technology
Product Finishing
Tooling
Work Study

2369 SCHILTROM PUBLICATIONS
4c, Lusset View
Radnor Street
Clydebank
Scotland

Schiltrom

2370 SCHOOL LIBRARY ASSOCIATION
Premier House
150, Southampton Row
London WC1B 5AR

School Librarian

2371 SCHOOL OF ORIENTAL & AFRICAN STUDIES
University of London WC1

Bulletin of the School of Oriental and African
Studies, University of London

2372 SCHOOLMASTER PUBLISHING CO. LTD.
Derbyshire House
St. Chad's Street
London WC1H 8AJ

Teacher

2373 SCHOOLS COUNCIL MODERN LANGUAGES PROJECT
University
York

Onwards

2374 SCHOOLS COUNCIL PUBLICATIONS
c/o College of Technology
Stafford

Computer Education

2375 SCHOOLS COUNCIL
Committee for Wales
129, Cathedral Road
Cardiff CF1 9SX

Wales Science Bulletin

2376 SCIENCE & TECHNOLOGY AGENCY
3, Dyer's Buildings
Holborn
London EC1

Atomic Absorption and Flame Emission Spec-
troscopy Abstracts
Gas-Chromatography Mass-Spectrometry
Abstracts
Laser-Raman Spectroscopy Abstracts
Neutron Activation Analysis Abstracts
Nuclear Magnetic Resonance Spectrometry
Abstracts
Thin-Layer Chromatography Abstracts
X-Ray Fluorescence Spectrometry Abstracts

2377 SCIENCE POLICY FOUNDATION
2A, Station Road
Frimley
Surrey

Science Policy

2378 SCIENTECHNICA LTD.
42-44, Triangle West
Bristol BS8 1EX

Comparative and General Pharmacology
Insect Biochemistry
International Journal of Biochemistry

2379 SCIENTIFIC & TECHNICAL GROUP OF THE ROYAL
PHOTOGRAPHIC SOCIETY
14, South Audley Street
London W1Y 5DP

Photographic Abstracts

2380 SCIENTIFIC ERA PUBLICATIONS
5/6, Malden Lane
Stamford
London PE9 2AZ

Scientific Era

2381   SCIENTIFIC INFORMATION CONSULTANTS LTD.
      661, Finchley Road
      London NW2 2HN

         Corrosion Control Abstracts
         Cybernetics Abstracts
         Czechoslovak Science and Technology Digest
         Index to Forthcoming Russian Books
         Mechanical Sciences Abstracts
         Russian Metallurgy

2382   SCIENTIFIC SURVEYS LTD.
      11A, Gloucester Road
      London SW7

         Corrosion Prevention and Control
         Natural Gas and L.P.G.
         Pipes and Pipelines International

2383   SCIENTOLOGY FOUNDATION
      Saint Hill Manor
      East Grinstead
      Sussex RH19 4JY

         Change

2384   SCOLAR PRESS LTD.
      20, Main Street
      Menston
      Yorks. LS29 6E2

         Archiuum Linguisticum

2385   SCOTIA
      33a, Huddart Street
      Wick
      Caithness

         Scotia Review

2387   SCOTS INDEPENDENT (NEWSPAPERS) LTD.
      16, Upper Bridge Street
      Stirling FK8 1ER

         Scots Independent

2388   COLIN SCOTT
      1, Saint Paul's Close
      Clitheroe
      Lancs.

         European Grocery Letter

2389   J.C. MEREDITH SCOTT
      Lagan nam Bann
      Ballachulish
      Argyll
      Scotland

         Envoi

2390   SCOTT POLAR RESEARCH INSTITUTE
      Cambridge CB2 1ER

         Polar Record
         Geological Society Special Reports
         Journal of the Geological Society
         Liturgical Studies
         Quarterly Journal of Engineering Geology
         University of Edinburgh Journal

2391   SCOTTISH ACADEMIC PRESS LTD.
      25, Perth Street
      Edinburgh EH3 5DW

2392   SCOTTISH AGRICULTURAL JOURNALS CO. LTD.
      39, York Street
      Glasgow C2

         Scottish Farmer

2393   SCOTTISH CATHOLIC HISTORIES ASSOCIATION
      25, Finlas Street
      Glasgow N2

         Innes Review

2394   SCOTTISH CIVIC TRUST
      24, George Square
      Glasgow G2 1EF

         Grapevine

2395   SCOTTISH COMMITTEE OF THE COMMUNIST
   PARTY OF GREAT BRITAIN
      Gallacher House
      69, Albert Road
      Glasgow S2

         Scottish Marxist

2396   SCOTTISH COUNCIL (DEVELOPMENT & INDUSTRY)
      1, Castle Street
      Edinburgh EH2 3AJ

         Scotland
         Scotland 72
         Sources of Finance

2397   SCOTTISH COUNCIL FOR RESEARCH IN EDUCA-
   TION
      16, Moray Place
      Edinburgh EH3 6DR

         Research in Education

2398   SCOTTISH DANCE ARCHIVES
      50, Wicks Crescent
      Formby
      Liverpool

         Scottish Dance Archives

2399   SCOTTISH DECORATORS FEDERATION
      14, Craigleith Hill Avenue
      Edinburgh EH4 2JA

         Scottish Decorators Quarterly Review

2400   SCOTTISH ESPERANTO FEDERATION
      2, Lady Helen Street
      Kirkcaldy
      Fife

         Esperanto en Skotlando

2401   SCOTTISH FARM BUILDINGS INVESTIGATION UNIT
      Craibstone
      Bucksburn
      Aberdeen

         Farm Building Progress
         Farm Building R & D Index
         Farm Building R & D Studies

2402   SCOTTISH FARMER PUBLICATIONS LTD.
      39, York Street
      Glasgow G2 8JL

         Horse & Pony

2403   SCOTTISH GENEALOGY SOCIETY
      16, Charlotte Square
      Edinburgh 2

         Scottish Genealogist

2404   SCOTTISH GEORGIAN SOCIETY
        41, Castle Street
        Edinburgh EH2 3BH

        Bulletin of the Scottish Georgian Society

2405   SCOTTISH INFORMATION OFFICE
        St. Andrew's House
        Edinburgh EH1 3DQ

        Newsletter from Scotland

2406   SCOTTISH INLAND WATERWAYS ASSOCIATION
        c/o Manse of Premnay Insch
        Aberdeen

        Scottish Inland Waterways Association
        Newsletter

2407   SCOTTISH INSTITUTE OF MISSIONARY STUDIES
        Dept. of Religious Studies
        University
        King's College
        Taylor Building
        Aberdeen AB9 2UB

        Bulletin of the Scottish Institute of Missionary
        Studies

2408   SCOTTISH INTERNATIONAL REVIEW LTD.
        23, George Square
        Edinburgh EH8 9LD

        Scottish International Review

2409   SCOTTISH LIBRARY ASSOCIATION
        Dept. of Librarianship
        University of Strathclyde
        Livingstone Tower
        Richmond Street
        Glasgow C1

        SLA News

2410   SCOTTISH MILK MARKETING BOARD
        Underwood Road
        Paisley
        Renfrew

        SMMB Bulletin

2411   SCOTTISH NATIONAL COMMITTEE OF
        OPHTHALMIC OPTICIANS
        38, Chalmers Street
        Dumfermline

        Scottish Optician

2413   SCOTTISH ORNITHOLOGISTS' CLUB
        21, Regent Terrace
        Edinburgh EH7 5BT

        Scottish Birds

2414   SCOTTISH PATRIOTS
        31, Howard Place
        Edinburgh E3 5JY

        Patriot

2415   SCOTTISH PHARMACIST
        5, London Street
        Mauchline KA5 5BD
        Ayr

        Scottish Pharmacist

2416   SCOTTISH PIPE BAND ASSOCIATION
        45, Washington St.
        Glasgow G3 8AZ

        Pipe Band

2417   SCOTTISH ROCK GARDEN CLUB
        Langfauld
        Glenfarg
        Perth

        Journal of the Scottish Rock Garden Club

2418   SCOTTISH SCHOOLMASTERS ASSOCIATION
        41, York Place
        Edinburgh 1

        Scottish Schoolmaster

2419   SCOTTISH SCHOOLS SCIENCE EQUIPMENT
        RESEARCH CENTRE
        103, Broughton Street
        Edinburgh EH1 3RZ

        Scottish Schools Science Equipment Research
        Centre Bulletin

2420   SCOTTISH SECONDARY TEACHERS ASSOCIATION
        15, Dundas Street
        Edinburgh EH3 6QG

        Scottish Secondary Teachers' Association
        Bulletin

2421   SCOTTISH SKI CLUB
        17, Elmbank Street
        Glasgow C2

        Scottish Ski Club Journal

2422   SCOTTISH SOCIETY FOR INDUSTRIAL
        ARCHAEOLOGY
        c/o Dept of Technology
        Royal Scottish Museum
        Edinburgh

        Newsletter of the Scottish Society for
        Industrial Archaeology

2423   SCOTTISH SPECIAL HOUSING ASSOCIATION
        15/21 Palmerston Place
        Edinburgh EH12 5AJ

        SSHA Journal

2424   SCOTTISH SUB-AQUA CLUB
        1, Windmill Road
        Hamilton
        Scotland ML3 6LX

        Scottish Diver

2425   SCOTTISH SUNDAY SCHOOL UNION FOR
        CHRISTIAN EDUCATION
        70, Bothwell Street
        Glasgow G2 7JE

        Scottish Primary Quarterly
        Scottish Sunday School Teacher
        Seniorscope

2426   SCOTTISH TARTANS SOCIETY
        Broughty Castle Museum
        Broughty Ferry
        Dundee DD5 2BE

        Proceedings of the Scottish Tartans Society

2427   SCOTTISH TEXTILE RESEARCH ASSOCIATION
        Kinnoull Road
        Kingsway West
        Dundee

        Bulletin of the Scottish Textile Research
        Association

2428 SCOTTISH THEATRE PUBLICATIONS
Thornfield House
Kirknewton
Midlothian
Scotland

Pointe
Scottish Theatre

2429 SCOTTISH TOURIST BOARD
2, Rutland Place
Edinburgh

Travel Trade Guide, Scotland

2430 SCOTTISH TYPOGRAPHICAL JOURNAL
136, West Regent Street
Glasgow C2

Scottish Typographical Journal

2431 SCOTTISH WILDLIFE TRUST LTD.
8, Dublin Street
Edinburgh EH1 3PP

Scottish Wildlife Trust Newsletter

2432 SCOTTISH WOODLAND OWNERS ASSOCIATION
6, Chester Street
Edinburgh EH3 7RD

Scottish Woodland Owners Association
Newsletter

2433 SCOTTISH YOUTH REVIEW
8, Palmerston Place
Edinburgh EH12 5AA

Scottish Youth Review

2434 SCOUT ASSOCIATION
25, Buckingham Palace Road
London SW1

Scouter

2435 SCUNTHORPE MUSEUM SOCIETY
Museum & Art Gallery
Oswald Road
Scunthorpe
Lincs

Journal of the Scunthorpe Museum Society

2436 SEAFARERS EDUCATION SERVICE
Mansbridge House
207, Balham High Road
London SW17 7BH

Seafarer

2437 SECHABA PUBLICATIONS
49, Rathbone Street
London W1A 4NL

Sechaba
South African Studies

2438 SECOND AEON PUBLICATIONS
3, Maplewood Court
Maplewood Avenue
Llandaff North
Cardiff CF4 2NB

Second Aeon

2439 SECURITY GAZETTE LTD.
326, St. John Street
London EC1V 4QD

Security Gazette

2440 SEED
8A, All Saints Road
London W11

Seed

2441 SEED PUBLICATIONS
88, Boileau Road
Ealing
London W5

Seed

2442 SELBOURNE SOCIETY
57, Carlton Road
Ealing
London W5

Selbourne Magazine

2443 ANDREW & WENDY SELKIRK
9, Nassington Road
London NW3 2TX

Current Archaeology

2444 SEMINAR PRESS/ACADEMIC PRESS
24-28, Oval Road
London NW1 7DD

International Journal of Nautical Archaeology
and Underwater Exploration
Journal of European Studies
Journal of Phonetics

2445 SERCK AUDCO VALUES
Newport
Shropshire

Seal

2446 SERVICE POINT
St. James Branch Library
Laird Street
Birkenhead

Service Point

2447 SERVITE PRIORY
Benburb
Co. Tyrone
N. Ireland

Aquarius

2448 SEYMOUR PRESS
334, Brixton Road
London SW9

Air Pictorial
Opera

2449 SHAKESPEAREAN AUTHORSHIP SOCIETY
25, Montagu Square
London W1H 1RE

Shakespearean Authorship Review

2450 SHAW PUBLISHING CO. LTD.
180, Fleet Street
London EC4

Electrical Equipment

2451 SHAW SOCIETY
125, Markyate Road
Dagenham
Essex

Shavian

2452 SHAW'S PRICE GUIDES LTD.
4, The Broadway
London N8 9SP

Shaws Price Guide

2453 A. L. SHEARN
11, Ember Gardens
Thames Ditton
Surrey

Flowers From the Printshop

2454 SHEFFIELD CONSUMER GROUP
548, Loxley Road
Loxley
Sheffield S6 6RT

Sheffield Consumer

2455 SHEFFIELD JUNIOR CHAMBER OF COMMERCE
Cutlers' Hall
Sheffield 1

Hub

2456 SHELL INTERNATIONAL PETROLEUM CO.
Shell Centre
London SE1 7NA

London Shell

2457 SHELL TANKERS (UK) LTD.
Shell Centre
London SE17 NA

British Fleet News

2458 SHETLAND COUNCIL OF SOCIAL SERVICE
46, Market Street
Lerwick
Shetland

New Shetlander

2459 SHETLAND PONY STUD-BOOK SOCIETY
8, Whinfield Road
Montrose
Angus

Shetland Pony Stud-Book Society Magazine

2460 K. SHINGLER
10, Fentiman Road
London SW8

Portuguese and Colonial Bulletin

2461 SHIP STAMP SOCIETY
33A, Ridgway Road
Timperley
Cheshire

Log Book

2462 SHIRLEY INSTITUTE
Manchester M20 BRX

Textiles

2463 SHOE AND ALLIED TRADES RESEARCH
ASSOCIATION
Satra House
Rockingham Road
Kettering

SATRA Bulletin
Footwear Digest
Shoe Materials Progress

2464 SHORTHORN SOCIETY OF THE U.K. & G.B. &
IRELAND
Green Lodge
Great Bowden
Market Harborough
Leics

Dairy Shorthorn Journal

2465 SHROPSHIRE ARCHAEOLOGICAL SOCIETY
20, Garmston Road
Shrewsbury

Shropshire Newsletter

2466 SHROPSHIRE ARCHAEOLOGICAL SOCIETY
Attingham Park
Shrewsbury

Transactions of the Shropshire Archaeological
Society

2467 SIGFORD LTD.
52, Hagley Road
Stourbridge
Worcs

Mode Magazine

2468 SIMON COMMUNITY TRUST
Simon House
Grange Road
Ramsgate
Kent

Social Action

2469 SIMON POPULATION TRUST
141, Newmarket Road
Cambridge CB5 8HA

Bibliography of Family Planning and Population

2470 SINO BRITISH TRADE COUNCIL
25, Queen Anne's Gate
London SW1H 9BU

Sino British Trade

2471 SIR JOHN HALL
29, Embercourt Road
Thames Ditton
Surrey KT7 0CH

Antique Records

2472 SIR THOMAS BEECHAM SOCIETY
46, Wellington Avenue
Westcliff-on-Sea
Essex

Le Grand Baton
Sir Thomas Beecham Society Newsletter

2473 SKEFCO BALL BEARING CO. LTD.
Leagrave Road
Luton
Beds

Ball Bearing Journal
Skefco News

2474 SKI CLUB OF GREAT BRITAIN
118, Eaton Square
London SW1 W9AF

Ski Survey

2475 SKYLINK LTD.
6, Adam Street
London WC2

Skytrader and Air Marketing International

2476 SLEEP-LEARNING ASSOCIATION
14, Belsize Crescent
London NW3 5QU

Quarterly Journal of the Sleep-Learning
Association

2477 SLIMMING MAGAZINE LTD.
16, Caxton Street
London SW1

Slimming

2478 SMALL INDUSTRIES COUNCIL FOR RURAL AREAS
OF SCOTLAND
27, Walker Street
Edinburgh EH3 7HZ

Craftwork

2479 SMITH'S INDUSTRIES
Aviation Division
Kelvin House
Wembley Park Drive
Wembley
Middlesex

Aviation Review

2480 SMOOTHIE PUBLICATIONS
67, Vere Road
Brighton

Datr

2481 SOCIAL SCIENCE RESEARCH COUNCIL
State House
High Holborn
London WC1R 4TH

SSRC Newsletter

2482 SOCIALIST COMMENTARY PUBLICATIONS LTD.
11, Great Russell Street
London WC1

Socialist Commentary

2483 SOCIALIST INTERNATIONAL
88a, St. John's Wood High St.
London NW8

Socialist Affairs

2484 SOCIALIST PARTY OF GREAT BRITAIN
52, Clapham High Street
London SW4

Socialist Standard

2485 SOCIALIST REVIEW PUBLISHING CO. LTD.
6, Cottons Gardens
London E2

International Socialism

2486 SOCIALIST WOMAN
182, Pentonville Road
London N1

Socialist Woman

2487 SOCIETY FOR ANALYTICAL CHEMISTRY
9/10 Savile Row
London W1X 1AF

Analyst
Proceedings of the Society for Analytical
Chemistry. Analytical Division, Chemical
Society

2488 SOCIETY FOR ARMY HISTORICAL RESEARCH
c/o The Library
Old War Office Building
Whitehall
London SW1

Journal of the Society for Army Historical
Research

2489 SOCIETY FOR CO-OPERATIVE STUDIES
Stanford Hall
Loughborough
Leics

Bulletin [of the] Society for Co-operative
Studies

2490 SOCIETY FOR EDUCATION IN FILM AND
TELEVISION
63, Old Compton Street
London W1V 5PN

Screen

2491 SOCIETY FOR EDUCATION THROUGH ART
29, Great James Street
London WC1

Athene

2492 SOCIETY FOR MEDIEVAL ARCHAEOLOGY
c/o University College
Gower Street
London WC1

Medieval Archaeology

2493 SOCIETY FOR PROCLAIMING BRITAIN IS ISRAEL
87, St. Barnabas Road
Woodford Green
Essex

Bible Impact
Brith

2494 SOCIETY FOR PSYCHICAL RESEARCH
1, Adam & Eve Mews
London W8

Journal of the Society for Psychical Research
Proceedings of the Society for Psychical
Research

2495 SOCIETY FOR RESEARCH INTO HIGHER
EDUCATION
25, Northampton Square
London EC1V 0HL

Research into Higher Education Abstracts

2496 SOCIETY FOR THE BIBLIOGRAPHY OF NATURAL
HISTORY
c/o British Museum (Natural History)
Cromwell Road
London SW7 5BD

Journal of the Society for the Bibliography of
Natural History

2497 SOCIETY FOR THE PROMOTION OF HELLENIC
STUDIES
31-34, Gordon Square
London WC1H 0PP

Journal of Hellenic Studies

2498 SOCIETY FOR THE PROMOTION OF NATURE
RESERVES
The Manor House
Alford
Lincs

Conservation Review

2499 SOCIETY FOR THE PROMOTION OF ROMAN
STUDIES
31-4, Gordon Square
London WC1

Britannia
Journal of Roman Studies

2500 SOCIETY FOR THE STUDY OF ALCHEMY AND
EARLY CHEMISTRY
Dept. of Hist. & Phil. of Science
University College
Gower Street
London WC1

Ambix

2501 SOCIETY FOR THE STUDY OF LABOUR HISTORY
University of Sheffield
Dept. of Extramural Studies
85, Wilkinson Street
Sheffield S10 2GS

Society for the Study of Labour History Bulletin

2502 SCOIETY FOR WATER TREATMENT AND
EXAMINATION
North Derbyshire Water Board
West Street
Chesterfield
Derbys S4O 4T2

Water Treatment and Examination

2503 SOCIETY OF ANALYTICAL PSYCHOLOGY LTD.
30, Devonshire Place
London W1

Journal of Analytical Psychology

2504 SOCIETY OF ANTIQUARIES OF NEWCASTLE UPON
TYNE
Black Gate
Newcastle upon Tyne 1

Archaeologia Aeliana

2505 SOCIETY OF ANTIQUARIES OF SCOTLAND
National Museum of Antiquities
Queen Street
Edinburgh

Proceedings of the Society of Antiquaries of
Scotland

2506 SOCIETY OF ARCHER-ANTIQUITIES
'Ascham'
14, Grove Road
Barnes
London SW13 0HQ

Journal of the Society of Archer-Antiquities

2507 SOCIETY OF ARCHITECTURAL HISTORIANS OF
GREAT BRITAIN
8, Belmount Avenue
Melton Park
Newcastle-upon-Tyne NE3 5QD

Architectural History

2508 SOCIETY OF ARCHIVISTS
Guildhall Library
Basinghall Street
London EC2P 2EJ

Journal of the Society of Archivists

2509 SOCIETY OF AUTHORS
84, Drayton Gardens
London SW10 9SD

Author

2510 SOCIETY OF CHEMICAL INDUSTRY
14, Belgrave Square
London SW1X 8PS

Chemistry and Industry

2511 SOCIETY OF CHIROPODISTS
8, Wimpole Street
London W1M 8BX

Chiropodist

2512 SOCIETY OF CIVIL ENGINEERING TECHNICIANS
1/7, Great George Street
London SW1P 3AA

Civil Engineering Technician

2513 SOCIETY OF CIVIL SERVANTS
19, Surrey Street
London WC2

Civil Service Opinion

2514 SOCIETY OF COMMERCIAL ACCOUNTANTS
40, Tyndalls Park Road
Bristol 8

Commercial Accountant

2515 SOCIETY OF DAIRY TECHNOLOGY
172A, Ealing Road
Wembley
Middlesex HA0 4QD

Journal of the Society of Dairy Technology

2516 SOCIETY OF DYERS AND COLOURISTS
PO Box 244
82, Gratton Road
Bradford BD1 2JB

Journal of the Society of Dyers and Colourists
SDC News

2517 SOCIETY OF ENDOCRINOLOGY
Biochemical Society (Publications)
PO Box 32
Commerce Way
Whitehall Industrial Estate
Colchester
Essex

Journal of Endocrinology

2518 SOCIETY OF ENGINEERS
Abbey House
Victoria Street
London SW1H 0ND

Society of Engineers Journal

2519 SOCIETY OF FILM AND TELEVISION ARTS LTD.
80, Great Portland Street
London W1N 6JJ

Journal of the Society of Film and Television
Arts

2520 SOCIETY OF GLASS TECHNOLOGY
Thornton
Hallam Gate Road
Sheffield S10 5BT

Glass Technology

2521 SOCIETY OF GRAPHICAL & ALLIED TRADES
13-16, Borough Road
London SE1

SOGAT Journal

2522 SOCIETY OF INDEXERS
c/o Barclays Bank Ltd
1, Pall Mall East
London SW1

Indexer

2523 SOCIETY OF INDUSTRIAL ARTISTS AND
DESIGNERS
12, Carlton House Terrace
London SW1

Designer

2524 SOCIETY OF INVESTMENT ANALYSTS
21, Godliman Street
London EC4

Investment Analyst

2525 SOCIETY OF LEATHER TRADES CHEMISTS
52, Crouch Hall Lane
Redbourn
Herts

Journal of the Society of Leather Trades
Chemists

2526 SOCIETY OF LICENSED AIRCRAFT ENGINEERS &
TECHNOLOGISTS
Grey Tiles
Kingston Hill
Kingston-upon-Thames
Surrey KT2 7LW

Tech Air

2527 SOCIETY OF MASTER GLASS PAINTERS
6, Queen Square
London WC1

Journal of the British Society of Master Glass
Painters

2528 SOCIETY OF POST OFFICE ENGINEERS
14, King Street
London EC2

Post Office Engineer

2529 SOCIETY OF RADIOGRAPHERS
14, Upper Wimpole Street
London W1M 8BN

Radiography

2530 SOCIETY OF RELAY ENGINEERS
10, Avenue Road
Dorridge
Solihull
Works

Relay Engineer

2531 SOCIETY OF ST. JOHN CHRYSATOM
Marian House
Holden Avenue
London N12

Chrysastom

2532 SOCIETY OF TEACHERS OF SPEECH AND DRAMA
St. Bride Institute
Bride Lane
London EC4

Speech and Drama

2533 SOCIETY OF UNIVERSITY CARTOGRAPHERS
Dept. of Geography
Social Studies Building
PO Box 147
University
Liverpool L69 3BX

SUC Bulletin

2534 SOLICITORS LAW STATIONERY SOCIETY
Breams Buildings
London EC4

Oyez Notes

2535 SOLIDARITY (LONDON)
c/o Sandringham Road
London NW11

Solidarity

2536 SOMAN-WHERRY PRESS
Norwich

Transactions of the Norfolk and Norwich
Naturalists Society

2537 SOMERSET ARCHAEOLOGICAL & NATURAL
HISTORY SOCIETY
Taunton Castle
Taunton

Somerset Archaeology and Natural History
Proceedings

2538 SONOSTRIPS LTD.
49B, Station Road
Edgware MA8 7HX

AD Magazine
Insite
LPG

2539 SOUTH EASTERN ELECTRICITY BOARD
Queen's Gardens
Hove
Sussex BN3 2LS

SeaBoard

2540 SOUTH-EASTERN REGIONAL HOSPITAL BOARD
11, Drumsheugh Gardens
Edinburgh EH3 7QQ

SERHB News

2541 SOUTH LANCASHIRE NEWSPAPERS LTD.
164, College Street
St Helens
Lancs

Rugby Leaguer

2542 SOUTH OF SCOTLAND ELECTRICITY BOARD
Cathcart House
Glasgow S4

SSEB News

2543 SOUTH PLACE ETHICAL SOCIETY
Red Lion Square
London WC1R 4RL

Ethical Record

2544 SOUTH STAFFORDSHIRE ARCHAEOLOGICAL &
HISTORICAL SOCIETY
c/o 58, Wednesbury Road
Walsall WS1 3RS

Transactions of the South Staffordshire
Archaeological & Historical Society

2545 SOUTH WALES INSTITUTE OF ENGINEERS
Park Place
Cardiff

Proceedings of the South Wales Institute of
Engineers

2546 SOUTHEND-ON-SEA CONSUMER GROUP
501, Sutton Road
Southend-on-Sea SS2 5PR

Value

2547 SOUTHERN ARTS ASSOCIATION
78, High Street
Winchester

Southern Arts

2548 SOUTHERN ELECTRIC GROUP
28, Hill View Road
Orpington
Kent

Live Rail

2549 SOUTHERN NEWSPAPERS LTD.
45, Above Bar
Southampton

Echoing Times

2550 SPARE RIB
9, Newburgh Street
London W1A 4XS

Spare Rib

2551 E. SPARKS
      Norwood Technical College
      Knight's Hill
      London SE27

      Black Outcry

2552 SPASTICS INTERNATIONAL MEDICAL PUBLICA-
      TIONS
      20-22, Mortimer Street
      London W1

      Developmental Medicine and Child Neurology

2553 SPASTICS SOCIETY AND THE ASSOCIATION FOR
      SPECIAL EDUCATION
      12, Park Crescent
      London W1N 4EQ

      Special Education

2554 SPEARHEAD PUBLICATIONS LTD.
      2, Fife Road
      Kingston on Thames
      Surrey

      Offshore Services

2555 SPEARHEAD PUBLICATIONS LTD
      Kinnard Lodge
      Kinnard Avenue
      Bromley
      Kent

      Hydrospace

2556 SPECIAL INTEREST PUBLICATIONS LTD.
      196, Shaftesbury Avenue
      London WC2

      Computer Digest
      Computer Management
      Export Direction

2557 SPECTATOR LTD
      99, Gower Street
      London WC1

      Spectator

2558 SPIRITUALIST NEWS AGENCY CO. LTD.
      Bankside
      42, High Street
      Barnet
      Herts.

      Spiritualist News

2559 SPOOK ENTERPRISES
      38, Woodfield Avenue
      London W5

      Quest

2560 SPORTS ACADEMY LTD.
      Walmar House
      288, Regent Street
      London W1R 5NF

      Football Academy

2561 SPORTS TURF RESEARCH INSTITUTE
      Bingley
      Yorkshire BD16 1AU

      Journal of the Sports Turf Research Institute
      Sports Turf Bulletin

2562 SPOTLIGHT PUBLICATIONS LTD.
      12, Sutton Row
      London W1V 5FH

      Good Listening and Record Collector
      Record Collector for Good Listening

2563 SPOTLIGHT
      43, Cranbourn Street
      London WC2H 7AP

      Spotlight Casting Directory
      Spotlight Contacts

2564 SPRING RESEARCH ASSOCIATION
      Henry Street
      Sheffield S3 7EQ

      Spring Journal

2565 STACEY PUBLICATIONS
      1, Hawthorndene Road
      Hayes
      Bromley
      Kent

      Amateur Stage

2566 STAINES LOCAL HISTORY SOCIETY
      413, Stroude Road
      Virginia Water
      Surrey

      Staines Local History Journal

2567 STAINLESS STEEL DEVELOPMENT
      ASSOCIATION
      65, Vincent Square
      London SW1P 2NY

      Stainless Steel

2568 STAMP COLLECTING LTD.
      42, Maiden Lane
      London WC2E 7LL

      Stamp Collecting

2569 STANBOROUGH PRESS LTD.
      Alma Park
      Grantham
      Lincs.

      Good Health

2570 STAND
      58, Queen's Road
      Newcastle on Tyne
      NE2 2PR

      Stand

2571 STANDARD CATALOGUE CO. LTD.
      26, Bloomsbury Way
      London WC1A 2SS

      Architectual Design

2572 STANDBROOK PUBLICATIONS LTD.
      Elm House
      Elm Street
      London WC1

      Family Circle
      Living

2573 STANLEY GIBBONS MAGAZINES LTD.
      Drury House
      Russell Street
      London WC2B 5HD

      Stamp Monthly

2574 STAPLES LTD.
      94, Wigmore Street
      London W1

      Journal of Tropical Medicine and Hygiene

2575 STATESMAN AND NATION PUBLISHING CO. LTD.
Great Turnstile
London WC1V 7HJ

News Statesman

2576 STATISTICAL RECORD
149, Fleet Street
London EC4

Statistical Record

2577 PHILIP STEADMAN
85, Norwich Street
Cambridge

Form

2578 STEAM BOAT ASSOCIATION OF GREAT BRITAIN
12, Marlborough Road
Ashford
Middx. TW15 3PW

Funnel

2579 STEAM MAN PUBLICATIONS
Stag House
Lowlands Crescent
Great Kingshill
High Wycombe
Bucks.

Steam Man

2580 NINA STEANE
31, Headlands
Kettering
Northants.

All In

2581 STEEL CASTINGS RESEARCH AND TRADE
ASSOCIATION
East Bank Road
Sheffield S2 3PT

Journal of Research of the Steel Castings
Research and Trade Association
Steel Castings Abstracts
SCRATA Journal of Research

2582 STEERING WHEEL PUBLICATIONS LTD.
Fulwood House
High Holborn
London WC1

Steering Wheel

2583 STEINER SCHOOLS FELLOWSHIP

4, Cavendish Avenue
London NW8 9JE

Child and Man

2584 STELLAR PRESS
Huggins Lane
Welham Green
Hatfield
Herts.

Printing Art

2585 STEPHENSON LOCOMOTIVE SOCIETY
49, Acfold Road
Handsworth Wood
Birmingham B20 1HG

Journal of the Stephenson Locomotive Society

2586 STEVENS ASSOCIATED BOOK PUBLISHERS
11, New Fetter Lane
London EC4P 4EE

British Journal of Criminology
Common Market Law Review

Journal of Business Law
Law Quarterly Review
Modern Law Review
Public Law

2587 STOCKER HOCKNELL LTD.
4, Market Square
Amersham
Bucks.

Bonus
Earth and Sky
Private Wire
Spirax Topics

2588 STOCKMARK PUBLICATIONS
Suite 13
St. Martin's House
29, Ludgate Hill
London EC4M 7BQ

Financial European

2589 STOKE-ON-TRENT LIBRARIES
Horace Barks Reference Library
Bethseda Street
Hanley
Stoke-on-Trent ST1 3RS

Current Bibliography of Published Material
Relating to North Staffordshire and South
Cheshire

2590 STOKES AND LINDLEY-JONES LTD.
21, Montpelier Row
Blackheath
London SE3 0SR

Export Courier

2591 STONE AND COX LTD.
44, Fleet Street
London EC4

Policy

2592 STREET FARM COLLECTIVE
63, Patshull Road
London NW5

Street Farmer

2593 STREET RESEARCH
32, Birchdale Street
Moss Side
Manchester M14 4JD

Street Research

2594 STRODE PUBLICATIONS LTD.
MAP House
243, Caledonian Road
London N1 1ED

Builder and Decorator
Decorating Contractor

2595 STUART THOMSON LTD.
1, Tahara Lodge
Lubbock Road
Chislehurst
Kent

Selling

2596 STUD AND STABLE LTD.
149, Fleet Street
London EC4A 2BU

Stud and Stable

2597 STUDIES IN EDUCATION
  Nafferton
  Driffield
  Yorks.

  Studies in Design Education and Craft

2598 SUFFOLK INSTITUTE OF ARCHAEOLOGY
  Bury St. Edmunds
  Suffolk

  Proceedings of the Suffolk Institute of
    Archaeology

2599 SYMATRA RESEARCH COUNCIL
  c/o Centre for South-East Asian Studies
  University of Hull
  Hull HU6 7RX

  Berita Kadjian Sumatera

2600 SUNRISE BAND
  26, Woodside Park Road
  London N12 8RR

  Sunrise News

2601 SURREY NATURALISTS TRUST LTD.
  96A, Brighton Road
  South Croydon CR2 6AD

  Newsletter of the Surrey Naturalists' Trust
  Surrey Naturalist

2602 SURVEY OF LANGUAGE AND FOLKLORE
  Department of English Language
  The University
  Sheffield S1D 2TN

  Lore and Language

2603 SUSSEX ARCHAEOLOGICAL SOCIETY
  Barbican House
  Lewes
  Sussex

  Sussex Archaeological Society Newsletter

2604 SUTHERLAND PUBLISHING CO. LTD.
  30, Princes Street
  Southport
  Lancs.

  Painting & Decorating Journal

2605 D. A. SUTTON
  194, Station Road
  Birmingham B14 7TE

  Shadow

2606 SWEET AND MAXWELL LTD.
  11, New Fetter Lane
  London EC4P 4EE

  British Tax Review
  Conveyancer and Property Lawyer
  Criminal Appeal Reports
  Criminal Law Review
  Current Law
  Industrial Law Journal
  Journal of Planning and Property Law
  Law Librarian
  Law Teacher
  Nigerian Law Journal
  Patent Law Review
  Programmed Learning and Educational
    Technology
  Property and Compensation Reports
  Sweet and Maxwell's Student's Law Reporter

2607 SWIFTS (LUTON) LTD.
  Stewart Street
  Luton
  Beds.

  Journal of the Institute of Engineers and
    Technicians Ltd.

2608 SWIMMING TIMES LTD.
  2, George Street
  Croydon
  Surrey

  Swimming Times

2609 SWINTON CONSERVATIVE COLLEGE
  Masham
  Ripon
  Yorks.

  Swinton Journal

2610 T S B ASSOCIATION
  Knighton House
  52-66, Mortimer St.
  London W1

  T S B Gazette

2611 T & A CONSTABLE LTD.
  Hopetoun Street
  Edinburgh

  Journal of the Gypsy Lore Society

2612 TTG PUBLICATIONS LTD.
  Adelphi
  John Adam Street
  London WC2

  Conferences and Exhibitions and Executive
    Travel
  Groundsman

2613 T & T CLARK
  38, George Street
  Edinburgh EH2 2LQ

  Expository Times

2614 TABLET PUBLISHING CO. LTD.
  48, Great Peter Street
  London SW1P 2NB

  Tablet

2615 TALBOT PRESS
  Dublin 1

  Studies

2616 TALYLLYN RAILWAY PRESERVATION SOCIETY
  Wharf Station
  Towyn
  Merioneth

  Narrow Gauge Telegraph
  Talyllyn News

2617 TARA TELEPHONE PUBLICATIONS
  30, Thorncliffe Park
  Rathgar
  Dublin 14

  Capella

2618 TARMAC LTD.
  Ettingshall
  Wolverhampton WV4 6JP

  Tarmac World

2619   TATE AND LYLE GROUP
        Leon House
        High Street
        Croydon CR9 3NH

            Tate and Lyle News
            Tate and Lyle Times

2620   TAXATION PUBLISHING CO. LTD.
        98, Park Street
        London W1Y 4BR

            Taxation

2621   TAYLOR AND FRANCIS LTD.
        10-14, Macklin Street
        London WC2B 5NF

            Advances in Physics
            Annals of Science
            Avicultural Magazine
            Contemporary Physics
            Ergonomics
            Ergonomics Abstracts
            International Journal of Control
            International Journal of Electronics
            International Journal of Production Research
            International Journal of Radiation Biology
            International Journal of Systems Science
            Journal of Natural History
            Molecular Physics
            Optica Acta
            Philosophical Magazine
            Xenobiotica

2622   TAYLOR WOODROW SERVICES LTD.
        345, Ruislip Road
        Southall
        Middx.

            Taywood News

2623   TECHNITRADE JOURNALS LTD.
        11-13, Southampton Row
        London WC1

            Heating and Ventilating Engineer

2624   TEESDALE PUBLISHING CO. LTD.
        Standard House
        Bonhill Street
        London EC2

            Motor Sport
            Motorcycle Sport

2625   TEILARD CENTRE FOR THE FUTURE OF MAN
        3, Cromwell Place
        London SW7 2JE

            Teilhard Review

2626   TELEPHONE RENTALS LTD.
        197, Knightsbridge
        London SW7

            TR Journal

2627   TELEVISION MAIL LTD.
        31, St. George Street
        London W1

            International Broadcast Engineer

2628   TELLTIME LTD.
        7, Carnaby Street
        London W1

            Easy Listening

2629   TEMPLE PRESS LTD.
        40, Bowling Green Lane
        London EC1

            Freight Management
            Motor
            Motor Boat and Yachting
            Railway Magazine
            Yachting World

2630   TENNYSON SOCIETY
        City Library
        Free School Lane
        Lincoln

            Tennyson Research Bulletin

2631   TENSOR SOCIETY OF GREAT BRITAIN
        66, South Terrace
        Surbiton
        Surrey

            Matrix and Tensor Quarterly

2632   TERMINUS PUBLICATIONS LTD.
        Speedway House
        Quarry Hill Parade
        Tonbridge
        Kent

            Tanker and Bulk Carrier

2633   TERTIARY RESEARCH GROUP
        c/o 4, Yewdale Close
        Bromley
        Kent BR1 4JJ

            Tertiary Times

2634   TEXTILE BUSINESS PRESS LTD.
        Stratham House
        Talbot Road
        Stretford
        Manchester M32 0EP

            Textile Month
            Textile News

2635   TEXTILE BUSINESS PRESS LTD.
        91, Kirkgate
        Bradford

            Wool Record and Textile World

2636   TEXTILE INSTITUTE
        10, Blackfriars Street
        Manchester M3 5DR

            Journal of the Textile Institute
            Textile Institute and Industry
            Textile Progress

2637   TEXTILE MANUFACTURER
        11, Albert Square
        Manchester M2 5ND

            Textile Manufacturer

2638   TEXTILE MERCURY LTD.
        1, Ford Lane
        Salford
        Lancs. M6 6PX

            British Knitting Industry

2639   TEXTILE TRADE PUBLICATIONS LTD.
        20, Soho Square
        London W1

            British Clothing Manufacturer
            Drapers' Record

2640 THAMES AND HUDSON LTD.
   30, Bloomsbury Street
   London WC1

   British Journal of Aesthetics

2641 THEOLOGICAL ABSTRACTING AND BIBLIO-
   GRAPHICAL SERVICES
   22, Dragon Terrace
   Harrogate
   Yorks, HG1 5DN

   Theological and Religious Index

2642 THEOLOGICAL STUDENTS FELLOWSHIP
   39, Bedford Square
   London WC1B 3EY

   RE Bulletin
   TSF Bulletin

2643 THEORETICAL CHEMICAL ENGINEERING
   ABSTRACTS
   PO Box No. 146
   Liverpool L69 2BL

   Theoretical Chemical Engineering Abstracts

2644 THEOSOPHICAL SOCIETY IN ENGLAND
   50, Gloucester Place
   London W1H 3HJ

   Theosophical Journal

2645 THIMBLE PRESS
   Weaver's
   Amberley
   Glos. GL5 5BA

   Signal

2646 THIRTY PRESS LTD.
   19, Draycott Place
   London SW3 2SJ

   Crusade Magazine

2647 THIS ENGLAND LTD.
   PO Box 62
   Cheltenham
   Glos.

   This England

2648 THOMAS REED PUBLICATIONS LTD.
   36/7, Cock Lane
   London EC1A 9BY

   Reed's Aircraft and Equipment News
   Reed's Marine Equipment News
   Ship and Boat International

2649 THORESBY SOCIETY
   23, Clarendon Road
   Leeds LS8 9NZ

   Publications of the Thoresby Society

2650 THOROTON SOCIETY OF NOTTINGHAMSHIRE
   c/o The Honorary Secretary
   21, Mappesley Hall Drive
   Nottingham NG3 5EY

   Transactions of the Thoroton Society of
   Nottinghamshire

2651 THOROUGHBRED BREEDERS ASSOCIATION
   26, Bloomsbury Way
   London W1A 2SP

   Statistical Abstract

2652 THORPE AND PORTER LTD.
   135/141, Wardour Street
   London W1V 4AP

   Mad

2653 PROFESSOR LEWIS THORPE
   The University
   Nottingham

   Bibliographical Bulletin of the International
   Arthurian Society

2654 THREE CANDLES
   Aston Place
   Dublin 2

   Irish Sword

2655 THUNDERBIRD ENTERPRISES LTD.
   102, College Road
   Harrow
   Middx. HA1 1BQ

   Effluent and Water Treatment Journal

2656 TIMBER GROWERS' ORGANISATION LTD
   National Agricultural Centre
   Kenilworth
   Warwickshire CU8 2LG

   Timber Grower

2657 TIME AND TIDE
   Classified House
   New Bridge Street
   London EC4

   Time and Tide

2658 TIME OUT IN LONDON LTD.
   374, Grays Inn Road
   London WC1X 8BB

   Time Out

2659 TIMES NEWSPAPERS LTD.
   Printing House Square
   London EC4

   Times Educational Supplement
   Times Higher Education Supplement
   Times Literary Supplement

2660 TIN PUBLICATIONS LTD.
   7, High Road
   London W4 2NE

   Tin International

2661 TIN RESEARCH INSTITUTE
   Fraser Road
   Perivale
   Greenford
   Middx.

   Tin and its uses

2662 TITUS WILSON AND SON LTD.
   28, Highgate
   Kendal

   Past and Present
   Transactions of the Cumberland and Westmorland
   Antiquarian and Archaeological Society

2663 TOC H
   15, Trinity Square
   London EC3

   Point Three

2664 TOFTS AND WOLFE (PUBLISHERS) LTD.
   64A, Lansdowne Road
   South Woodford
   London E18

   Keyboard
   Music Industry

2665   TOLKIEN SOCIETY
       31, Great Dell
       Welwyn Garden City
       Herts.

          Anduril
          Mallorn

2666   TOUCAN PRESS
       Mount Durand
       St. Peter Port
       Guernsey C.I.

          Literary Repository

2667   TOWN AND COUNTRY PLANNING ASSOCIATION
       28, King Street
       London WC2

          Town and Country Planning

2668   TOWN AND COUNTRY PLANNING ASSOCIATION
       17, Carlton House Terrace
       London SW1

          Bulletin of Environmental Education

2669   TOY PUBLICATIONS
       7c, Carlton Drive
       London SW15

          How to Buy Toys

2670   TRADE PAPER (LONDON) LTD.
       157, Hagden Lane
       Watford WD1 8LW

          Piano World & Music Trades Review
          Radio and Electrical Retailing

2671   TRADE AND TECHNICAL PRESS LTD.
       Crown House
       Morden
       Surrey

          Church and School Equipment News
          Hydraulic Pneumatic Power
          Pumps

2672   TRADE CHRONICLES LTD.
       Mercury House
       Waterloo Road
       London SE1

          Furnishing World
          Woodworking Industry

2673   TRADE NEWS LTD.
       203/9, North Gower Street
       London NW1

          ICHCA Monthly Journal
          Electrical and Electronics Manufacturer
          Toys International

2674   TRADE NEWS LTD.
       Pembroke House
       Campsbourne Road
       Hornsey
       London N8

          Security and Protection

2675   TRADE PRESS (FMB) LTD.
       33, John Street
       London WC1

          Master Builder's Journal

2676   TRADEN PUBLICATIONS
       Charlton Place
       Downing Street
       Manchester

          Market Place

2677   TRAMWAY AND LIGHT RAILWAY SOCIETY
       102, Marlborough Lane
       London SE7

          Bulletin of the Tramway and Light Railway
          Society

2678   TRAMWAY MUSEUM SOCIETY
       29, Old Hall Avenue
       Duffield
       Derbys.

          Journal of the Tramway Museum Society

2679   TRANSATLANTIC REVIEW
       33, Ennismore Gardens
       London SW7 1AE

          Transatlantic Review

2680   TRANSPORT AND GENERAL WORKERS' UNION
       Transport House
       Smith Square
       London SW1

          Record

2681   TRANSPORT TICKET SOCIETY
       18, Villa Road
       Luton LU2 7NT

          Journal of the Transport Ticket Society

2682   TRAVEL AND TRANSPORT LTD.
       4, Milk Street
       London EC2V 8AT

          Coaching Journal and Bus Review

2683   TREHARNE PUBLICATIONS (HULL) LTD.
       Midland Bank Chambers
       9, Lairgate
       Beverley
       E. Yorks.

          East Riding Bystander
          Humberside Export News

2684   TRIBUNE PUBLICATIONS LTD.
       24, St. John Street
       London EC1

          Tribune

2685   R. TRILLO LTD.
       Broadlands
       Brockenhurst
       Hants

          Air-Cushion and Hydrofoil Systems
          Bibliography Service

2686   TRIUMPH MOTOR CO. LTD.
       Canley
       Coventry

          Triumph News

2687   TROUP PUBLICATIONS LTD.
       76, Oxford Street
       London W1N 0NH

          Steam and Heating Engineer

2688   TRUMAN LTD.
       92, Brick Lane
       London E1 6QN

          Truman Times

2689   TRUSTEES OF MUCKROSS HOUSE
       Killarney
       Co. Kerry

          ROS

2690 ALAN AND JOAN TUCKER
The Bookshop
Station Road
Stroud
Glos.

Format

2691 TUDOR PRESS LTD.
75, Carter Lane
London EC4V 5ET

Insurance Record
Packaging

2692 TUESDAY PRESS LTD.
8, Garrick Street
London WC2E 9BH

Tuesday Paper

2693 JOHN TUNSTILL
36, Kennington Road
London SE1

Miniature Warfare and Model Soldiers

2694 TUPPERWARE CO. LTD.
43 Upper Grosvenor Street
London SW1

Prospect

2695 TURF NEWSPAPERS LTD.
55, Curzon Street
London W1

British Racehorse

2696 TURNMILL PRESS LTD.
65/66, Turnmill Street
London EC1

Materials Handling and Management

2697 TURRET PRESS LTD.
65/66, Turnmill Street
London EC3M 5RA

Baltic Exchange Magazine
British Clayworker
Ceramics
Energy Digest
Journal of Fuel and Heat Technology
Mulling
Storage Handling Distribution

2698 TURRET PRESS LTD./TURRET PRESS (HOLDINGS) LTD.
157, Hagden Lane
Watford WD1 8LW

Cleaning and Maintenance
Feed and Farm Supplies
Records of the Month

2699 TWEEDDALE PRESS LTD.
90, Marygate
Berwick-upon-Tweed
Northumberland

New Zealand News

2700 TYNDALE PRESS
39, Bedford Square
London WC1B 3EY

Tyndale Bulletin

2701 TYNE & WEAR CHAMBER OF COMMERCE
4, St. Nicholas Buildings
Newcastle-on-Tyne NE1 1RR

Industrial Tyneside

2702 UKCIS
University
Nottingham NG7 2RD

UKCIS Macroprofiles
Ukcis Macroprofiles ESR-Chemical Aspects
Ukcis Macroprofiles: Gas Chromatography
Ukcis Macroprofiles NMR-Chemical Aspects
Ukcis Macroprofiles Paper and Thin-layer
    Chromatography
Ukcis Macroprofiles: Steroids

2703 UML LTD.
Lever House
Port Sunlight
Wirral
Cheshire

Port Sunlight News

2704 UNISAF PUBLICATIONS LTD.
Dudley Road
Tunbridge Wells
Kent

Fire
Fire International

2705 UKRAINIAN REVIEW
49, Linden Gardens
Notting Hill Gate
London W2

Ukrainian Thought

2706 ULSTER ARCHAEOLOGICAL SOCIETY
7, Sans Souci Park
Belfast 9

Ulster Journal of Archaeology

2707 ULSTER LIBERAL PARTY
5, Windsor Avenue
Belfast BT9 6EE

Northern Radical

2708 ULSTER MEDICAL SOCIETY
PO Box 222
City Hospital
Belfast 9

Ulster Medical Journal

2709 UNDERCURRENTS PARTNERSHIP
34, Cholmley Gardens
Aldred Road
London NW6

Undercurrents

2710 UNIGATE LTD.
34, Palace Court
London W2 4HX

Unigate News

2711 UNILEVER LTD.
Unilever House
Blackfriars
London EC4

Unilever International

2712 UNILEVER EXPORT LTD.
Lever House
Port Sunlight
Wirral
Cheshire

Export News

2713 UNION MOVEMENT
76a, Rochester Row
London SW1

Alternative

2714 UNION OF LIBERAL AND PROGRESSIVE
SYNAGOGUES
28, St. John's Wood Road
London NW8

Pointer

2715 UNION OF MODERN FREE CHURCHMEN
c/o 79, Friern Watch Avenue
London N12

Modern Free Churchman

2716 UNION OF SHOP, DISTRIBUTIVE AND ALLIED
WORKERS
188, Wilmslow Road
Fallowfield
Manchester M14 6LJ

New Dawn

2717 UNION OF WELSH INDEPENDENTS
11, St. Helens Road
Swansea

Y Tyst

2718 UNION OSLOBODJENJE
53, Hawthorn Drive
Harrow
Middx. HA2 7NU

Nasa Rec

2719 UNITARIAN
c/o 27, Gladstone Road
Altrincham
Cheshire

Unitarian

2720 UNITARIAN HISTORICAL SOCIETY
c/o 13, Devonshire Road
West Bridgford
Nottingham

Transactions of the Unitarian Historical
Society

2721 UNITED COMMERCIAL TRAVELLERS ASSOCIATION
LTD.
Bexton Lane
Knutsford
Cheshire WA16 9DA

Do it Yourself Retailing
Exchange & Mart
Selling Today

2722 UNITED KINGDOM ATOMIC ENERGY AUTHORITY
11, Charles II Street
London SW1Y 4QP

Atom News

2723 UNITED KINGDOM ATOMIC ENERGY RESEARCH
ESTABLISHMENT
Harwell
Didcot
Berks.

Harlequin

2724 UNITED KINGDOM PROVIDENT
33, Gracechurch Street
London EC3P 3DY

Ukapian

2725 UNITED KINGDOM READING ASSOCIATION
63, Laurel Grove
Sunderland
Co. Durham SR2 9EE

Reading

2726 UNITED NEWSPAPERS PUBLICATIONS LTD.
127, Fishergate
Preston PR1 2DN

Farmers Guardian

2727 UNITED REFORMED CHURCH
86, Tavistock Place
London WC1H 9RT

Reform

2728 UNITED TRADE PRESS LTD.
42-43, Gerrard Street
London W1V 7LP

Manufacturing Clothier

2729 UNITED TRADE PRESS LTD.
9, Gough Square
Fleet Street
London EC4

Biomedical Engineering
Computer Survey
Dairy Industries
Electronic Components
Industrial Safety
Instrument Practice
Laboratory Practice
Soap, Perfumery and Cosmetics

2730 UNITED WRITERS PUBLICATIONS
Trevail Mill
Zennor
St. Ives

Good Reading

2731 UNIVERSITY COLLEGE
Faculty of Education
Cardiff

Education for Development

2732 UNIVERSITY COLLEGE
School of Environmental Studies
Gower Street
London WC1E 6BT

Research Bulletin

2733 UNIVERSITY COLLEGE
Department of Music
Cardiff

Soundings

2734 UNIVERSITY COLLEGE
Computer Laboratory
Belfield
Dublin 4

Format

2735 UNIVERSITY COLLEGE, DUBLIN
Student Psychological Society
Thornfield Laboratory
Stillorgan Road
Dublin 4

Thornfield Journal

2736 UNIVERSITY COLLEGE HOSPITAL MEDICAL
SCHOOL
London WC1

Too Much

2737 UNIVERSITY MICROFILMS LTD.
      A Xerox Company
      Tylers Green
      High Wycombe
      Bucks.

      Ruma

2738 UNIVERSITY OF BRADFORD
      Library
      Richmond Road
      Bradford BD7 1DP

      Ace

2739 UNIVERSITY OF BRISTOL
      Dept. of Economics
      Bristol BS8 1HY

      History of Economic Thought Newsletter

2740 UNIVERSITY OF CALIFORNIA PRESS
      2-4, Brook Street
      London W1

      Viator

2741 UNIVERSITY OF DURHAM
      Old Ship Hall
      Durham DH1 3HP

      Durham University Journal

2742 UNIVERSITY OF EAST ANGLIA
      Students Union
      University Village
      Wilberforce Road
      Norwich NOR 88C

      Twice

2743 UNIVERSITY OF EDINBURGH
      Dept. of Educational Studies
      11, Buccleuch Place
      Edinburgh EH8 9JT

      Local History Bulletin for South-East Scotland

2744 UNIVERSITY OF EDINBURGH
      School of Scottish Studies
      27, George Square
      Edinburgh

      Scottish Studies

2745 UNIVERSITY OF EDINBURGH
      Philosophy Dept.
      David Hume Tower
      George Square
      Edinburgh 8

      Seed

2746 UNIVERSITY OF EDINBURGH
      Student Publications Board
      1, Buccleugh Place
      Edinburgh EH8 9LW

      New Edinburgh Review
      Throb

2747 UNIVERSITY OF ESSEX
      Dept. of Sociology
      Colchester
      Essex

      Oral History

2748 UNIVERSITY OF GLASGOW
      9, Southpark Terrace
      Glasgow W2

      Absees

2749 UNIVERSITY OF GLASGOW
      Dental Hospital and School
      378, Sauchiehall Street
      Glasgow 3

      Glasgow Dental Journal

2750 UNIVERSITY OF GLASGOW
      Dept. of Extra-Mural Education
      57-9, Oakfield Avenue
      Glasgow G12 8LE

      Proceedings of the Geological Society of
      Glasgow

2751 UNIVERSITY OF HULL
      Institute of Education
      173, Cottingham Road
      Hull HU5 4AY

      Aspects of Education

2752 UNIVERSITY OF KEELE
      Keele
      Staffs. ST5 5BG

      Sociological Review

2753 UNIVERSITY OF KEELE
      Dept. of Geography
      University of Keele
      Newcastle
      Staffs. ST5 5BG

      Iberian Studies

2754 UNIVERSITY OF KENT
      The Editor, Fuss
      Room 150
      The Registry
      University of Kent

      Fuss

2755 UNIVERSITY OF LANCASTER
      Dept. of Educational Research
      University
      Bailrigg
      Lancaster

      Higher Education Bulletin

2756 UNIVERSITY OF LANCASTER
      Dept. of Systems Engineering
      Bailrigg
      Lancaster

      Journal of Systems Engineering

2757 UNIVERSITY OF LEEDS
      Central Printing Services
      Woodhouse Lane
      Leeds LS2 9JT

      University of Leeds Gazette
      University of Leeds Reporter

2758 UNIVERSITY OF LEEDS
      Dept. of Education
      Leeds LS2 9JT

      Journal of Educational Administration and
      History

2759 UNIVERSITY OF LEEDS AND LEEDS POLYTECHNIC
      Students Union
      155, Woodhouse Lane
      Leeds 2

      Leeds Student

2760 UNIVERSITY OF LIVERPOOL
Dept. of Geology
Liverpool

Geological Journal
Geological Magazine

2761 UNIVERSITY OF LONDON
24, Russell Square
London WC1

University of London Bulletin

2762 UNIVERSITY OF LONDON
Goldsmith's College
Lewisham Way
New Cross
London SE14 6NW

Ideas

2763 UNIVERSITY OF LONDON
Institute of Education
London WC1

London Educational Review

2764 UNIVERSITY OF LONDON
Institute of Education Library
11-13, Ridgmount Street
London WC1E 7AH

Education Libraries Bulletin

2765 UNIVERSITY OF LONDON
School of Oriental and African Studies
London WC1E 7HP

African Language Studies

2766 UNIVERSITY OF LOUGHBOROUGH
Chemical Engineering Dept.
Loughborough
Leics.

Chemical Engineering Journal

2767 UNIVERSITY OF LOUGHBOROUGH
Social Science Society
Loughborough
Leics.

Feedback

2768 UNIVERSITY OF MANCHESTER
Dept. of Economics
Dover Street
Manchester M13 9PL

Manchester School of Economic and Social
Studies

2769 UNIVERSITY OF MANCHESTER
Dept. of Spanish and Portugese Studies
Manchester M13 9PL

Newsletter of the Luso-Brazilian Section
Association of British Hispanists

2770 UNIVERSITY OF MANCHESTER
Institute of Science and Technology
Sackville Street
Manchester M60 1QD

Advance

2771 UNIVERSITY OF NEWCASTLE
Institute of Education
Newcastle-on-Tyne NE1 7RU

Journal of the Institutes of Education of
Durham and Newcastle Universities

2772 UNIVERSITY OF NOTTINGHAM
University Park
Nottingham

Renaissance and Modern Studies

2773 UNIVERSITY OF NOTTINGHAM DEPT. OF ADULT
EDUCATION
14-22, Shakespeare Street
Nottingham

Local Population Studies

2774 UNIVERSITY OF NOTTINGHAM
Dept. of Geography
University
Nottingham

East Midland Geographer

2775 UNIVERSITY OF NOTTINGHAM
Students Union
Portland Building
Nottingham

Gangster

2776 UNIVERSITY OF NOTTINGHAM
School of Agriculture
Dept. of Agriculture and Horticulture
Sutton Bonington
Loughborough
Leics. LE12 5RD

Farming in the East Midlands

2777 UNIVERSITY OF OXFORD
Institute of Agricultural Economics
Dartington House
Little Clarendon Street
Oxford OX1 2HP

Oxford Agrarian Studies

2778 UNIVERSITY OF OXFORD
Liberal Society
Oxford

Fringe

2779 UNIVERSITY OF READING
Dept. of Geography
White Knights
Reading RG6 2AF

Reading Geographer

2780 UNIVERSITY OF ST. ANDREWS
St. Andrews
Fife

Philosophical Quarterly

2781 UNIVERSITY OF SHEFFIELD
Dept. of Sociological Studies
Sheffield S10 2TN

Sociological Analysis

2782 UNIVERSITY OF STIRLING
Publications Board
Stirling

Brig

2783 UNIVERSITY OF STRATHCLYDE
Glasgow

Metallurgical Journal

2784 UNIVERSITY OF STRATHCLYDE ABACUS
School of Architecture
University of Strathclyde
Glasgow G1 0NG

Bulletin of Computer Aided Architectural
Design

2785 UNIVERSITY OF SURREY
    Library
    Guildford

      Current Awareness Bulletin: Human Sciences
        and Management
      Current Awareness Bulletin for Mechanical
        Engineering

2786 UNIVERSITY OF WALES PRESS
    Merthyr House
    James Street
    Cardiff CF1 6EU

      Bulletin of the Board of Celtic Studies
      Efrydiau Athron Yddol
      Geiriadur Prifysaol Cymru
      Llen Cymru
      Studia Celtica
      Trivium
      Welsh History Review
      Y Gwyddonydd

2787 UNIVERSITY OF YORK
    Dept. of Economics
    Heslington
    York YO1 5DD

      Bulletin of Economic Research

2788 UNIVERSITY OF YORK
    Dept. of Philosophy
    Heslington
    York

      Locke Newsletter

2789 UPDATE PUBLICATIONS LTD.
    33-34, Alfred Place
    London WC1E 7DP

      Bulletin of the National Association of Clinical
        Tutors
      Teach-in
      Update

2790 UPLANDS PRESS LTD.
    1, Katharine Street
    Croydon CR9 1CB

      Filtration and Separation

2791 USHAW COLLEGE
    Durham

      Ushaw Magazine

2792 UP PRESS
    20, Droylsden Road
    Newton Heath
    Manchester M10 6HB

      Viewpoints

2793 VEGETARIAN SOCIETY (U.K.) LTD.
    Parkdale
    Dunham Road
    Altrincham
    Cheshire

      Vegetarian

2794 VEHICLE BUILDERS AND REPAIRERS ASSOCIATION
    13/14, Park Place
    Leeds 1

      Body

2795 VERNONS ORGANISATION
    Vermail House
    Ormskirk Road
    Liverpool

      Opportunity

2796 VETERAN CAR CLUB OF GREAT BRITAIN
    36, New England Road
    Haywards Heath
    Sussex

      Veteran Car

2797 VICKERS LTD.
    Vickers House
    Millbank Tower
    Millbank
    London SW1

      Vickers News

2798 VICTOR GREEN PUBLICATIONS LTD.
    44, Bedford Row
    London WC1R 4LL

      Fire Surveyor
      Security Surveyor

2799 VICTOR PRODUCTS LTD.
    PO Box 10
    Wallsend
    Northumberland

      Victor Magazine

2800 VICTORIA AND ALBERT MUSEUM
    South Kensington
    London SW7

      Victoria and Albert Museum Bulletin

2801 VICTORIA VERNON PUBLICATIONS LTD.
    54/55, Wilton Road
    London SW1

      Mother and Child

2802 VIETNAM SOLIDARITY CAMPAIGN
    182, Pentonville Road
    London N1

      Indochina

2803 VIKING SOCIETY FOR NORTHERN RESEARCH
    University College London
    Gower Street
    London WC1

      Saga Book of the Viking Society

2804 VILLIERS PUBLICATIONS
    Ingestre Road
    Tufnell Park
    London NW5

      Antacus

2805 VINCENT PRESS
    60, Cole Park Road
    Twickenham
    Middlesex

      Journal of World Trade Law

2806 VIOLA DA GAMBA SOCIETY
    123, Russell Lane
    London N20

      Chelys

2807 VISION
    17, Stratton Street
    London W1X 5FD

      Vision

2808 VISUAL PUBLICATIONS LTD.
    32, Liverpool Road
    Worthing
    Sussex

      Advertisement Parade

2809   VOICE OF THE PEOPLE
194, Hackney Road
London E2

    Voice of the People

2810   VOLUNTARY COMMITTEE ON OVERSEAS AID
AND DEVELOPMENT
Parnell House
25, Wilton Road
London SW1

    Internationalist

2811   VOLUNTARY COMMITTEE ON OVERSEAS AID
AND DEVELOPMENT
69, Victoria Street
London SW1

    Development News
    Vox

2812   W. GREEN & SON LTD.
St. Giles Street
Edinburgh EH1 1PU

    Juridical Review

2813   WB SAUNDERS CO. LTD.
12, Dyott Street
London WC1A 1DB

    Clinics in Endocrinology and Metabolism
    Clinics in Gastroenterology
    Clinics in Haematology

2814   W. CANNING & CO. LTD.
Great Hampton Street
Birmingham B18 6AS

    Canning Journal
    Canning Quarterly News

2815   W. KING LTD.
100, Grays Inn Road
London WC1

    Gas in Industry
    Gas Service

2816   W. D. & H. O. WILLS
East Street
Bedminster
Bristol BS99 TUJ

    Wills World

2817   W. H. SMITH & SON
Strand House
Portugal Street
London WC2A 2HS

    Smiths' Trade News
    Stationery Trade Review

2818   WPR LTD.
Rex House
Hampton Road West
Hanworth
Middx.

    Flambeau

2819   WALDENS & CO. LTD.
18, Station Approach
London SW11

    Proceedings of the Virgil Society

2820   WALES AND BORDER NEWSPAPERS
Caxton Press
Oswestry
Salop.

    Teacher in Wales

2821   WALKER ART GALLERY
William Brown Street
Liverpool L3 8EL

    Annual Report and Bulletin of the Walker Art
    Gallery, Liverpool

2822   WALLACE PRINTERS LTD.
44, Crook Street
Bolton
Lancs.

    Table Tennis News

2823   WALLPAPER, PAINT AND WALLCOVERINGS
ASSOCIATION OF GREAT BRITAIN
20, Huntingdon House
220, Cromwell Road
London SW5 05W

    Wallpaper, Paint and Wallcovering

2824   WARBURG INSTITUTE
Woburn Square
London WC1H 0AB

    Journal of the Warburg and Courtauld Institutes

2825   WARD LOCK EDUCATIONAL
116, Baker Street
London W1M 2BB

    Children's Literature in Education

2826   WARWICKSHIRE LOCAL HISTORY SOCIETY
47, Newbold Terrace
Leamington Spa
Warwickshire

    Warwickshire History

2827   WATCH TOWER BIBLES AND TRACT SOCIETY
Watch Tower House
The Ridgeway
London NW7 1RN

    Awake
    Watchtower

2828   WATER POLLUTION RESEARCH LABORATORY
Elder Way
Stevenage
Herts. SG1 1TH

    Notes on Water Pollution

2829   WATER RESEARCH ASSOCIATION
Ferry Lane
Medmenham
Marlow
Bucks. SL7 2HO

    WRA Digest
    Library List

2830   WATERLOW & SONS
12, Vandy Street
London EC2

    Bankers' Magazine

2831   WATERWAY RECOVERY GROUP
c/o 4, Wentworth Court
Wentworth Avenue
Finchley
London N3 1YD

    Navires

2832   WATERWAYS PRODUCTIONS LTD.
26, Chaseview Road
Alrewas
Burton-on-Trent
Staffs.

    Waterways World

2833 WATFORD AND DISTRICT INDUSTRIAL HISTORY
SOCIETY
49, Longcroft Road
Maple Cross
Rickmansworth
Herts.

Journal of the Watford and District Industrial
History Society

2834 WATMOUGHS LTD.
Idle
Bradford
Yorks.

Fur and Feather

2835 WATNEY MANN LTD.
Palace Street
London SW1

Watneys News

2836 WAVERLEY PRESS
Hilton Place
Aberdeen AB9 1FA

Education in the North

2837 WEALD OF KENT PUBLICATIONS (TONBRIDGE)
LTD.
3, Castle Street
Tonbridge
Kent

International Vending Times

2838 WEALDEN PRESS LTD.
Quarry Hill Parade
Tonbridge
Kent

Pollution Monitor

2839 WEBB SOCIETY
Wildrose
Church Road
Winkfield
Windsor

Webb Society Quarterly Journal

2840 WEBSTERS PUBLICATIONS LTD.
79, Temple Chambers
Temple Avenue
London EC4

Racing and Football Outlook
Soccer Star
World Soccer

2841 WEIR GROUP LTD.
Cathcart
Glasgow G44 4EX

Weir Bulletin

2842 WELDING INSTITUTE
Abington Hall
Abington
Cambridge CB1 6AL

Welding Research International

2843 WELLCOME INSTITUTE OF THE HISTORY OF
MEDICINE
183, Euston Road
London NW1

Current Work in the History of Medicine
Medical History

2844 WELLENS PUBLISHING
The Sun
Guilsborough
Northampton NN6 8PY

Industrial and Commercial Training

2845 WELMAR PUBLICATIONS LTD.
8, Marwell
Westerham
Kent

Elevator Lift and Ropeway Engineering

2846 R. W. WELSH
2, Coates Crescent
Edinburgh 3

Scottish Circular

2847 WELSH BIBLIOGRAPHICAL SOCIETY
National Library of Wales
Aberystwyth SY23 3BU

Journal of the Welsh Bibliographical Society

2848 WELSH LIBRARY ASSOCIATION
Central Library
The Hayes
Cardiff CF1 2QU

Y Ddolen

2849 WELSH MEDICAL PRESS LTD.
23, Blenheim Road
Cardiff

Welsh Medical Gazette

2850 WELSH THEATRE ASSOCIATION
Waterloo Street
Bangor
Caernarvonshire

Llwyfan

2851 WELSHPOOL AND LLANFAIR LIGHT RAILWAY
PRESERVATION CO. LTD.
20, The Terraces
Morda
Oswestry
Salop.

Llanfair Railway Journal

2852 WELSHPOOL PRINTING COMPANY
Severn Street
Welshpool

C. P. R. W. Newsletter

2853 WELWYN HALL RESEARCH ASSOCIATION
Church Street
Welwyn
Herts

Welwyn Newsletter

2854 WESLEY HISTORICAL SOCIETY
c/o A. A. Taberer Ltd.
Bankhead
Broxton
Chester

Proceedings of the Wesley Historical Society

2855 WESLEY HISTORICAL SOCIETY
Lancashire and Cheshire Branch
4, Brecon Close
Royton
Oldham
Lancs.

Journal of the Lancashire and Cheshire
Branch of the Wesley Historical Society

2856 WESLEYAN REFORM UNION
Wesleyan Reform Church House
123, Queen Street
Sheffield
Yorks. S1 2DU

Christian Words

2857 WEST INDIA COMMITTEE
18, Grosvenor Street
London W1X 0HP

West Indies Chronicle

2858 WEST LONDON FREE PRESS
22, Cedars Drive
Hillingdon
Middx.

West London Free Press

2859 WEST OF ENGLAND PRESS PUBLISHERS LTD.
Tavistock
Devon

Army Quarterly and Defence Journal

2860 WEST WALES NATURALIST TRUST
4, Victoria Place
Haverfordwest
Pembroke

Nature in Wales

2861 WESTBOURNE PUBLISHING GROUP
Crown House
Morden
Surrey

Decor and Contract Furnishing
Educational and Church Equipment
Shop Equipment and Shopfitting News
Shopfitting and Equipment Monitor
Wood and Equipment News

2862 WESTERN REGIONAL HOSPITAL BOARD
351, Sauchiehall Street
Glasgow G2 3HT

Regional Review

2863 WESTERN SPORTING PRESS LTD.
28, Church Road
Whitchurch
Cardiff

Welsh Rugby

2864 WESTMINSTER ABBEY
London SW1

Wesminster Abbey Occasional Paper

2865 WESTMINSTER CATHEDRAL
Archbishop's House
London SW1

Westminster Cathedral Journal

2866 WESTMINSTER PRESS LTD.
Blair House
Vine Street
Uxbridge
Middx.

Funeral Service Journal

2867 WESTWOOD PUBLISHING GROUP LTD.
Morden
Surrey

DIY and Woodworking Information

2868 WHEATLAND JOURNALS LTD.
157, Hagden Lane
Watford
Herts.

Blinds & Shutters
Brushes
Brushes International
Contractors Plant Review
Cordage, Canvas and Jute World
Electroplating and Metal Finishing
Industrial Finishing and Surface Coatings
Jeweller
Motor Cycle and Cycle Trader
Pram & Nursery Trader
Toy Trader

2869 WHERE TO GO LTD.
191, Kings Cross Road
London WC1

Where to Go in London...

2870 J. L. WHITE
Falkland Cottage
Mottram Street
Andrew
Nr. Macclesfield
Cheshire SK10 4RA

Commercial Teacher

2871 WHITE CRESCENT PRESS LTD.
Crescent Road
Luton
Beds.

Bedfordshire Magazine
C & T: Luton Commerce and Trade Journal

2872 WHITE FISH AUTHORITY
Lincoln's Inn Chambers
2/3, Cursitor Street
London EC4A 1NQ

Fish Industry Review

2873 THE WHITE HOUSE
Church Road
Croydon
Surrey

Pilot

2874 WHITEFRIARS PRESS

Health and Social Service

2875 WHITEHALL MUSICAL AND DRAMATIC SOCIETY
135, Griffith Avenue
Dublin 9

Anthos

2876 WHITEHALL PRESS LTD.
Wrotham Place
Wrotham
Sevenoaks
Kent

DIY Trade
Book Trade
Electronics Today International
Shipbuilding and Marine Engineering
International

2877 WHITEHALL PRESS LTD.
29, Palace Street
London SW1

Hospital Management

2878   WHITEHORN PRESS LTD.
      Thomson House
      Withy Grove
      Manchester M60 4BL

          Cheshire Life
          Lancashire Life
          Yorkshire Life

2879   WHITELANE PUBLICATIONS LTD.
      52, Whitehorse Lane
      South Norwood
      London S2 25

          Drag Racing & Hot Rod Magazine

2880   WHOLESALE PHOTO FINISHERS ASSOCIATION
      50, Great Russell Street
      London WC1

          Photo Finisher

2881   D. WILD
      20, Chalcot Road
      London NW1 8LL

          Architects for a Really Socialist Environment

2882   PETER WILD
      Pheasant Walk
      High Legh
      Mere
      Cheshire

          Worldwide Newspaper Collecting and Press
          History

2883   WILDLIFE & COUNTRY PHOTOS LTD.
      Orcombe
      Peckham Bush
      Tonbridge
      Kent

          Defend Kent

2884   WILDFOWL TRUST
      Slimbridge
      Glos. GL2 7BT

          Wildfowl

2885   WILDFOWLERS ASSOCIATION OF GREAT BRITAIN
      & IRELAND
      104, Watergate Street
      Chester

          WAGBI Magazine

2886   WILKINSON BROS. LTD.
      12-16, Laystall Street
      London EC1R 4PB

          Handy Shipping Guide

2887   WILLIAM BLACKWOOD & SONS LTD.
      32, Thistle Street
      Edinburgh EH2 1EN

          Blackwood's Magazine

2888   WILLIAM CLOWES & SONS LTD.
      Hawkins Road
      The Hythe
      Colchester
      Essex

          Behavioural Technology

2889   WILLIAM COLLINS SONS & CO. LTD.
      144, Cathedral Street
      Glasgow C4 0NB

          Education 3-13
          Journal of Curriculum Studies

2890   WILLIAM MALLINSON & DENNY MOTT LTD.
      130, Hackney Road
      London E27 QR

          Journal of William Mallinson & Denny Mott
          Ltd.

2891   WILLIAM MORRIS SOCIETY
      25, Lawn Crescent
      Kew
      Surrey

          Journal of the William Morris Society

2892   WILLIAM PRESS GROUP
      Publicity Dept.
      22, Queen Anne's Gate
      London SW1

          Expression

2893   WILLIAM REED LTD.
      19, Eastcheap
      London EC3

          Grocer
          International Brewing and Distilling
          Off Licence News
          Scottish Licensed Trade News

2894   KEMBLE WILLIAMS
      South Bank
      Spring Road
      Ipswich
      Suffolk

          Samphire

2895   WILTON PUBLICATIONS LTD.
      8, Buckingham Street
      London WC2

          Tunnels and Tunnelling

2896   WILTSHIRE ARCHAEOLOGICAL AND NATURAL
      HISTORY SOCIETY
      41, Long Street
      Devizes
      Wilts.

          Bi-Annual Bulletin of the Wiltshire
            Archaeological & Natural History Society
          Wiltshire Archaeological and Natural History
            Magazine

2897   WIMPY INTERNATIONAL LTD.
      214, Chiswick High Road
      London W

          Wimpy Times

2898   WINCHESTER COLLEGE
      Winchester
      Hants

          Caliban

2899   WINCHESTER CONSUMER GROUP
      Mrs S. Cope
      10, Hubert Road
      Winchester
      Hants.

          Target

2900   WINE & FOOD PUBLICATIONS LTD.
      1, Hanover Square
      London W1

          Wine and Food

2901 WINE & SPIRIT PUBLICATIONS LTD.
Victoria House
Southampton Row
London WC2

Wine Magazine

2902 WINSOR & NEWTON LTD.
Wealdstone
Harrow
Middx.

Colour Review

2903 WIRE INDUSTRY LTD.
157, Station Road East
Oxted
Surrey RH8 0QE

Wire Industry

2904 WOKING REVIEW LTD.
1, Duke Street
Woking
Surrey

Guildford and District Outlook
Review for Addlestone, Byfleet, Chertsey,
New Haw, Weybridge
Woking Review

2905 WOLVERHAMPTON POLYTECHNIC
Arts Department
Polytechnic
Wolverhampton

Forge

2906 WOMEN'S ENGINEERING SOCIETY
25, Fouberts' Place
London W1V 2AL

Woman Engineer

2907 WOMEN'S GAS FEDERATION
29, Great Peter Street
London SW1

Scope

2908 WOMEN'S LITERATURE COLLECTIVE
27, Deeds Grove
High Wycombe
Bucks.

Women's Liberation Review

2909 WOMEN'S REPORT
Fawcett House
27, Wilfred Street
London SW1

Women's Report

2910 WOMEN'S ROYAL VOLUNTARY SERVICE
17, Old Park Lane
London W1Y 4AJ

WRVS Magazine

2911 A & B WOOD
14, Stoke Road
Guildford
Surrey

Books For Your Children

2912 WOOL INDUSTRIES RESEARCH ASSOCIATION
Headingley Lane
Leeds LS6 IBW

WIRA News
WIRASCAN
WIRASCAN for Clothier's

2913 WOOLHOPE NATURALISTS FIELD CLUB
Chy an Whyloryon
Wigmore
Leominster
Herefordshire HR6 9UD

Transactions of the Woolhope Naturalists
Field Club

2914 WOOLWICH EQUITABLE BUILDING SOCIETY
Equitable House
Woolwich
London SE18 6AB

New Advance

2915 WOOTTEN PUBLICATIONS LTD.
150/152, Caledonian Road
London W1 9RD

Planned Savings

2916 WORCESTER CITY MUSEUM
Foregate Street
Worcester WR1 1DT

Worcestershire Archaeology Newsletter

2917 WORCESTERSHIRE NATURALISTS CLUB
202, Pickersleigh Road
Malvern
Worcs. WR14 2QX

Worcestershire Naturalists Club News Letter

2918 WORKERS ASSOCIATION FOR THE DEMOCRATIC
SETTLEMENT OF ONE NATIONAL CONFLICT IN
IRELAND
10, Athol Street
Belfast 12

Two Nations

2919 WORKERS EDUCATIONAL ASSOCIATION
Temple House
9, Upper Berkeley Street
London W1H 8BY

WEA News

2920 WORKSHOP PRESS LTD.
2, Culham Court
Granville Road
London N4 4JB

Workshop New Poetry

2921 WORLD ATHLETICS & SPORTING PUBLICATIONS
LTD.
344, High Street
Rochester
Kent

Athletics Weekly

2922 WORLD EDUCATION FELLOWSHIP
55, Upper Stone Street
Tunbridge Wells
Kent

New Era

2923 WORLD EXPEDITIONARY ASSOCIATION
22, Beauchamp Place
London SW3

Expedition News

2924 WORLD JEWISH CONGRESS
55, New Cavendish Street
London W1M 8BT

World Jewry

2925 WORLD PLOUGHING ORGANISATION
Alfred Hall
Foulsyke
Loweswater
Cockermouth
Cumberland

Bulletin of News and Information

2926 WORLD REFRIGERATION
11A, Gloucester Road
London SW7

World Refrigeration and Air Conditioning

2927 WORLD TRADE CENTRE
52, St. Katharine's Way
London E1

Tower Times

2928 WORLD TRADE MAGAZINE LTD.
13, New Bridge Street
London EC4V 6HH

Achievement

2929 WORLD WILDLIFE FUND
7, Plumtree Court
London EC4

World Wildlife News

2930 WORLD'S FAIR LTD.
P. O. Box 57
Union Street
Oldham OL1 1DY

World's Fair

2931 WRESTLER LTD.
Caxton House
Ham Road
Shoreham-by-Sea
Sussex BN4 6QD

Wrestler

2932 WRIGHT & ROUND LTD.
Parliament Street
Gloucester

Brass Band News

2933 WRITER'S FORUM
262, Randolph Avenue
London W9

Writer's Forum

2934 WRITERS PUBLISHING ASSOCIATION
BCM Buildings
London WC1

Topical Dates & Facts Newsletter

2935 WYNN WILLIAMS LTD.
Centenary Buildings
King Street
Wrexham

Educational Broadcasting International

2936 YACHTING PRESS LTD.
196, Eastern Esplanade
Southend-on-Sea
SS1 3AA

Yachts and Yachting

2937 YOGA RESEARCH ASSOCIATION
79, Addison Way
London NW11

Yoga Quarterly Review

2938 YORK ART GALLERY
Exhibition Square
York YO1 2DR

Preview

2939 YORK POETRY SOCIETY
90, Manor Cottage
Museum Gardens
York YO 1 2DR

York Poetry

2940 YORKSHIRE ARCHAEOLOGICAL SOCIETY
Claremont
Clarendon Road
Leeds LS2 9N2

Yorkshire Archaeological Journal

2941 YORKSHIRE ARTS ASSOCIATION
Clyde House
Clydegate
Bradford 5

Ahead in Yorkshire
Month in Yorkshire

2942 YORKSHIRE DIALECT SOCIETY
School of English
The University
Leeds
Yorkshire LS2 9JT

Transactions of the Yorkshire Dialect Society

2943 YOUNG WRITER GROUP
(Sponsored by the Ashford Community)
2A, Chertsey Road
Ashford Common
Middx.

Young Writer

2944 YOUNG ZOOLOGISTS CLUB
Zoological Society of London
Regents Park
London NW1 4RY

Zoo Magazine

2945 YOUR ENVIRONMENT
10, Roderick Road
London NW3

Your Environment

2946 YOUTH CAMPING ASSOCIATION
The Office
Upper Flat
14, East Road
Enfield
Middx.

Lightweight Camper

2947 YOUTH CRUSADE WORLDWIDE
Bulstrode
Gerrard's Cross
Bucks. SL9 8S2

Purpose

2948 YOUTH HOSTELS ASSOCIATION
Trevelyan House
St. Albans
Herts.

Hostelling News

2949   YOUTH SERVICE INFORMATION CENTRE
        37, Belvoir Street
        Leicester LE1 6SL

        Youth Service

2950   YR ACADEMI GYMREIG
        [The Welsh Academy of Letters]
        c/o The Secretary
        The Welsh Academy
        St David's College
        Lampeter
        Cards.

        Taliesin

2951   ZINC DEVELOPMENT ASSOCIATION
        34, Berkeley Square
        London W1X 6A5

        Zinc Abstracts

2952   ZODIAC PUBLISHING CO. LTD.
        Mercury House
        Theobolds Road
        London WC1X 8RX

        Mercury
        Zodiac

2953   ZULULAND SWAZILAND ASSOCIATION
        c/o The Rectory
        Hanwood
        Shrewsbury
        Salop.

        Net

2954   NICHOLAS ZURBRUGG
        Church Steps
        Kersey
        Ipswich
        Suffolk

        Stereo Headphones

INDEX

All titles follow presentation of title page—no inversions are employed.